Security Management
for Sports
and Special Events

An Interagency Approach to Creating Safe Facilities

Stacey A. Hall, PhD

Walter E. Cooper, EdD

Lou Marciani, EdD

James A. McGee, MS

National Center for Spectator Sports Safety and Security
University of Southern Mississippi, Hattiesburg

Human Kinetics

Library of Congress Cataloging-in-Publication Data

Security management for sports and special events : an interagency approach to creating safe facilities / Stacey A. Hall ... [et al.].
    p. cm.
  Includes bibliographical references and index.
  ISBN-13: 978-0-7360-7132-1 (hard cover)
  ISBN-10: 0-7360-7132-6 (hard cover)
  1. Sports facilities--United States--Management. 2. Sports facilities--Security measures--United States. 3. Sports facilities--United States--Safety measures. 4. Sports administration--United States. 5. Sports--United States--Management. I. Hall, Stacey A.
  GV401.S44 2012
  796.068--dc23

                    2011028525

ISBN: 978-0-7360-7132-1 (print)

The web addresses cited in this text were current as of May 2011, unless otherwise noted.

Acquisitions Editor: Myles Schrag; **Developmental Editor:** Katherine Maurer; **Assistant Editors:** Steven Calderwood, Derek Campbell, Anne Rumery, and Tyler Wolpert; **Copyeditor:** Bob Replinger; **Indexer:** Andrea Hepner; **Permissions Manager:** Dalene Reeder; **Graphic Designer:** Fred Starbird; **Graphic Artist:** Denise Lowry; **Cover Designer:** Keith Blomberg; **Photographer (cover):** David Joles/Star Tribune/ZUMA Press; **Photos (interior):** p. 12 Pics United/Icon SMI, p. 14 PA Photos, p. 51 Roni Galgano/Union-Tribune/ZUMA Press, p. 1, 23, 43, 61, 81, 101, 119, 133, and 155 © Human Kinetics; **Photo Asset Manager:** Laura Fitch; **Visual Production Assistant:** Joyce Brumfield; **Photo Production Manager:** Jason Allen; **Art Manager:** Kelly Hendren; **Associate Art Manager:** Alan L. Wilborn; **Illustrations:** © Human Kinetics; **Printer:** Total Printing Systems

Printed in the United States of America   10 9 8 7 6 5 4 3 2

The paper in this book is certified under a sustainable forestry program.

Human Kinetics
Web site: www.HumanKinetics.com

United States: Human Kinetics, P.O. Box 5076, Champaign, IL 61825-5076
800-747-4457
e-mail: info@hkusa.com

Canada: Human Kinetics, 475 Devonshire Road Unit 100, Windsor, ON N8Y 2L5
800-465-7301 (in Canada only)
e-mail: info@hkcanada.com

Europe: Human Kinetics, 107 Bradford Road, Stanningley, Leeds LS28 6AT, United Kingdom
+44 (0) 113 255 5665
e-mail: hk@hkeurope.com

For information about Human Kinetics' coverage in other areas of the world,
please visit our website: www.HumanKinetics.com

                                                          E4221

Contents

Preface

Sport and special events are an integral part of most cultures, and millions of spectators attend such events annually. The provision of a safe, secure environment for patrons is critical. Subsequently, individuals, agencies, and private contractors face the significant challenge of providing a safe environment and enjoyable experience.

Over $2 billion is spent on sport security efforts each year, and during years of international mega sporting events this figure rises to more than $6 billion. Although substantial resources are expended on ensuring safe and secure events, the authors note that little information is available pertaining specifically to sport and special event security. The sport industry has embraced best practices and technological tools to aid their efforts, but we recognize that professionals in the field and current students lack access to new knowledge in this relatively new field of sport and special event safety and security. We want to provide a basic overview of key topics related to multiagency collaboration, risk management, training, planning, exercising, and emergency management.

To familiarize readers with current safety concerns, chapter 1 provides an overview of the sport and special event industry. Practical examples of sporting disasters from various countries are included. Threats and risks to sport and special events are presented, ranging from extreme terrorists attacks to less extreme cases such as vandalism and theft.

Many stakeholders are involved in the safety and security planning of major events, including but not limited to the following: facility or event management, law enforcement, emergency management, fire and HAZMAT, emergency medical services, local and state agencies, local community entities, public health, and public relations. Coordination between all these entities is essential for effective planning and response to safety and security threats. Chapter 2 focuses on multiagency collaboration and addresses the training and leadership of stakeholders in a multiagency working environment. Chapter 3 explores incident management strategies in the context of the U.S. Department of Homeland Security and the roles of various jurisdictions and agencies in responding to terror attacks, natural disasters, riots, and other dangerous incidents.

Venue and event managers must act in a prudent manner by identifying risks and instituting plans, policies, procedures, and protective measures to combat all-hazard potential incidents that can be harmful to assets—human, physical, and financial. Chapters 4, 5, and 6 walk the reader through the processes of risk assessment, security planning and policy design, and emergency response and emergency planning. Along the way, the text offers a range of practical application tools, forms, and reference materials. After security plans and procedures are in place, training and exercises are essential for them to work effectively. Chapters 7 and 8 provide detailed information on training needs for security staff. The text explains how both discussion-based exercises and operations-based exercises are used to test plans. Finally, chapter 9 explores the future of sport and special event security and refers the reader to additional resources.

In each chapter, a case study presents a real-world scenario relevant to the topics discussed in the chapter and points out lessons learned and issues for further reflection and discussion. Sidebars throughout the text highlight important current issues in sport and event security management and provide examples. At the back of the book, organized by chapter, you will find numerous appendixes that provide additional examples, as well as forms and templates to aid in developing security plans.

Readers will notice that much of this book is based on United States guidelines, directives, and entities. This bias reflects the fact that much of our research has been based in the United States, in the context of the U.S. government's emphasis on increased security over the past decade. But the security threats discussed and the importance of assessing risk, creating security and emergency response plans, and training and exercising plans will be the same wherever spectator sport is popular or wherever people gather for large events. If you are working in sport or event security outside the United States, you will need to be familiar with local laws, incident response guidelines, and jurisdictions to have a context in which to apply the principles in this book. To serve as a starting point, in chapter 3 we've provided a section that provides an overview of common types of national agencies involved in major event security and information on a few international security organizations. A variety of examples interspersed throughout the rest of the book reflect the importance of sport and special event security throughout the world.

Although this book draws on many examples related to sporting events, the same principles are applicable to all types of venues and events. In addition, managers for venues that host concerts, rallies, and other types of events will find examples throughout the text to illustrate the applicability of the concepts to a variety of non-sport events and nontraditional sport events.

For the first time, a book dedicated solely to explaining the safety and security system for sport and special events is available. This text aims to communicate all aspects of planning, managing, and implementing safety and security for sport and special events. The book provides an overview of the major steps involved in the process including assessing risks, training staff, and conducting exercises to test plans and procedures.

Acknowledgments

I would like to thank my colleagues, Walter E. Cooper, James A. McGee, and Lou Marciani at the University of Southern Mississippi for their support and contributions in making this book a reality. Walter provided much needed mentorship; Jim's extensive experience proved valuable for real-world applications within the text; and Lou provided insight on innovative sport security technology solutions.

I must also acknowledge our hard-working staff at the National Center for Spectator Sports Safety and Security: Lauren Cranford, Nick Nabors, Luca Giardino, Rickey Bradley, Hobbie Reagan, Young Lee, and Steve Miller. They continuously strive to do the best job possible. I thank them for their dedication to the Center.

Last but not least, I would like to thank my family in Northern Ireland for their unconditional love and support in all my personal and professional endeavors.

Stacey A. Hall, PhD, MBA

CHAPTER 1

Safety and Security Environment for Sports and Special Events

CHAPTER GOALS

- Understand the importance of sport event security planning efforts.
- Discuss potential threats to sport and special events (terrorism, crowd management, natural disasters).
- Define terrorism and discuss terrorist motivations, hazards, and indicators.
- Discuss the legal and economic implications of threats to stadium owners and operators.
- Provide an overview of the sport event security aware (SESA) system.

Providing a safe and secure environment is a priority for all stakeholders involved in delivering a sporting or special event. The increasing profile of sport and event properties has resulted in increased exposure to risks that affect spectators, participants, and other entities (Stevens, 2007). Risks associated with sporting and special events are terrorism, hooliganism, crowd disorder, assault, vandalism, logistical failure, fraud, theft, and inclement weather (Stevens, 2007; Fried, 2005).

Terrorism has been cited as one of the most common risks associated with the security of sport and event venues (Stevens, 2007). This chapter provides an overview of the safety and security environment, including all-hazard risks facing sport and event facilities. Emphasis is placed on terrorism, crowd management issues, and natural disasters, as well as the legal and economic implications of sporting and special event incidents.

Sport and event stadia operators implement safety and security measures to prepare for and mitigate consequences of potential all-hazard risks (natural and manmade). The terms *safety* and *security* are sometimes used interchangeably, but they are two separate activities. In essence, safety is concerned with protection against accidental incidents (e.g., slip and fall, severe storm), whereas security is concerned with protection against intentional damages (e.g., suicide bomber). Certain safety measures have been enforced in the workplace through government standards, such as those enforced by the Occupational Safety and Health Administration (OSHA) in the United States. The safety of spectators and patrons has long been a concern for facility managers. In contrast, the concept of security, especially securing venues against manmade threats such as terrorism, is more recent. Since the tragic events of September 11, 2001, the concept of security has been propelled to the forefront, especially in the United States. Security measures vary from venue to venue depending on facility structure, capacity, event, and available resources.

Sport event organizers around the world spend over $2 billion each year on security efforts, although during years when major global sporting events occur (FIFA World Cup and Olympics) the figure can rise to $6 billion (Culf, 2006). Security costs are associated with implementing protective measures, including staffing, physical protection systems, perimeter control, access control, risk management, emergency management, crowd management, and traffic control. The following list provides examples of sport security related costs for major sport events:

- 1992 Barcelona Olympic Games: $66 million.
- 1996 Atlanta Olympic Games: $108 million.
- 2000 Sydney Olympic Games: $179 million.
- 2002 Salt Lake City Winter Olympic Games: $500 million.
- 2004 Athens Summer Olympic Games: $1.5 billion. The International Olympic Committee (IOC) also had a $170 million insurance policy in the event the Games were cancelled because of terrorism.
- 2008 Beijing Summer Olympic Games: $6.5 billion.
- 2010 Vancouver Winter Olympic Games: $1 billion.
- 2012 London Summer Olympic Games security costs are estimated at $2.2 billion.

The terrorist attacks in the United States on September 11, 2001, had a major effect on the financial commitment to safety and security at major sporting and special events. As evident from the examples provided, safety and security costs increased dramatically after 9/11. Security costs rose from Barcelona ($66 million) to Beijing ($6.5 billion) and will continue to rise given the ongoing threat of terrorism worldwide and crowd management problems inherent with hosting mega sporting events. As a result, sport and event managers must implement risk mitigation measures using additional resources, such as police and military personnel, new or emerging technological solutions, and the latest intelligence gathering and communication methods.

For an in-depth discussion of security concerns and methods for sport and special events, see the transcript of a presentation by Janet Napolitano at the NCS[4] (National Center for Sports Spectator Safety and Security) conference in appendix 1.1.

Major Sport and Special Event Threats

The following section specifically addresses the threat of terrorism, crowd management issues, and natural disasters in the global sport and event industry. Examples of sport-related incidents are also provided. High-profile sport events provide a perfect target for terrorists; therefore, sport managers responsible for safety and security planning must be able to detect, deter, respond to, and recover from a catastrophic incident, be it natural or manmade. Besides terrorism, fan violence and inclement weather are concerns for event managers. Player and fan violence has become a problem in the United States in recent years, although it has been prevalent in Europe for many decades. Natural disasters must also be considered. The onset of unexpected weather could create chaos at a stadium or arena that needs to be evacuated without warning. An incident could have a devastating effect that results in mass casualties and catastrophic social and economic consequences. Potential consequences of unexpected disasters at sport or special events may include mass casualties or fatalities, destruction of infrastructure, liability issues, and higher insurance premiums.

Terrorism

The United States Federal Bureau of Investigation (FBI) defines two primary categories of terrorism—domestic terrorism and international terrorism:

> Domestic terrorism is the unlawful use, or threatened use, of force or violence by a group or individual based and operating entirely within the United States and its territories without foreign direction, and whose acts are directed at elements of the U.S. Government or its population, in furtherance of political or social goals. (Texas Engineering Extension Service, 2005, pp. 2–4)

> International terrorism is the unlawful use of force or violence against persons or property committed by a group or individual who has some connection to a foreign power or whose activities transcend national boundaries. (Texas Engineering Extension Service, 2005, pp. 2–4)

The 1996 Atlanta Olympic Games Centennial Park bombing is an example of a domestic terrorist incident. Eric Rudolph, a U.S. citizen acting alone, planted a backpack bomb at an open-air concert at Centennial Park. The pipe-bomb device detonated among thousands of spectators, killing 1 person and injuring 110 (this incident is highlighted in the case study on page 19). The September 11, 2001, attacks on the U.S. World Trade Center and Pentagon were international terrorist attacks, because the attackers had connections to a foreign-based terrorist group. This incident changed the security landscape of sporting and special events. Terror attacks, however, have been a threat all over the world for many decades. Here are some other notable acts of domestic and international terrorism:

- **Rajneeshee cult:** In 1984 in Oregon, salad bars were contaminated with salmonella before election day in an effort to influence local elections. Over 750 people became seriously ill.

- **World Trade Center**: In 1993 an Islamic terrorist groups attacked the World Trade Center in New York City. The terrorists placed a 1,500-pound (675 kg) urea-nitrate bomb in a van, parked it in the basement of one of the buildings, and set the timer. The bomb exploded, killing 6 people and injuring over 1,000 innocent victims.

- **Tokyo subway**: In 1995 a terrorist group released the nerve agent sarin in the Tokyo subways, killing 12 and sickening thousands.

- **Oklahoma City bombing**: In 1995 domestic terrorist Timothy McVeigh parked a truck loaded with explosives outside the Alfred P. Murrah government building in Oklahoma City. This attack killed 168 people and wounded over 500 others.

- **U.S. Embassies, Africa**: In 1998 a coordinated attack was executed on two U.S. embassies in Kenya and Tanzania. A total of 224 people were killed and over 5,000 were injured. Osama Bin Laden was held responsible for these attacks.

- **USS Cole**: In 2000 in Yemen, a group of suicide bombers used a skiff to pull alongside the *USS Cole*. They detonated a bomb that killed 17 and wounded 39. This attack was also attributed to Osama Bin Laden.

- **World Trade Center and Pentagon**: On September 11, 2001, terrorists hijacked four commercial airplanes to use as weapons of mass destruction. One plane crashed into Trade Center Tower One, and another crashed into Trade Center Tower Two. Both towers eventually collapsed, resulting in the deaths of approximately 3,000 men, women, and children.

- **Anthrax mailings**: In October 2001 anthrax was mailed to several individuals and entities in the United States. Targets included an NBC television station and the U.S. Congress. One person died from contracting anthrax from a letter sent to American Media in Florida.

- **Madrid subway**: In 2004 subways in Madrid, Spain, were attacked with explosives, killing 191 people. This incident is believed to have changed the course of presidential elections in Spain.

- **London bombings**: The attack on the British underground system in London in July 2005 killed 52 people and injured over 700.

Sporting events are considered part of a nation's critical infrastructure and key assets. The major goal of terrorist activity is to destroy or incapacitate critical infrastructure and key resources, cause mass fatalities, weaken the economy, and damage the nation's morale and confidence. The U.S. Department of Homeland Security therefore identified major sport stadia as likely terrorist targets because of the potential for mass casualties, widespread media coverage, and social impact. Target objectives for terrorists are highlighted in figure 1.1. The terrorists' primary goal is

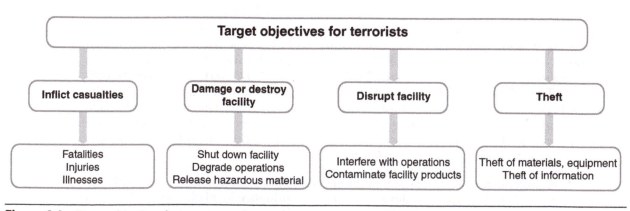

Figure 1.1   Target objectives for terrorists and examples.

to inflict harm by killing or injuring as many people as possible. Attaining this objective is feasible at a sporting event because of the number of spectators who attend sporting events each year. For example, 106 million people attended college sporting events in the United States in 2008. Furthermore, sport is an enormous industry in the United States, estimated at $410 billion in 2009. An incident at a major sport event that causes a cancellation, postponement, or relocation can potentially have a catastrophic effect on the local community, state, and nation.

Terrorist Motivations

Spangler (2001) explained that modern terrorism comes in many shapes and forms, from organized groups to a single individual acting on his or her own agenda. According to Arquilla, Ronfeldt, and Zanini (1999), terrorism appeals to its perpetrators for three principal reasons: (1) to harm and defeat superior forces, (2) to assert identity and command attention, and (3) to achieve a new future order by wrecking the present. Terrorist motivations provide insight to specific sites that may be considered targets. These motivations are key considerations when analyzing the potential for a group or individual to commit an act of terrorism at a sporting or special event. The FBI established five major classifications for threat motivations: (1) political, (2) religious, (3) racial, (4) environmental, and (5) special interest (U.S. Department of Homeland Security, 2009c) (see table 1.1). Although sport is highlighted only in the religious category, sport events are susceptible to attacks from all groups depending on the event, size, location, function, and attendance by certain individuals, such as political figures or celebrities. The same applies to special events, such as concerts, festivals, political rallies, historical events, and conferences or exhibitions. Attendance at events by dignitaries or U.S. or foreign officials may create interest among adversaries who are trying to publicize their cause to the masses. The sheer size of an event, such as a papal visit that may draw over 100,000 people, can attract the attention of terrorists and criminals. Likewise, the historical or political significance of an event may attract terrorists and criminals.

Table 1.1   Terrorism Motivations and Likely Targets

Threat motivation	Likely targets
Political	Government institutions Government or national leadership or authority figures Icons and symbols of government (historical facilities)
Religious	Financial institutions Media Large public venues (sport stadia, concert halls, churches) Women's health facilities
Racial	Minority churches Facilities and symbols of racial groups or organizations
Environmental	Construction projects Mining Logging or exploration sites Potential sources of pollution of air or water
Special interest	Women's health facilities Animal research laboratories Technology companies University research facilities

Political motivations include various theories and ideologies. Political groups are classified as right wing or left wing depending on their view of the government. Right-wing groups are normally associated with the militia movement or groups that are opposed to government control and power. Left-wing groups are normally associated with a socialist ideology, such as communism (U.S. Department of Homeland Security, 2009c). Political activist groups are likely to target government institutions, government leaders, and icons or symbols of government such as historical facilities. Examples of political activist groups include Armed Forces of National Liberation (FALN), Mountaineer Militia, Anarchists, Sons of the Gestapo, and Patriots Council (Texas Engineering Extension Service, 2005). The bombings by the extremist Somalia militant group al-Shabab (with connections to Al-Qaeda) during the 2010 World Cup Final celebrations in Uganda is an example of a politically motivated attack because a justification was declared—retaliation for Ugandan troops' participation in the African Union peacekeeping mission in Mogadishu.

Religious groups are considered the most dangerous because of their willingness to die for their cause. Organizational affiliations range from formal religions to doomsday cults. Adherents believe that they are doing the work of God or are on a holy mission. The motivations and beliefs of these individuals or groups tend to extend to rewards after death. Therefore, religious groups are more likely to choose suicide terrorism as a method to carry out their attacks. Suicide terrorism is an effective means for terrorists to achieve their goal of mass casualties and mass humiliation through media coverage. According to Kennedy (2006), suicide attacks accounted for 3 percent of all terrorist attacks from 1980 to 2003 but were responsible for 48 percent of all fatalities. As table 1.1 highlights, sport stadia are likely targets for religious extremists. In addition, religious extremists are likely to target financial institutions, media outlets, and churches. Religious activist groups include fundamentalist and extremist groups such as Al-Qaeda. In 2008 an Iraqi female suicide bomber targeted soccer fans who were watching the national team play China in the town marketplace. At least 29 people were injured.

Racial groups are often referred to as hate groups. They believe in a social order based on the supposed superiority of a particular race, and they often advocate separatism, persecution, or the elimination of other races. Racially motivated groups target individuals or facilities that represent other races, such as minority churches. Examples of racially motivated groups include National Black United Front, Aryan Nations, National Alliance, and Ku Klux Klan (Texas Engineering Extension Service, 2005). Environmentalist groups are dedicated to hindering development deemed invasive or damaging to the environment. These groups tend to target activities and businesses that they believe are destroying or damaging the environment, such as construction projects, mines, and logging sites. Examples of environmentally charged groups include Earth First and Earth Liberation Front (ELF). In 1998 ELF members set fire to various structures in Vail, Colorado, resulting in $12 million damage to ski lifts and construction projects (Texas Engineering Extension Service, 2005). In 2003 ELF members attacked four SUV dealers in the Los Angeles area, causing $2.4 million in damage. Special interest groups are those that support a variety of causes with a single focus that are not included in the previous categories, such as Animal Liberation Front (ALF) and groups opposed to abortion and technology (U.S. Department of Homeland Security, 2009c). These groups are likely to target research laboratories, technology companies, and health facilities. Eric Rudolph, the 1996 Atlanta Olympics bomber, can be classified under the special interest motivation category because he was also indicted for the bombing of a Planned Parenthood clinic in Birmingham, Alabama.

Despite the terrorists' diversity in motive of attack, terrorist organizations are shaped by several factors: underlying conditions, international environment, states, organization, and leadership (U.S. Department of Homeland Security, 2003a). Underlying conditions include poverty, religious conflict, corruption, and ethnic strife, which terrorists use to justify their actions and gain support. The international environment influences how terrorist strategies evolve. Open borders provide access to support, such as safe havens and capabilities. States around the world, intentionally and unintentionally, offer physical (training grounds) and virtual (communication networks) havens for terrorists to plan, train, and organize their operations. Organization and leadership determine membership, resources, and capabilities, and provide direction for terrorist action. Some terrorist organizations have decentralized command with autonomous cells. Terrorist groups aim to ensure secrecy of operations and tend to operate underground, concealed from authorities and informants. To maintain secrecy, groups are organized into cells separate from others in the organization, but all work in harmony toward a common goal. A terrorist cell can include two to three people or many people, and only one member may know someone in another cell. In the event that authorities locate a member of one cell, they will obtain information about the activities of only one cell or an adjacent cell but not information about the overall organization. Terrorists therefore prefer this organizational structure of interconnected cells. The structure narrows in a pyramid style toward the group's leader at the top, to whom few members have access (U.S. Department of Homeland Security, 2006).

Terrorist-Related Hazards

Terrorist threats, such as explosives, suicide bombers, weapons of mass destruction (WMDs), hostage taking, and active shooters, are a major concern to sport stadia operators (Hall, Marciani, & Cooper, 2008). The methods used by modern-day terrorists range from the simple to the elaborate (Johnson, 2005). Conventional means such as knives, guns, and explosives are frequently used, but in recent years the probability that terrorists will use weapons of mass destruction such as chemical, biological, radiological, nuclear, or high-yield explosives (CBRNE) has significantly increased. The knowledge, technology, and materials needed to build WMDs are more accessible and widespread than ever before, and the proliferation of these weapons increases the probability that terrorists will use them. The Commission on the Prevention of WMD Proliferation and Terrorism (2008) believes that it is more likely than not that a WMD will be used in a terrorist attack somewhere in the world by the end of 2013.

For purposes of criminal prosecution, the U.S. Department of Justice defines WMD (title 18 USC Section 2332a) as

> any weapon or device that is intended, or has the capability, to cause death or serious bodily injury to a significant number of people through the release, dissemination, or impact of toxic or poisonous chemicals or their precursors; a disease organism; or radiation or radioactivity.

> (a) Any explosive, incendiary or poison gas, bomb, grenade or rocket having a propellant charge of more than four ounces, or a missile having an explosive or incendiary charge of more than one quarter ounce, or mine or device similar to the above; (b) poison gas; (c) any weapon involving a disease organism; or (d) any weapon that is designed to release radiation or radioactivity at a level dangerous to human life. (Texas Engineering Extension Service, 2005, pp. 2–19)

Chemical weapons are extremely lethal and capable of producing mass casualties. Unfortunately, they are easily manufactured because the constituent materials normally have legitimate purposes. Chemicals could be transported by a vehicle or a hijacked aircraft to a sport or event facility or nearby site. Chemical agents fall into four categories: nerve agents (neurotoxins), blister agents (skin irritants), blood agents (asphyxiants), and choking agents (respiratory irritants). Chemical agents can enter the body in four ways: ingestion, inhalation, absorption, and injection. Chemical agents were used extensively during World War I. One of the first cases involved German forces who released chlorine gas, resulting in thousands of casualties (Texas Engineering Extension Service, 2005).

Biological weapons release large quantities of disease-causing microorganisms and can be extremely dangerous. Biological agents fall into five categories: anthrax, cholera, plague, tularemia, and salmonella. Anthrax was first weaponized in the United States during the 1950s. The U.S. Postal Service proved to be a highly effective means of deploying anthrax in October 2001 after the 9/11 attacks, and five deaths resulted. Cholera is a disease deployed through contaminated food and water. Pneumonic and bubonic plague is transmitted through infected flea bites or exposure to an infected person's cough and sneezing. Tularemia is spread through the feces of insects. Salmonella is a common form of food poisoning. The most effective means of disseminating a biological agent is by dispersing a fine mist or spray that victims inhale or by contaminating water or food sources. People do not know immediately that they are being attacked, so the biological agent has time to spread and cause serious harm (Texas Engineering Extension Service, 2005). The U.S. Department of Homeland Security (2005) released a document that described 15 potential threat scenarios to the United States. One scenario addressed the potential of a biological attack on a sport arena. The document stated that the spreading of pneumonic plague in the bathrooms of a sport arena could potentially kill 2,500 people (Hall, Marciani, & Cooper, 2008).

Radiological dispersion devices (RDD) combine radioactive material with conventional explosives and can cause widespread panic in densely populated areas (U.S. Department of Homeland Security, 2002). The short-term dangers of an RDD, or dirty bomb, are radiation burns and acute poisoning; the long-term effect is various forms of cancer. Radioactive materials are readily available and can be found in medical or industrial equipment. In fall 2006 the National Football League (NFL) received a radiological dirty bomb threat against several NFL stadiums.

Nuclear weapons can cause enormous destruction and devastation. Nuclear weapons are not easily acquired, and working with such a weapon requires a high degree of technical ability. Explosives, on the other hand, have been the weapon of choice for terrorists because the materials needed for manufacturing are easily available. Improvised explosive devices (IEDs) can be constructed of commonly used materials. For example, ammonium nitrate and fuel oil (ANFO) are sometimes located at sport facilities in unprotected areas, providing an opportunity to assemble an IED onsite. A suicide bomber could also carry an IED into a facility or place it near a facility for later detonation. In 2005 a University of Oklahoma student prematurely detonated a bomb strapped to his body outside the school's football stadium, which was filled to its 82,000-seat capacity (Hagmann, 2005). Vehicle-borne improvised explosive devices (VBIED) are explosives loaded into a car, truck, or motorcycle that can be driven into a facility or parked near a facility where large crowds gather.

Other forms of terrorism may include cyber attacks on electronic and computer networks that are linked to critical infrastructures such as energy, financial, and security networks (U.S. Department of Homeland Security, 2002).

Terrorist enemies are constantly looking for new ways to attack by finding areas of vulnerability. Most countries with large, diverse, highly mobile populations provide an infinite number of potential targets. People congregate at schools, sporting arenas, malls, concert halls, office buildings, high-rise residences, and places of worship, presenting targets with the potential for many casualties. The sidebar describes potential threats and strategies at some additional non-sport venues.

Convention Centers

Possible Threats

Convention centers play host to events that frequently attract crowds exceeding 100,000. In many cases, convention centers are located in highly congested urban areas. The type of convention held in these venues may enhance the threat. For example, conventions that address medical research often attract the attention of terrorist organizations like the Animal Liberation Front (ALF), who are opposed to research that uses animals for testing. Conventions associated with economic summits frequently attract anarchist groups such as the Ruckus Society.

Security Strategies

In an effort to bring more control to owners of convention centers and to enhance security, many of the services traditionally performed by outside contractors are now being handled internally. In this way, owners can ensure that *all* employees, regardless of their job duties, receive adequate, frequent, and accurate training on emergency management procedures and reporting of suspicious activities. This becomes a force multiplier in terms of numbers of trained employees present during events. It also ensures that all employees are vetted, credentialed, and held accountable according to employee guidelines.

Shopping Malls

Possible Threats

Shopping malls are venues where large crowds gather on a consistent basis. As such, shopping malls are viable targets for attack by crazed shooters or terrorists. Such was the case on December 5, 2007, at the Westroads Mall in Omaha, Nebraska, when Robert Hawkins stepped out of the elevator on the third floor of the Von Maur department store and opened fire. He killed eight people and wounded four others

over the course of six minutes before dying from a self-inflicted gunshot wound to the head.

Security Strategies

Robert Hawkins represented the dilemma referred to as the lone wolf offender. This dynamic presents a unique challenge to security specialists because individuals of this type frequently do not appear on the radar in terms of prior behavior indicating that they are a threat and capable of such an attack. To assist with addressing this danger, security personnel must be trained to recognize behavioral characteristics indicating a potential threat. This includes outward nervousness, erratic behavior, and unusual inquiries. Anything that arouses suspicion from security should be pursued and addressed.

Casinos

Possible Threats

Casinos are a venue of mass gathering that represent immorality and indulgence to some potential terrorist groups. In addition to the terrorist threat, casinos may be targeted by disgruntled employees or by patrons who have lost large sums of money.

Security Strategies

Casinos traditionally have sophisticated security systems, and this can help with monitoring the large numbers of people attracted to casinos nationwide. Casinos employ internal security departments that include both uniformed security personnel and stand-alone surveillance departments that electronically monitor all activity in the casinos and resort areas.

Airports

Possible Threats

Airports continue to be a target of terrorists, as demonstrated by the Domodedovo Airport bombing in Russia on January 24, 2011. The aviation industry continues to be targeted

(continued)

Other Venues of Mass Gathering at Risk of Attack   *(continued)*

because of the global attention inherent with any attack in such an environment. Terrorists recognize that attacks outside the designated security checkpoints can result in high casualties and receive extensive media coverage. This further demonstrates the need for well-trained personnel who are security conscious and recognize potential threats.

Security Strategies

In addition to passenger scanning and access and traffic control, airport authorities attempt to detect these types of threats by implementing methodologies that focus on identifying behavioral characteristics that provide insight into a person's nefarious intent. As in the shopping mall environment, recognizing a potential threat based on behavioral characteristics is not the same as profiling. Behavior that is unusual, clothing that is out of place, nervousness, profuse sweating, and avoiding eye contact are just some of the behavioral characteristics that trained security can recognize and then exploit to determine whether there is a need for further questioning or investigation. In addition, the establishment of secure buffer zones, located at a safe distance from airport terminals, is highly recommended.

Terrorist Indicators

Sport and event facility operators and staff members should be able to recognize potential terrorist threats and know how to respond to them. Terrorist acts are usually planned with much attention to detail. Substantial planning and preparation are required to carry out a successful attack. With this being the case, the public has many opportunities to identify or recognize suspicious behavior. Therefore, the citizenry should be familiar with the potential indicators of terrorist activity. Kennedy (2006) presents seven signs of terrorist activity that can be adapted to any facility:

1. **Surveillance**: People may observe the event site to determine security strengths and weaknesses and the number of personnel that may respond to an incident. Event management staff should take note of anyone recording activities, taking notes, or using video, cameras, or observation devices.

2. **Elicitation**: People may attempt to gain information about event security operations. For example, terrorists may acquire knowledge about a stadium structure, access control procedures, and the location of security personnel before, during, and after game time.

3. **Test of security**: Security tests are conducted to measure reaction times to breaches of security and to test physical security barriers for weaknesses. For example, people may try to access unauthorized areas of a sport or event facility.

4. **Acquiring supplies**: Someone may purchase or steal explosives, weapons, or ammunition near the event site; they may also try to acquire security passes or uniforms that make it easier for entrance to prohibited areas of the facility.

5. **Suspicious people**: Someone from outside the sport or event organization or on the facility staff may not fit in because he or she behaves strangely, uses unusual language, or asks odd questions.

6. **Trial run**: Before the final attack, terrorists normally conduct a dry run to address any unanticipated problems. This trial may include recording emergency response times.

7. **Deploying assets**: Perpetrators position themselves and supplies to conduct the attack. This is the final stage and last opportunity to thwart an attack.

Sporting events are desirable targets for many reasons, such as (1) large crowds that make it difficult to identify terrorists, (2) presence of high-profile national or international athletes, (3) national or international media audience, (4) known date, time, and location of events, and (5) proximity of major venues to transportation hubs for quick escape routes ("Security and Policing," 2005; Tarlow, 2002). One hundred and sixty-eight sport-related terrorist attacks were reported from 1972 to 2004 (Toohey & Taylor, 2008). Examples of sport-related terrorist incidents include the following:

- **1972 Olympic Games**: During the Munich Olympic Games 11 Israeli athletes were held hostage by the Palestinian Black September Group. All 11 hostages, 5 terrorists, and a police officer were killed.
- **1992 Barcelona Olympic Games**: Spanish terrorist groups vowed to disrupt the Opening Ceremony by bombing utility supply routes.
- **1996 Atlanta Olympic Games**: One died and 110 were injured from a pipe-bomb blast at Centennial Olympic Park during an open-air concert.
- **2000 Australian Olympic Games**: New Zealand police thwarted an extremist plot to target a nuclear reactor during the Olympic Games.
- **2002 FBI alert**: Al-Qaeda's *Manual of Afghan Jihad* proposed U.S. college football stadiums as a possible terrorist target. People with links to terrorist groups were downloading stadium images.
- **2002 Madrid car bomb**: Sixteen people were injured when a car bomb exploded outside a Madrid soccer stadium before a European Champions League match.
- **2004 English soccer threat**: A suicide bomb plot to kill thousands of soccer fans at a Manchester United versus Liverpool FC match was thwarted. Old Trafford stadium seated 67,000 fans, and terrorists had already purchased tickets around the stadium, where Al-Qaeda fanatics planned to blow themselves up.
- **2004 Spanish soccer bomb threat**: A bomb threat caused the evacuation of 70,000 people during a soccer match at Bernabeu Stadium in Madrid.
- **2005 U.S. college suicide bomber**: A University of Oklahoma student killed himself by prematurely detonating a bomb strapped to his body outside an 84,000-seat stadium.
- **2006 NFL dirty bomb threat**: The NFL received a radiological dirty bomb threat that several stadiums were subject to attack. Fortunately, the threat was a hoax.
- **2007 bombings of Iraqi soccer fans**: Two suicide bombings killed 50 people celebrating the Iraqi national team victory in the Asian Cup finals.
- **2008 Iraqi suicide bomber**: A female suicide bomber in northern Iraq targeted soccer fans who had just watched the national team play China. At least 29 people were injured when the bomber detonated her suicide vest in the town marketplace.
- **2009 Sri Lanka cricket team attack**: Twelve gunmen coordinated a commando-style ambush on the Sri Lankan cricket team bus while the team was traveling in Pakistan.

Special planned events (such as a papal visit) or places of mass gathering such as shopping complexes, entertainment venues, cultural facilities, hotels and convention centers, public transport hubs, and business districts are also vulnerable to terrorist attacks. Recent incidents include the Mumbai hotel attacks, the New York City Times Square bombing attempt, and the numerous Iraqi shopping mall suicide attacks.

Soccer fans are evacuated from Bernabeau Stadium in Madrid in December 2004, following a bomb threat.

Crowd Management

Doukas (2006) defined crowd management as "every component of the game or event from the design of the stadium or arena to the game itself and the protection of patrons from unforeseeable risk of harm from other individuals or the actual facility itself" (p. 1). Crowds need to be managed for several reasons. Large gatherings of people increase the odds that something will happen, and people within a crowd mostly assume that others have responsibility. Large crowds make changes in action slower to accomplish and more complex. Communication also becomes slower and more complicated than normal. More important, in the event of an incident at a mass gathering, the number of possible victims increases (Marsden, 1998). Thousands of people are harmed or killed every year at stadiums and arenas around the world from crowd crushes, fires, bombs, heat exhaustion, stage collapses, overcrowding, and rioting (Doukas, 2006). Crowd congestion has been associated with many stadium tragedies. The primary causes have been crowd size exceeding venue capacity, excessive alcohol consumption, inadequate access control, or inadequate design of facility structure (Schwarz, Hall, & Shibli, 2010).

Spectator violence in and around stadiums has been a longstanding problem for authorities. Incidents can occur wherever fans congregate, including sport events and entertainment venues (e.g., concert halls). Acts of fan violence are less frequent in the United States than they are in European countries such as England and Italy. Fan violence in Europe is most commonly referred to as hooliganism, which has been an ongoing problem for policing authorities at major soccer stadia in Europe for decades. Hooliganism involves disorderly fans who engage in criminal activity before and after games. Incidents may be organized or spontaneous. Organized hooliganism, the more serious form, involves gangs who attend events specifically to cause a disturbance (Pearson, 2006). Hooligan activities include fighting with rival supporters and police, causing disruption at the event, or destroying property (Stevens, 2007). U.S. events tend to experience spontaneous forms of violence that result from an intoxicated or overzealous crowd who might, for example, rush the field. Failure to prevent acts of violence at events can produce negative consequences, including injury to spectators, participants, or staff; decreased public confidence and future attendance; and property destruction. The following are examples of crowd management disasters at sport events:

- **1964 soccer riot**: Three hundred spectators were killed and 500 were injured during a riot at a Peru versus Argentina soccer match in Lima, Peru.
- **1985 European Cup soccer**: At a soccer match between English and Italian teams at Heysel Stadium in Brussels, Belgium, 41 persons died when a crowd barrier collapsed under the weight of people trying to escape from the rioting between rival fans.
- **1985 Bradford fire**: Fifty-six fans burned to death and over 200 were injured when a fire burned through the main stand at Bradford's soccer stadium in England.
- **1989 Hillsborough Stadium disaster**: Crushing took place in a standing area of the stadium when fans entering the stadium through a vomitory were unaware that the pushing was crushing people at the fence line of the terrace. Officials were slow to detect the crush and relieve the pressure. Ninety-six people were killed.
- **1993 college football crowd rush**: Twelve thousand fans rushed the field in Madison at a college football game between Michigan and Wisconsin at Camp Randall Stadium. Fans were hurt when chain-link and rail fences collapsed under a wave of jubilant Wisconsin fans pushing toward the field after the game.
- **1996 soccer crowd crush**: One hundred died in a crowd crush at a tunnel leading to soccer stadium seating in Guatemala City at a World Cup qualifying match. Too many tickets had been sold.
- **2002 fan violence**: A father and son attacked Major League Baseball (MLB) Kansas City Royals first-base coach Tom Gamboa at Comiskey Park.
- **2004 fan and player violence**: Mayhem broke out at a National Basketball Association (NBA) Indiana Pacers game when fans and players exchanged punches in the stands.
- **2004 crowd celebrations**: A street reveler was killed at a Boston Red Sox celebration when she was hit in the eye by a projectile filled with pepper spray.
- **2005 fan violence**: Louisiana State University (LSU) Tigers fans pelted beer bottles at a University of Tennessee bus after the Volunteers came from behind to defeat the Tigers 30–27 in overtime.
- **2006 college football player violence**: A major on-field altercation between Florida International University and University of Miami football players led to the suspension of 31 players. Two dozen police officers were needed to control the situation.
- **2006 NBA player violence**: Ten players were ejected following a brawl between the Knicks and Nuggets.
- **2007 soccer riots**: A police officer was killed in Sicily, Italy, when fans rioted at a Serie A soccer game, leading to the suspension of all league matches and a safety assessment of all stadiums.
- **2007 Australian Open**: More than 150 Serbian and Croatian fans attacked each other with flagpoles and bottles.
- **2009 Australian Open**: Fans from the Serbian and Croatian communities clashed again, hurling chairs and missiles at each other during Serbian Novak Djokovic's win over Bosnian-born Amer Delic, who now represents the United States.
- **2010 Kenyan football stampede**: Seven people were killed in a stampede at a football stadium in the Kenyan capital, Nairobi.

Fans struggle to escape the fatal crowd crush during the 1989 Hillsborough Stadium disaster.

Nonsport events such as concerts and rallies are vulnerable to many of the same threats as sport events. The sidebar describes one tragic example that occurred at a 1979 Who concert in Cincinnati, Ohio.

Madensen and Eck (2008, p. 3) identified six common forms of spectator aggression:

1. **Verbal**: singing, chanting, and yelling taunts or obscenities
2. **Gesturing**: signaling to others with threatening or obscene motions
3. **Missile throwing**: throwing items such as food, drinks, bricks, bottles, broken seats, and cell phones
4. **Warming**: rushing the field or stage and trying to crash the gates to gain entry, or rushing the exit, both of which may result in injury or death from trampling
5. **Property destruction**: knocking down sound systems, tearing up the playing field, and burning or damaging the venue
6. **Physical**: spitting, kicking, shoving, fist fighting, stabbing, and shooting

Natural Disasters

The sudden onset of storms, tornadoes, or lightning can pose real problems for facility operators. Mass evacuations or shelter in place at stadiums and arenas may be required. Researchers have acknowledged the existence of a severe storm threat to large venues. According to Edwards and Lemon (2002), massive casualties are a real risk if a sporting venue is hit by tornado, large hail, violent winds, flash flooding, or cloud-to-ground lightning during an event (even with a warning in effect). Severe weather or natural disasters can also cause dangerous crowd disorder. On March 12, 1988, 80 soccer fans were crushed to death following a stampede to seek cover during a hailstorm at Nepal's national stadium.

Several other notable incidents have occurred:

- **May 1975**: A violent (F4) tornado struck Ak Sar Ben horse track in Omaha, Nebraska.
- **December 1987**: An F3 tornado passed within .25 mi (.4 km) of a dog-racing track in West Memphis, Arkansas, where 7,000 spectators had assembled.

The Who Concert Tragedy

On December 3, 1979, 11 fans were crushed to death and dozens were injured as they tried to enter a sold-out rock concert by The Who in Cincinnati, Ohio.

More than 18,500 fans showed up for a sold-out concert. Fans began to gather at 1:30 p.m. for the 8:00 p.m. show at Riverfront Coliseum. The concert was using a general-admission ticket policy, known as festival seating (standing room). At 7:05 p.m. just 5 of the coliseum's 134 doors were opened and fans began to push forward. Crowd surges and rippling human waves of pressure knocked people down and rendered them trapped and fighting for their lives.

At 7:30 p.m. a police lieutenant asked the coliseum manager to open additional doors, but he was told that no more ticket takers were available. Only nine had been hired, and enlisting ushers would be a union violation. The 25 police officers assigned to the concert to keep order did not have authority to open more doors; only the security staff could do so.

Besides the forced competition among fans that festival seating brought to the event, other crowd safety lapses appeared. The situation was made worse by an absence of communication between event organizers, security, and the crowd; a lack of crowd management of any kind, including queuing; and a refusal by those in charge to respond to a police call to open a sufficient number of main entrance doors to relieve the crowd crushing.

Ron Duristch, one of the many Who fans caught in the crowd, describes the horror of the situation:

> A wave swept me to the left and when I regained my stance I felt that I was standing on someone. The helplessness and frustration of this moment sent a wave of panic through me. I screamed with all my strength that I was standing on someone. I couldn't move. I could only scream. Another wave came and pushed me further left towards the door. I felt my leg being pulled to the right. The crowd shifted again and I reached down and grabbed an arm at my leg. I struggled for a while and finally pulled up a young girl who also had a young boy clinging to her limbs. They were barely conscious and their faces were filled with tears.

Following the tragedy, the City of Cincinnati immediately established the Task Force on Crowd Control and Safety to analyze and recommend ways to make future concerts safe at Riverfront Coliseum and at other city venues. The task force's report, *Crowd Management*, was submitted on July 8, 1980, and it remains a landmark document in the field of crowd management. Many of the task force suggestions became incorporated into legislation and public assembly planning in the United States.

Reference: *Crowd management: Report of the task force on crowd control and safety.* (1980). Available at www.crowdsafe.com/taskrpt/.

- **April 1998**: An F3 tornado in Nashville, Tennessee, hit the incomplete Adelphia Coliseum, now called LP Field, home to the Titans of the NFL.
- **May 1998**: An F5 tornado suspended play at a minor league baseball game in Alabama.
- **August 1999**: An F2 tornado travelled through downtown Salt Lake City, Utah, striking a large outdoor convention center and damaging the Delta Center, the arena used by the NBA's Utah Jazz (Edwards & Lemon, 2002).

In 1989 an earthquake occurred in San Francisco during Game 3 of the World Series between the San Francisco Giants and Oakland A's at Candlestick Park. Fortunately, the stadium remained intact, and no fans received serious injuries. In August 2005

Hurricane Katrina, the worst natural disaster in U.S. history, caused mass devastation to the U.S. Gulf South region and New Orleans area. Both professional sport and collegiate sport organizations in the affected areas suffered major destruction and financial loss (Hall, Marciani, & Cooper, 2008). For example, the New Orleans Saints football team relocated to Baton Rouge, Louisiana, for the 2005 season, and renovation of the Superdome facility for the team's return in 2006 cost an estimated $180 million (Steinbach, 2006).

Weather-related concerns also affect nonsport events, such as concerts and political events. For example, in September 2010, the Jonas Brothers concert at the 1-800-ASK-GARY Amphitheatre in Tampa, Florida, was canceled because of flooding from heavy rains. An estimated 2 to 3 inches (5 to 7.5 cm) of rain fell in a few hours, flooding the backstage area and the orchestra seating at the front of the theater. A Jay-Z concert was cancelled in Atlanta in 2009 because of severe storms and lightning. In October 2008 John McCain and Sarah Palin had to cancel a preelection rally at Memorial Stadium in Philadelphia.

Some venue operators have stated that weather-related incidents are considered an act of God, absolving them from responsibility. Because of these passive responses, many venues at risk have done nothing to prepare for severe weather disasters. Some type of action is needed to encourage and persuade venue owners and operators to prepare for such dangers (Edwards & Lemon, 2002).

Legal and Economic Implications

Safety and security threats have potential legal and economic implications for facility owners and operators. The threat of terrorism is a growing concern for major stadia operators. Safety issues include managing crowds and protecting athletes, staff, and patrons from harm during an event (Chen, 2009). Facility management can significantly reduce liability exposure by successfully managing risks and foreseeable actions that lead to injuries (Schwarz, Hall, & Shibli, 2010). Legal issues related to event security management include inadequate security, negligent employment practices, and handling disturbances, ejections, and arrests (Kinney, 2003). According to Chen (2009), the monitoring of fans is critical because they represent the most costly potential liability. Addressing unlawful activity, such as unruly or violent fan behavior, can lead to accusations and allegations of manhandling upon rejection from a facility. These types of liabilities represent potentially significant money lost to litigation activities.

Currently, there is little legislation that forces stadium owners and operators to abide by international or even national safety and security standards (Chen, 2009). Nevertheless, the threats covered earlier in this chapter vary from country to country, event to event, and depend on the facility's capacity and location, so facility operators must set a certain standard for security (Chen, 2009; Hall et al., 2010). European countries such as England, because of a history of hooliganism, have enacted safety legislation that requires each football club to hold a stadium safety certificate. Every soccer club in the top four divisions of the English Football Association (FA) must acquire the safety certificate to operate (Hall et al., 2010). Furthermore, the Union of European Football Association (UEFA) requires stadiums to be fully compliant with its safety and security rules and regulations if they are to host high-profile soccer games (Chen, 2009).

In the United States, the standard of care that facility operators must exert when providing security at their venues is increasing, leading to the possibility of liability following a terrorist attack (Marciani, Hall, & Finch, 2009). A recent U.S. court decision (April 29, 2008) established higher security requirements for facilities said to be on notice of an attack. The Port Authority of New York and New Jersey was found to be 68 percent liable for liability damages suffered in the 1993 terrorist bombing of the World Trade Center. The New York Supreme Court decision against the Port Authority was viable on two issues: (1) whether the facility owner was on notice of the possibility of an attack (foreseeability) and (2) what mitigation steps were reasonable or necessary in light of that knowledge. The term *notice* refers to when a defendant knew or should have known that a terrorist attack was possible. This decision ultimately changed the liability landscape for any entity that owned a potential terrorist target (Finch, 2008).

Sport and event facility owners and operators are possibly on notice of a terrorist attack taking place at their property, especially given the Department of Homeland Security (DHS) warning and identification of major stadia as likely terrorist targets. So what can facility operators do in light of the threat? The first step is being proactive. According to Appenzeller (2000), sport managers tend to react to events and circumstances rather than take proactive steps to prevent catastrophic losses. Facility owners and operators must investigate what hazard mitigation measures they currently have in place and what similar facilities are doing to prevent terrorist acts. Benchmarking will help facility managers assess their degree of preparedness compared with others in the business, and expose their organization to industry best practices. Facility owners in the United States should also consider applying for DHS Support Anti-Terrorism by Fostering Effective Technologies (SAFETY) Act protection. The DHS SAFETY Act is federal law designed to minimize or eliminate liability arising from terrorist activities (Finch, 2008). The SAFETY Act was enacted in 2002 in response to the multibillion dollar lawsuits filed after the September 11, 2001, attacks. The SAFETY Act protection extends to companies' products and services that DHS has approved as being effective against terrorism. Additionally, facility owners must possess adequate insurance coverage. According to Finch (2008), the average victim's family from the 9/11 attacks received $3 million in compensation. The 9/11 attacks also had an effect on insurance rates for sport entities. Insurance premiums for the New York Giants Stadium, Continental Airlines Arena, and other New Jersey Sports and Exhibition holdings increased 343 percent to $3.2 million in 2002 (Livingstone, 2008).

Given the multitude of threats to sporting and special events and the legal and economic implications, sport and event managers need to be concerned with the safety and security of their venues. This text provides an overview of strategies for facility managers to assess threats and risks, identify vulnerabilities, develop protective security measures, implement security plans, train staff, and conduct planning activities.

Sport Event Security Aware System: A Continuous Improvement Model

The education and training of security personnel is critical to ensure that effective security measures are implemented and that an all-hazards approach to emergency planning is employed (Sauter & Carafano, 2005). An effective management system for sport event security requires the involvement and commitment of many agencies and individuals, such as professionals, volunteers, public agencies, and outsourced contractors. Acknowledging the industry need to educate and train sport security professionals and provide consistency in security management practices, the National Center for Spectator Sports Safety and Security Management (NCS[4]) developed a continuous improvement process for the effective security management of sport venues—the sport event security aware (SESA) system. The SESA system involves four key processes including (1) risk assessment, (2) training, (3) exercise, and (4) validation (see figure 1.2 on page 18). The ultimate goal of the proposed SESA model is to ensure consistent security practices at sporting venues.

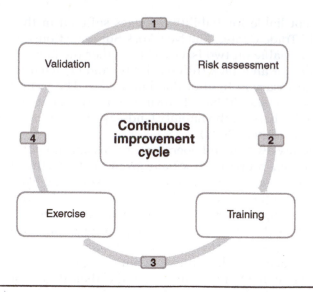

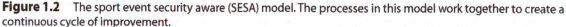

Figure 1.2   The sport event security aware (SESA) model. The processes in this model work together to create a continuous cycle of improvement.

• **Risk assessment**: Sport venue owners, managers, and stakeholders must be aware of risk assessment methodologies to assess threats, identify vulnerabilities, and minimize consequences through the implementation of risk reduction strategies. This process includes (1) identifying a command group (CG) to oversee event security operations, (2) characterizing assets, (3) conducting a threat assessment, (4) conducting a vulnerability assessment, (5) evaluating consequences, (6) calculating risk levels, and (7) developing consequence reduction proposals. This process is covered in chapter 4.

• **Training**: Effective staff training is a key component of protecting critical infrastructure such as sport stadiums and arenas. The sport organization should provide adequate resources for the recruitment, training, and evaluation of personnel responsible for venue security. The three key levels of staff training are (1) multiagency leadership, (2) supervisory staff, and (3) security line (event) staff. This process is covered in chapter 5.

• **Exercise**: Sport organizations should conduct exercises to test plans in place and enhance the staff's awareness of roles and responsibilities during an incident scenario. The seven types of exercises defined by the Homeland Security Exercise and Evaluation Program (HSEEP) are considered either discussion based or operations based. This process is covered in chapter 7.

• **Validation**: The sport organization should assess the organization's sport event security aware system process, which includes a review of threats and risks, improvement plans relative to countermeasure recommendations, staff training, and exercises.

The SESA system exemplifies a continuous improvement process, as indicated by the circular shape of figure 1.2 requiring individuals or agencies to self-assess continuously to enhance their safety and security system. This method is applicable at all levels of the safety and security planning process.

Sport managers should be proactive and take the necessary steps to secure their venues. By doing so, they can help their sport organizations accomplish the following:

• Fulfill their moral and legal responsibility to protect spectators, officials, competitors, employees, and community stakeholders.

• Facilitate compliance with the regulatory requirements of municipal, county, state, and federal agencies.

- Enhance a facility's ability to recover from financial losses, regulatory fines, loss of market share, damage to equipment or products, or business interruptions.
- Avoid exposure to civil or criminal liability in the event of an incident.
- Enhance image and credibility with spectators, competitors, employees, suppliers, and the community.
- Provide documentation that may reduce venue insurance premiums.

CASE STUDY

Centennial Olympic Park Bombing

The city of Atlanta, Georgia, hosted the 1996 Olympic Games. Hosting the event resulted in the rejuvenation of the downtown area. Specifically, the Centennial Olympic Park was constructed in the heart of the downtown area amid abandoned lots and was considered the town square of the Olympics. It contained a large stage where bands could perform and large screens on which video images of the events at the various Olympic venues could be projected. On Friday, July 26, the ninth day of the Olympics, the R&B band Jack Mack and the Heart Attack was performing a concert at the Centennial Olympic Park before over 50,000 spectators. At approximately 1:20 a.m., a pipe bomb inside a military backpack exploded underneath a bench near the concert sound tower. One person was killed and more than 100 people were injured.

The timeline of events leading up to this explosion was as follows:

- **Midnight–12:45 a.m.**: Eric Rudolph plants a green U.S. military backpack containing three pipe bombs surrounded by nails underneath a bench in the park area. Weighing over 40 pounds (18 kg), the device was the largest pipe bomb in U.S. history.

- **12:45 a.m.**: The suspicious backpack is found by security guard Richard Jewell, who notified the Georgia Bureau of Investigation. Federal explosive experts rush to the area.

- **12:58 a.m.**: An anonymous 911 call warns authorities about the bomb 22 minutes before detonation, but confused 911 operators couldn't determine the location. Centennial Olympic Park had been renamed for the Olympics, causing confusion about which park the caller was referring to.

- **1:08 a.m.**: An explosive specialist identifies wires and a pipe within the backpack. It is suggested that the contents were slightly moved during this examination. An evacuation of the surrounding area near the backpack begins, but people were slow to move because of excessive alcohol consumption and lack of information about why they were being moved.

- **1:20 a.m.**: The device explodes, causing debris, nails, screws, and shrapnel to fly everywhere. One person is killed and 111 are injured. Law enforcement officers attempting to clear the area were among the wounded. Some people thought that the noise was part of the show. The movement of the device during the examination likely shifted the contents, and ultimately the bomb blast direction, which could have been much worse.

- **2:00 a.m.**: Downtown Atlanta is sealed.

(continued)

Case Study   *(continued)*

LESSONS LEARNED

- The Atlanta Games hosted 5,000 athletes representing 197 countries. Two million visitors came to Georgia, and 3.5 billion people watched on television. This high-profile event and the global media audience provided a perfect target for causing mass casualties and generating publicity.

- The suspicious device was found at 12:58 a.m. and was examined at 1:08 a.m., but the evacuation of spectators was not completed before detonation occurred at 1:20 a.m. Officials were reluctant to conduct a mass evacuation of the entire area because of the size of the crowd. A bomb scare could lead to panic, which could result in a stampede and further injuries, so officials focused on clearing people away from the backpack area. The response timeline and activities were evidently stretched because of the huge crowd and the limited assets and capabilities available to coordinate an effective response. This incident clearly indicated the need to have a standard bomb threat response protocol and evacuation procedures. In addition, event managers need to have sufficient resources and personnel to deal with a mega sport event such as the Olympics.

- Crowd management and crisis communication appear to have been problems. Spectators were slow to react to calls for evacuation because of excessive alcohol consumption and the lack of communication from law enforcement about why they were being moved. Crowd management plans must be developed, including a communication protocol among responding agencies as well as effective communication with a large crowd that does not cause unnecessary panic.

- Emergency operators did not know where Centennial Olympic Park was located, resulting in critical time being lost during the response efforts. A preevent briefing should be conducted with representatives from all potential responding agencies in the area to address safety and security plans to familiarize individuals and agencies with the event.

- Law enforcement and response personnel were among the wounded, a circumstance that could have inhibited recovery efforts. Therefore, additional backup resources should be made available. Event managers should develop community and recovery plans to include mutual aid agreements in the event that additional resources are needed.

QUESTIONS TO CONSIDER

1. Identify five potential terrorist targets in your community.
2. Identify potential terrorist groups in your community and their respective motivations.

REFERENCE

Noe, D. (2009). *Eric Rudolph: Serial bomber. The crime library*. Retrieved from www.trutv.com/library/crime/terrorists_spies/terrorists/eric_rudolph/1.html

Key Chapter Points

- The increasing profile of sports on a global scale has resulted in increased exposure to risks that affect all stakeholders in the delivery of sporting and special events.
- Terrorism has been cited as one of the most common risks associated with the security of sport events.

- The five major terrorist threat motivations are political, religious, racial, environmental, and special interest.
- The seven signs of terrorist activity are (1) surveillance, (2) elicitation, (3) test of security, (4) acquiring supplies, (5) suspicious persons, (6) trial run, and (7) deploying assets.
- Crowds need to be managed for several reasons: 1) Large gatherings raise the odds that something will happen, 2) changes in action tend to be slower and more complex, and 3) communications are slower and more complicated than normal.
- The sudden onset of storms, tornadoes, or lightning can pose real problems for facility operators resulting in mass evacuations or shelter in place at stadiums and arenas.
- Legal issues related to event security management include inadequate security, negligent employment practices, and handling disturbances, ejections, and arrests.
- Owners and operators of major sporting and event venues must be aware of risk management strategies and implement industry best practices.
- Sport venues should complete the sport event security aware (SESA) continuous improvement system proposed by the National Center for Spectator Sports Safety and Security (NCS[4]). This includes conducting a risk assessment, training staff, exercising plans, and validating the system.

Application Questions

1. In your own words, define terrorism. Is terrorism something new?
2. What kinds of threats should sport and event managers be aware of? Can you provide any examples from local venues in your city or community?
3. Should sport and event managers, facility operators, and owners be held culpable for sporting and special event incidents?

Activity

Research a sporting event incident and provide a summary of the event details, including the lessons learned by the sporting entity and the sport industry as a whole. Use the case study earlier in the chapter as a guide to present your review.

CHAPTER 2

Leadership and Multiagency Collaboration

CHAPTER GOALS

- Identify the key stakeholders in the sport or event security command group responsible for event security planning efforts.
- Discuss the importance of multiagency collaboration and describe how a sport or event manager can enhance collaborative efforts.
- Discuss teamwork principles and describe characteristics of a mature team.
- Define leadership and compare various leadership styles.
- Describe strategies to build high levels of trust among team members.
- Define transformation leadership and discuss the characteristics of dysfunctional leadership.
- Discuss the problem-solving process and identify attributes of an effective decision maker.
- Discuss the importance of communicating in a crisis and explain various communicating strategies.

The provision of safety and security at sport and special events requires the collaboration and coordination of many individuals and agencies. Sport and event organizations need to cultivate a working relationship among key stakeholders involved in planning and implementing security plans, policies, and protective measures. This chapter highlights the key stakeholders involved in securing events from all-hazard risks. The concept of multiagency collaboration and the importance of establishing partnerships with response agencies are addressed. Teamwork characteristics, communication strategies, crisis leadership, and decision-making principles are covered. Teamwork and leadership management must be established before an incident occurs to ensure effective response and recovery efforts. To develop teamwork concepts, the organization should first identify its command group (CG), which will essentially be responsible for security planning.

Sport and Event Security Command Group

A command group (CG) encompasses key players from multiple agencies that collaborate to provide a safe and secure environment for spectators, athletes or entertainers, and officials. Individuals included in the command group should represent the following key areas: facility management, law enforcement, emergency management, fire and hazardous materials (HAZMAT), and emergency medical services (EMS) (see figure 2.1). This group serves as the core functional group for all security efforts, including managing incidents (chapter 3), assessing risk (chapter 4), conducting training initiatives (chapter 5), implementing protective measures (chapter 6), conducting exercises (chapter 7), and coordinating response, recovery, and continuity plans (chapter 8). Here is an example of the people who might be included in a command group for a university sport event:

- Athletic director or assistant athletic director of operations
- Campus police chief
- Local county emergency management director
- Fire chief
- Medical supervisor

Besides the command group, other entities and people that may play a role in security operations include state and federal government security, public health and safety,

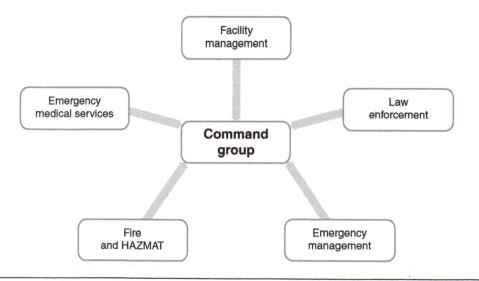

Figure 2.1 Organizations represented in the security command group.

media and public relations, public utilities, contractors, vendors, and temporary employees.

Establishing a multidiscipline team can ensure collaborative planning and response efforts. The group should be established before the sport or event season and meet regularly, especially following events for debriefing discussions and making future recommendations. Input from the command group during the risk assessment process is critical to ensure that all information and intelligence are shared about threats and vulnerabilities inside and outside the organization. The facility manager and security director provide insight into daily operations and event management. Local law enforcement and emergency management provide information on community situations and threats. The command group is the primary group for developing, updating, and implementing security operations. They coordinate efforts before the event and work together on event day in the venue's command center. The command center logistics and operations on event day will be covered in chapter 3.

Multiagency Collaboration

A fully functional group whose members trust and respect each other's role and purpose in the overall security program is critical. Therefore, the command group should advocate the concept of multiagency collaboration. Multiagency refers to all agencies, individuals, and stakeholders who are involved in the various processes of the security management system. Multiagency collaboration is the process that might well determine the degree of effectiveness relative to the level of preparedness, prevention, response, and recovery capabilities in an emergency incident.

Multiagency collaboration is critical because emergency incidents usually require the capabilities of agencies and specialists working effectively together to achieve optimal results (U.S. Department of Homeland Security, 2009c). Collaboration (integration) is a win–win situation for both parties; both parties are fully satisfied with the outcome (DuBrin, 2002). According to Ross (1982), collaboration is one of several processes or behaviors related to conflict resolution. Collaboration aims to satisfy the needs and concerns of all interested parties. Collaborating involves several elements:

1. Acknowledging that there are (or will be) disagreements and conflicts relative to problem solving and challenges faced
2. Identifying and respecting each other's needs, concerns, and objectives
3. Identifying possible alternative solutions and the consequences for each party, having a win–win solution as the desired result
4. Selecting and agreeing on a solution that addresses mutual goals
5. Implementing the agreed-upon solution and evaluating results for continuous improvement

Effective multiagency collaboration is achieved only though the development and practice of high-level trust, communicating directly and clearly, leading, creating positive climates, and proposing a win–win teamwork environment (U.S. Department of Homeland Security, 2009c). Trust is the foundation and relationship skill of effective collaboration and mature teamwork. According to Drucker (1999, p. 72),

> Organizations are no longer built on force but on trust. The existence of trust between people does not necessarily mean they like one another. It means they understand one another. Taking responsibility for relationships is, therefore, an absolute necessity. It is a duty.

Sporting and other special events usually have a designated time and duration, and they normally require a temporary workforce to manage security operations. A challenge arises in that the majority of staff involved are part-time and do not work together on a regular or full-time basis (temporary and volunteer workforce issues are discussed in chapter 7). Therefore, leadership-level staff must put in place training that builds high-level trust and teamwork skills. This approach assures a well-coordinated effort toward disaster planning, prevention, response, and recovery. Without multiagency collaboration capabilities, the security management system will never approximate optimal effectiveness.

Teamwork Principles

Team conflict may arise for various reasons and can be functional or dysfunctional. Functional conflict is good for overall security operations because this type of confrontation enhances organizational performance as disagreements arise on the method to achieve program goals. For example, members of the command group may disagree on the best method to prevent unauthorized persons from accessing restricted areas of the facility; one argues that law enforcement should be present at access points, and another wants to use access control technology with an electronic card entry system. This type of conflict leads to optimal solutions and facilitates positive change and innovation (Ivancevich & Matteson, 1999). Dysfunctional conflict can have negative effects on group dynamics and ultimately the event security management system. Dysfunctional conflict wastes time and places personal interests above the interests of the sport or event organization (Ivancevich & Matteson, 1999). For example, a security supervisor disgruntled with his or her salary may orchestrate a strike among security workforce members. The ability to exercise conflict management is needed in every organization.

Collaboration or interaction is the process by which team members build trust and respect for each other. Transforming a group of individuals into a high-performing team can be a difficult task for everyone involved. Highly effective leaders seem to agree that rigid organizational structures and chains of command are barriers to effective communication and team building. A team can be defined as a group of individuals pulled together to pursue a common purpose. In this particular situation, the common purpose is to develop an effective security management system for sport or special events. Simply forming a team does not guarantee effectiveness or high performance. Certain specific characteristics are common to mature teams as contrasted with immature teams or teams in other stages of development. Mature teams have several characteristics:

- The team discusses the undiscussible.
- Members give up the need to fix or control.
- Interpersonal differences are appreciated.
- A commitment to coexist is established.
- No sides are taken.
- The group is comfortable with decision making.
- A full range of emotions is acceptable.
- Authority is totally decentralized.
- A win–win climate is established.
- The group acknowledges fear of the unknown.

The ultimate goal is to build mature command groups characterized by a sense of community. Peck (1988, p. 58) defined true community as

> a group of individuals who have learned how to communicate honestly with each other, whose relationships go deeper than their masks of composure, and who have developed some significant commitment to rejoice together, mourn together, to delight in each other and make other's conditions their own.

Leocioni (2002) identified issues related to building teamwork or multiagency collaboration. Five potential dysfunctions of a team are absence of trust, fear of conflict, lack of commitment, avoidance of accountability, and inattention to results. The ultimate desired result of multiagency collaboration is a shared mind-set that has been built on trust and respect by a wide variety of interactions, such as briefings, training, and exercises. Those who come together for event security management have learned to work effectively together, sharing power and leadership to optimize protection of the human asset.

Leadership

Leadership is vital in security management, emergency preparedness, prevention, response, and recovery efforts, because a lack of it may result in loss of life, property, and public confidence. Ivancevich and Matteson (1999) defined leadership as "the process of influencing others to facilitate the attainment of organizationally relevant goals" (p. 409). Various definitions of leadership have been developed, but three main themes commonly emerge—people, task, and environment. Bennis (1997) concluded that all leaders share four characteristics: (1) they provide direction (remind staff what is important and that their contributions are making an important difference), (2) they generate trust, (3) they are risk takers and are proactive, and (4) they reinforce the notion that success will be attained. Note that although leadership is a major function of management, it is not the same thing (DuBrin, 2002). Some managers may or may not possess leadership qualities. Kotter (1990) described the key difference between managers and leaders—managers preserve order and consistency, whereas leaders deal with change in a rapidly changing competitive environment. Leaders also formulate a vision for the future and persuade, inspire, and motivate others to follow the direction of the vision. Ivancevich and Matteson (1999) highlighted the following characteristics in leaders and managers:

- **Leaders**: visionary, passionate, creative, flexible, inspiring, innovative, courageous, imaginative, experimental, independent
- **Managers**: rational, consulting, persistent, problem solving, tough minded, analytical, structured, deliberate, authoritative, stabilizing

Among the many theories about leadership and the role of the leader are contingency theory, servant leader, and situational leadership. This text focuses on the situational leadership model and building trust among the sport and event security command group. Situational leadership theory (SLT) has been applied in both large and small business contexts and is endorsed by many managers because of its practicality in dealing with leadership problems on a daily basis (Ivancevich & Matteson, 1999). Paul Hersey and Kenneth Blanchard (1988) developed a practical model—the situational leadership model—to help leaders select the most appropriate leadership behavior given certain situations and knowledge of the followers' developmental and maturity levels.

Readiness is defined as the ability and willingness or confidence of the follower to accomplish a specific task. The concept of readiness is not a characteristic, motive, or trait; it is the ability to accomplish a task (DuBrin, 2002). Two dimensions measure follower readiness—job maturity (technical ability) and physiological maturity (level of self-confidence and self-respect) (Slack & Parent, 2006). The key question is how much the followers know about what the leader is asking them to do, and how willing they are to do it. Leaders can select from three styles of behaviors (see figure 2.2 on page 28). (U.S. Department of Homeland Security, 2009c, p. 103):

- **Directing or telling behavior:** The leader defines roles and tells followers what, where, how, and when to perform specific tasks. They essentially say, "Here's what

I want you to do and here's exactly how I want you to do it." This approach is most appropriate for new employees, for those who have never performed the requested task before, and even sometimes for those who are highly unwilling.

- **Participating or selling behavior**: The leader involves the ideas and concerns of followers. The leaders might say, "Here's what I think we should do. What do you think?" In return, the leader must be willing to listen and clarify. If the leader has a high level of confidence in followers, he or she might say, "Given this situation, what do you think we should do?" This style requires the leader to be self-confident because he or she is now sharing power; the followers' opinions are valued and possibly acted on.

- **Delegating behavior**: The leader provides little instruction or close direction. This behavior is useful when the leader is attempting to influence highly capable and highly willing followers or associates. The leader must be able to make clear assignments and be willing to give the authority to carry out the needed functions as the follower deems necessary. The leader might say, "Here's what needs to be solved or taken care of. You've been there before. I have full confidence in your abilities. If you need me, I'm available to help. Please keep me informed of progress." The caution here is that the leader may think that she or he is delegating but in fact expects the follower to carry out the tasks in a particular way (which is really a directing or telling style).

Members of the command group must be capable of relating effectively to those whom they supervise or report to in security operational efforts, such as part-time employees and volunteers, vendors, outsourced personnel, peers, and upper management. The goal is to earn the respect and confidence of peers and superiors in advance so that they seek assistance during times of crisis. Suppose that a sport or event security manager determines that his or her temporary workforce (checkers, ticket takers, ushers) has limited training and is not familiar with venue policies. These employees would have lower readiness to take charge, and the security manager would exercise a telling style of leadership to provide specific instructions and closely monitor performance. At the other end of the spectrum, for employees (fellow members of the command group) who are considered self-sufficient or provide an area of expertise, the security manager would exercise a delegating style of leadership because the employee would be considered to have higher readiness.

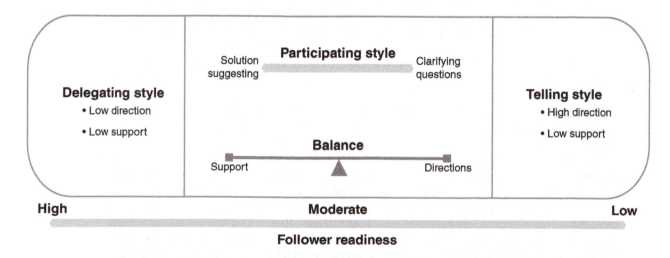

Figure 2.2 A continuum showing three types of leadership behavior—telling, participating, and delegating. These approaches vary in degree of direction and support and might be more or less appropriate depending on the employee and the task.

Reprinted from U.S. Department of Homeland Security, 2009, *Sport event risk management*.

Building Trust

The issue of trust and building trust among the command group and subsidiary security stakeholders is important. Trustworthiness is essential to leadership effectiveness. It is exhibited through behavioral integrity, that is, being reliable and predictable, and being honest and keeping promises (DuBrin, 2002). Trust is a state of mind; therefore, it develops not from what people say, but from what they do. To build trust, leaders must communicate honestly; respect the knowledge, skills, and abilities of others; maintain confidentiality; and keep interactions unguarded (Federal Emergency Management Agency, 2005a).

Trust is the core of leadership because followers must trust their leaders. Being able to facilitate change in an organization also requires a level of trust. Mutual trust must be present among all stakeholders. The benefits of creating a high-level trust environment include commitment and loyalty to the organization, program, or project and willingness to take action to achieve goals and accept change if necessary. A leader in security management has a complex role to build trust at multiple levels by (1) leading subordinates; (2) developing relationships with government agencies to ensure coordinated response in time of crisis; (3) working with other agencies in joint preparedness, response, recovery, and mitigation efforts, including threat and vulnerability analysis, planning exercises, and establishing mutual aid agreements; and (4) developing relationships with the media to ensure effective cooperation in public education and warning communications (Federal Emergency Management Agency, 2005a). Relationships among the event command group, government officials, media, and the public will affect the ability to manage an event incident successfully, and these relationships are built on a foundation of trust. Specific trust-enhancing behaviors are highlighted in the sidebar.

Trust-reducing behaviors may include concealing real motives, falsifying information, controlling and dominating, not discussing and meeting others' expectations,

Trust-Enhancing Behaviors

Do What You Say

- Establish boundaries
- Delegate appropriately
- Honor agreements
- Be consistent
- Meet expectations

Respect People's Knowledge, Skills, and Abilities

- Acknowledge their abilities
- Allow them to use their talents
- Reduce control; don't micromanage
- Include others on decisions by seeking their input
- Provide the resources they need to get the job done right

Demonstrate Unguarded Interactions

- Share information
- Be truthful
- Admit mistakes
- Give and receive constructive feedback
- Maintain confidentiality

Reference: Federal Emergency Management Agency. (2005). Building and rebuilding trust. In *Leadership and influence: Independent study*, p. 4.6.

accepting credit for the work of others, and not honoring agreements. If trust levels need to be restored, leaders should consider six steps to assist in recovering from damaged trust: (1) accept personal responsibility for actions, (2) publically acknowledge that they made a mistake, (3) apologize, (4) take action to deal with the consequences of a mistake, (5) make amends, (6) pay attention to those affected, ask for feedback, and be open to constructive criticism (Federal Emergency Management Agency, 2005a).

Transformative Leadership

Building and nurturing trust takes thinking and acting from a transformational leadership perspective (Federal Emergency Management Agency, 2005a, p. 4.7). Transformational leaders influence major changes in the attitudes and assumptions of staff members and are capable of building commitment for major changes in the organization's objectives and strategies (Yukl, 2002). Changes in organizational processes and structure may include downsizing, right sizing, reengineering, or refocusing. The transformational leader can develop new visions for the firm and inspire followers to exceed expectations in attaining those new visions (Chelladurai, 2006). Transformational leaders have several characteristics (DuBrin, 2002):

- **Vision**: communicates a clear and positive vision of the future to employees regarding safety and security
- **Staff development**: treats staff as individuals and supports and encourages their development in the workplace and in the area of safety and security
- **Supportive leadership**: provides encouragement and recognition to staff when it is due
- **Empowerment**: fosters trust, involvement, and cooperation among safety and security team members
- **Innovative thinking**: encourages thinking about safety and security problems in new ways
- **Lead by example**: expresses clearly personal values and practices what she or he preaches
- **Charisma**: instills pride and respect in others and inspires staff to be highly competent

According to DuBrin (2002), "A major contributing factor to transformational leadership is charisma, the ability to lead others based on personal charm, magnetism, inspiration, and emotion." (p. 194). A charismatic leader may be more successful in influencing follower behavior than a leader who does not have the trait that inspires support and acceptance (Griffin & Moorhead, 1986).

Charismatic leaders exude several key characteristics, which include their ability to establish an organizational vision (or lofty goal), communicate effectively, inspire trust, be energetic, and manage impressions adeptly. Charismatic leaders provide vision to the organization that extends beyond organizational goals. They are effective communicators and formulate achievable dreams and vision for the future. They usually use metaphors to inspire followers. Inspiring trust is also critical to getting followers to share their vision and make sacrifices upfront with the potential for great success (Conger & Kanungo, 1998; Gardner & Avolio, 1998).

Dysfunctional Leadership

According to Med Yones (2009) at the International Institute of Management, "Leadership is the most important competitive advantage of a company, not technology, finance, operations or anything else. . . . It is the most important asset of the company and can be its worst liability" (p. 1). Dysfunctional leadership includes several symptoms (Plochg Business Psychology Consulting, 2009; Yones, 2009):

- **Conflict avoidance**: Some managers need to be liked and approved of so they are unable or unwilling to make difficult decisions that might threaten their acceptance by others.
- **Micromanagement**: Managers may become detail oriented and controlling. Lacking trust in the capabilities of others has a negative effect on organizational processes and ruins morale.
- **Manic executives**: Some managers are possessed with boundless energy and push themselves and others to the limit. They are so hyperactive that they don't know what they are doing wrong.
- **Inaccessibility of leadership**: Some managers have no time for others, are unapproachable, or may hide behind secretaries, assistants, and closed-door policies.
- **Game players**: Managers may talk and think only about themselves and fail to be attentive when others talk. They refuse to let subordinates shine and use and abuse them rather than help them grow and develop. Game players experience high turnover among their employees.
- **No 360-degree feedback**: Managers may offer limited or no performance feedback.
- **Personal agendas**: Recruitment and promotion may be based on internal politics. For example, friends may be hired to guarantee personal loyalty at the expense of high-performing and more qualified candidates.
- **Inefficient use of resources**: Budgets may be allocated based on favoritism rather than business needs.

Organizations need to employ managers who do not practice the dysfunctional methods of leadership just described. Safety and security leaders should encourage multiagency collaboration among all stakeholders involved in the operation and response efforts of an event. Effective collaboration requires open communication, efficient use of resources, and trusting others to assume designated responsibilities during an emergency.

Problem Solving and Decision Making

The event command group needs to make sound, timely decisions during an emergency incident. Good problem-solving and decision-making skills can prevent catastrophic situations and enhance recovery processes. The reverse is also true; poor or untimely decisions can exacerbate the situation, causing further harm or damage. Problem solving involves analyzing a situation and generating, implementing, and evaluating solutions. Decision making is a mechanism for making choices at each stage of the problem-solving process (Federal Emergency Management Agency, 2005e).

Decisions can be categorized as either programmed or nonprogrammed. Programmed decisions are repetitive and routine and are made based on policies and experience (day-to-day decisions). Nonprogrammed decisions are new and unique and have no preestablished guidelines or clear alternatives to direct decision making (Ivancevich & Matteson, 1999). Such decisions may need to be made in response to an event incident, such as fans rushing the field. Effective decision makers make decisions with competence and confidence, and most of their decisions work out right (Federal Emergency Management Agency, 2005d). Attributes of an effective decision maker are presented in table 2.1 on page 32.

Table 2.1 Attributes of an Effective Decision Maker

Attribute	Description
Knowledge	Is well informed and has a deep understanding of all factors
Initiative	Assumes responsibility for the entire decision-making process from start to finish
Advice seeking	Seeks help from others when needed
Selectivity	Seeks pertinent information and avoids being distracted by extraneous facts
Comprehensiveness	Considers all possible alternatives before making a choice
Currency	Considers current conditions and takes advantage of opportunities that exist
Flexibility	Remains open minded about new concepts and ideas and is willing to change or try a different approach
Good judgment	Exercises judgment in considering factors related to the situation
Calculated risk taking	Weighs risks of various alternatives and accepts consequences, whether positive or negative
Self-knowledge	Knows own abilities, biases, and limitations

Reprinted from Federal Emergency Management Agency, 2005, Identifying decision-making styles and attributes.

The sport or event organization and its event command group should have developed standard operating procedures (SOPs) or other procedural documents for security operations (discussed further in chapter 6). These documents provide the foundation for decision making during a time of crisis. These kinds of documents will answer many questions upfront, such as the following: (1) who is responsible for what and who has the authority to make executive decisions? (2) what agencies should be used during incident response and recovery? (3) what is the communication protocol? (4) under what conditions is an evacuation issued? and (5) what provisions are in place for medical emergencies requiring mass care (Federal Emergency Management Agency, 2005e).

Obviously, there are advantages to having these documents in place and deciding on protocol before an incident rather than in the midst of an emergency. Decisions made under normal conditions can be deliberated without stress factors associated with a crisis and can use a group process to gather input from all stakeholders to achieve a consensus decision. This process also allows the group to consider all options, contingencies, and responses. Planning gives the group time to obtain the commitment of key stakeholders and to train and exercise the plan (Federal Emergency Management Agency, 2005e). Regardless of the types of decisions that will be needed to solve the problem (daily versus critical and time sensitive), a standard problem-solving model should be followed (see figure 2.3).

Problem identification is the most critical step in the problem-solving process because all subsequent steps depend on how one defines the problem. "A problem is a situation or condition of people or the organization that will exist in the future, and that is considered undesirable by members of the organization" (Federal Emergency Management Agency, 2005e, p. 2.13). Exploring alternatives involves generating and evaluating alternatives. Techniques for generating alternatives include brainstorming (individually and as a group), surveys, and discussion groups. After alternatives have

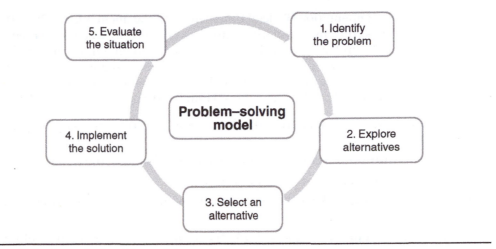

Figure 2.3   A standard problem-solving model.

Reprinted from Federal Emergency Management Agency, 2005, The decision-making process.

been identified they must be evaluated. Criteria for evaluating alternatives involves identifying constraints (e.g., limited equipment, legal restrictions, cost restrictions, human resources constraints, or time requirements), determining appropriateness, verifying adequacy, evaluating effectiveness, and identifying possible side effects. At this point an alternative (solution) should be selected, ideally the one with the most advantages and fewest restrictions. Selection of a solution will ultimately be governed by political, safety, financial, environmental, and ethical factors. The next step in the process is to implement the chosen solution, which requires an action plan, objectives, and needed resources. The final step in the problem-solving process is to evaluate the situation by monitoring progress and evaluating results (Federal Emergency Management Agency, 2005e).

For example, a stadium operator identifies a problem—the need for a new video surveillance system to assist in the identification of criminal behavior and disorderly fan conduct in the stands. Resolving this issue requires identifying alternatives by researching video surveillance companies that offer various packages and price structures. Management has provided only a limited budget to acquire new technology; therefore, the options available to the operator are restricted. The security team agrees that they need new cameras at the points of ingress and egress. Once identified, these constraints and priorities become the criteria for selecting an alternative. Potential technologies are identified, and members of the safety and security team conduct a brainstorming and evaluation session to ensure that they choose the most appropriate technology for their immediate purposes.

The sport or event command group is composed of representatives from various agencies. The goal of problem solving and decision making in a collaborative environment is to assure that all members have input and can envision themselves a part of agreed-upon policies and procedures, thereby assuring ownership. This time-consuming and difficult process requires committed team players who trust each other, are willing to share power and control, and are willing to put the well-being of the team above their own self-interest.

Blake and Mouton (1964) recommended making decisions by using consensus as a major component of team management. A consensus decision is defined by the Atlanta Consulting Group (2002) as one in which agreement on the decision is substantial (but not necessarily unanimous). The group reaches consensus status when all members can say that their personal views and ideas have been listened to and considered, that they have openly listened to and considered the ideas and views of others, and finally that they believe they can accept and support the decision and work toward its implementation (Federal Emergency Management Agency, 2005d). Voting is often labeled as consensus, but true consensus occurs only when team members talk things through, understand the issues, and reach agreement. Groups make decisions by a number of procedures, but the consensus model seems to be consistent in producing the most effective results. Listed here are some of the principles of consensus decision making (U.S. Department of Homeland Security, 2009c, p. 106):

- **Plan the session**: Establish ground rules of how the group is going to work together.
- **Inventory group resources**: What does each party bring to the table?
- **Stand up for convictions**: It's OK to disagree.
- **Don't agree for the sake of agreement**: Resolving conflict situations can produce innovative results.
- **Don't argue to win as an individual**: Trying to win an argument is often detrimental to reaching effective group decisions.
- **Listen for understanding**: Empathetic listening builds trust.
- **Be willing to change your mind**: When confronted with strong evidence and logic, be open minded.
- **Regulate participation**: Make sure that all members are heard. Quiet members tend not to speak up or may feel intimidated.
- **Explore all alternatives**: Use brainstorming to explore all possible alternatives.
- **Integrate facts, logic, and intuition**: The best results flow from an integration of facts, logic, and intuition based on experience.

The command group is composed of highly trained specialists, many of whom do not work together on a regular or full-time basis. Therefore, orientation activities and meetings should be scheduled so that members can build trust and respect for each other's specialties, develop plans, and eventually exercise those plans. Emergency responders all seem to agree that the time to pass out business cards is not when responding to an incident!

Communication and Information Sharing

Communication, or lack thereof, consistently emerges as a major area for improvement in organizations. Leaders and managers are responsible for planning, organizing, and controlling functions. These functions require giving and receiving instructions to complete tasks as expected. When questioned, managers agree that a major part of their time is spent giving instructions, yet when asked whether associates complete assignments as desired, the answer is a resounding "Never" (U.S. Department of Homeland Security, 2009c). Something is obviously missing between the sending of information, the accurate receipt of that information, and the correct implementation of the requested tasks.

Effective communication requires active listening, understanding of different communication styles, and creating a positive communication climate. Active listening involves several steps. The first is to listen and concentrate on the speaker. The listener then uses her or his imagination to enter the speaker's situation and try to imagine the speaker's frame of reference and point of view. Also, the listener should observe the speaker's vocal inflection, enthusiasm or lack thereof, and style of delivery. The listener should listen without interruption, use paraphrasing or clarifying questions to confirm that she or he received the intended message, and finally provide feedback to the speaker. Numerous variables are involved in the communication process, such as differences between the sender and receiver, differences in communication styles, difference in previous experiences, and cultural differences (Federal Emergency Management Agency, 2005b).

Normal day-to-day communications and emergency communications differ. Emergency information is vitally important and can mean the difference between life and death, or it can provide the calm reassurance that response and recovery efforts are underway. Timelines are essential because the rumor mill will begin and speculation may override accurate information that needs to be disseminated. Unfortunately, people find it difficult to hear messages during an emergency because of stress or change of routine (Federal Emergency Management Agency, 2005c). Additionally, many parties respond to an emergency, so information shared with the public should be consistent and relay the same intended message. When communicating in a crisis, the speaker should

- word the message precisely;
- avoid jargon, codes, or acronyms;
- use common names for all personnel and facilities;
- omit unnecessary information;
- speak in sync with other agencies; and
- keep messages consistent across all media outlets.

For example, a bomb threat was received at a sport venue, and local law enforcement deemed the threat credible. A search ensued within the venue to locate a suspicious package. Within 10 minutes a backpack containing explosive devices was located. Management decided to conduct a full evacuation of the venue. The following public address announcement was released: "Ladies and gentlemen, may I have your attention: Officials have chosen to suspend play on the field and are implementing a full evacuation of the stadium. Please remain calm and exit the venue as directed by officers and venue staff." This announcement is very clear, concise, and does not panic the fans by offering explicit directions to exit the venue. Identifying the problem to the public through such an announcement could potentially cause mass chaos or hysteria which may lead to further injury or harm.

Types of communication methods are highlighted in table 2.2. The most effective communication tool is one that reaches the intended target audience in a timely manner when they need it most, delivers the message reliably, enhances comprehension of the message content, and can be accessed within resource limitations.

Table 2.2   Types of Communication

Type of communication	Examples
Emergency alert system (EAS)	An established communication system that warns of impending dangers. All stakeholders should be aware of warning tones, crawling messages across TV screens, cable TV override, and National Oceanic and Atmospheric Administration (NOAA) weather radio.
Oral communication	Briefings, phone conversations, public speeches, on-air interviews, radio or TV public service announcements (PSA).
Print communication	Fax, e-mail, public notice, fact sheet or flier, press release, or feature article. **Documentation can always be consulted in the future, be reviewed and revised before delivery, and exist independent of human memory.*

Reprinted from Federal Emergency Management Agency, 2005, Communicating in an emergency.

Technology is not a communication solution, but the right technology can support and enhance communication capabilities (discussed further in chapter 6). Most often a combination of methods is used to deliver a message. The event command group should consider how they issue emergency communications, what areas of emergency communications can be improved, what steps need to be taken to improve communications, and whether they should collaborate with other agencies in this effort (Federal Emergency Management Agency, 2005c).

After basic communication skills are mastered, the ways of sharing critical information must be focused on. What is the chain of command for communication? Does information flow through a preset protocol (during day-to-day activities) or through an all-channel network to preestablished personnel (during an incident response). Communication climate is also a major concern in accurate sharing of information. "Communication climate can be defined as the internal environment of information exchange among people through an organization's formal and informal networks" (Buchholz, 2001, p.1). The climate is an intangible that determines the effectiveness of individuals and agencies relative to teamwork and collaboration. Communication climate can be based on what we say and do; therefore, it can be managed. Negative behavior (e.g., lack of full disclosure, keeping secrets, or rudeness) needs to be minimized. The communication climate is considered open when information flows freely and when employees feel comfortable expressing opinions, voicing complaints, and offering suggestions to management. An open communication climate has three distinct characteristics: It is supportive, participative, and trusting (Buchholz, 2001).

In supportive environments, employees communicate information to supervisors without hesitation, knowing that the information will be accepted, whether good or bad. For example, the best suggestions for improving plans, policies, and processes come from employees who work daily on the front line of event security operations, such as ticket takers, ushers, and parking attendants. These employees have valuable information that they should share with decision makers. "Employees know they are valued participants when their suggestions are implemented, their questions answered, and their concerns recognized" (Buchholz, 2001, p.2). All parties involved in exchanging information must be honest and convey accurate information. This approach ultimately establishes creditability and trust. Employees need to trust and believe their information sources if they are to be effective (Buchholz, 2001). A security director with a reputation for lying, deceit, or manipulation of the facts will have a difficult job of communicating to employees. For example, at weekly security debriefing meetings, the staff may hear contradictory information from the director of security operations about plans, decisions, or salary. In this case, employees are likely to dismiss all information because they do not know what to believe.

Many stories have been told about the inability of incident command teams to communicate in emergencies because of lack of basic skills or incompatible equipment. All parties need to work to alleviate this problem. In times of crisis, all parties must be trained and possess high levels of communication skills so that they can send, receive, and understand all information (U.S. Department of Homeland Security, 2009c). The World Trade Center attack in 2001 provides a good example. Soon after the first plane struck the north tower, New York City Office of Emergency Management (OEM) directed resources to the area. The OEM building, however, was damaged and evacuated when the north tower eventually collapsed resulting in limited to no communication capabilities. Command and control had to be established elsewhere.

The Department of Homeland Security (DHS) Office of Intelligence and Analysis has created state and local fusion centers to share information and intelligence within their communities. Sport and event organizations in the United States should be familiar with their state or local fusion center representatives because this type of support can assist in gathering information pertaining to potential threats or issues at upcoming events. This support is tailored to the unique needs of the locality and serves to help the flow of classified and unclassified information, provide expertise, coordinate with local law enforcement and other agencies, and provide local awareness and access. As of July 2009, there were 72 designated fusion centers in the United States (U.S. Department of Homeland Security, 2009d).

CASE STUDY

Building Multiagency Collaboration

Given the different world that emerged after 9/11, sport and event organizations have general concerns about their capability to respond effectively to a disaster incident, either natural or manmade, that occurs during an event. Coordinating the effort among numerous individuals and agencies—event coordinators, emergency management, law enforcement, fire, hazardous materials, EMS—is a critical challenge. Ways and means must be developed to convene all these key stakeholders for orientation meetings, training, and exercises before, during, and after events and seasons. Sporting events and other special events present a unique challenge relative to safety and security management because most of the workforce is part time, some may be volunteers, and others may be outsourced.

Xcell Sports is responsible for operations management of a major sporting venue that has a seating capacity of 40,000 for multiple events. Another season is approaching, and planning to improve the security management system is proceeding. Full-capacity crowds normally attend major events, of which about 80 are scheduled annually. The director of event operations has three full-time staff assistants but must depend heavily on a part-time and outsourced workforce for security operations.

Agencies used for emergency response include the local police department for off-duty officers, the local fire department, local jurisdiction emergency management, and EMS (the cost for off-duty personnel is between $30 and $50 per hour and thus is a major budget concern). Xcell has contracted with an external security company, PRE-vent, to provide ticket takers, bag checkers, ushers, and parking attendants (the hourly rate for these employees is $10 per hour and is another budget consideration). Another major consideration is that Xcell is legally responsible for assuring the safety and security of fans, players, performers, coaches, officials, and others.

Given the number expected to attend an event and the number of event staff needed (based on available standards and best practices), a budget of $4,000 is approved for hiring off-duty certified law enforcement agency (LEA) officers for security management at the event. The event director has calculated that this figure is about half of what is needed for full-venue coverage, so he or she must set priorities to assure protection of critical areas in and around the venue. Certified off-duty LEAs are positioned at critical points around the venue to provide preventive support and response capability should potential criminal behavior be observed. Examples of places where LEAs would be stationed are gates and field or court access that needs to be controlled, as well as locations where they can be called on by event staff should they be needed to deal with an incident (fights, overindulgence with alcohol, threats, or any inappropriate behavior that is getting out of control).

Positive relations among numerous individuals and agencies should be continually developed and nurtured. The challenge becomes developing a process to orient and train representatives from stakeholder agencies relative to teamwork capabilities for implementing incident command systems (ICS) should an incident occur. A sport event

(continued)

Case Study   *(continued)*

is categorized as a special event that has unique characteristics, such as the hiring of a part-time work force during a specific period. Therefore, many of the staff do not work together on a day-to-day basis and may not even know each other. And if they know each other, across multiple agencies and institutions, they may not respect or like each other!

People required to work together to implement an ICS may also have little training in common. For example, law enforcement officers are trained to respond to criminal behavior, firefighters to fires and rescue operations, emergency management to natural disasters, and so on. Given this specialized nature of training and capabilities, the challenge of security management is to build teamwork capabilities that assures the protection of critical assets—facilities and infrastructure, equipment, and, most important, the human asset. Responders are highly skilled in their specialties but often have received little or no training in collaborative capabilities.

In this case the director of operations has attended training and visited some sport venues similar to Xcell's. To assure the building and continuous improvement of teamwork and collaboration, she took the following actions:

- Scheduled preevent breakfast or lunch meetings to get everyone together to network ("meet and greet"). These interactions help build trust and respect.
- Planned and implemented off-season workshops or training sessions for key supervisors to assist in building leadership and collaboration capabilities.
- Developed and implemented training programs for the various levels of staff involved in the security management system.

Training was implemented for three levels of staff:

1. **Top management and administration**: These people are responsible for budget approval and decisions regarding cancellations, rescheduling, media briefings, and so forth.
2. **Supervisors**: These event staff have specific area assignments and include ticket takers, bag checkers, ushers, parking attendants, traffic control, field and court access, and so forth (off-duty LEA, fire, HAZMAT, and EMS would be included in supervisory training and orientation). Some persons designated as supervisor of concessions and vendors would also be in this category.
3. **Line staff**: These staff members are part-time hourly employees who generally have a specific assignment such as ticket taker at gate 6 or usher for section C. Training programs for the expanded event staff targeted the following:
   - Awareness of rules, policies, and regulations of the venue
   - Strategies used for credentialing
   - Communication system, specifically the procedure for reporting something or someone suspicious
   - Limits of authority and when and how to call for assistance in case of emergency
   - Appropriate behavior, dress, and focus of attention for the specific assignment
   - Orientation to any expected problems, such as threats received, gang activity, weather reports, and so on
   - Evacuation plan and procedures and role in the process

The time available for training is always limited, particularly for part-time employees, so the training program had to focus on the most critical knowledge needed for the specific assignment.

LESSONS LEARNED

- There was a need for improvement in collaboration and teamwork capabilities among all stakeholders involved in safety and security operations.
- Mature teamwork does not simply show up; rather, it is based on well-planned and coordinated efforts.
- The director of operations (sometimes an associate athletic director or a designated venue coordinator) should carefully calculate the number of event staff needed to cover an event based on experience and expected attendance and then project a budget needed to cover safety and security management. If the full budget needed is not available, then priorities must be determined to cover and protect as well as possible given limited resources.

QUESTIONS TO CONSIDER

1. How can the director of operations assure that all stakeholders involved in safety and security operations know each other and understand the importance of building trust and teamwork?
2. What trust- and team-building activities can the director implement or conduct at the scheduled sessions to assure development of effective multiagency collaboration capabilities?

Key Chapter Points

- The provision of safety and security at sporting events requires the collaboration and coordination of many individuals and agencies.
- The sport or event organization should identify a command group (CG) that will be responsible for security planning and include representatives of facility management, law enforcement, emergency management, fire and hazardous materials (HAZMAT), and emergency medical services (EMS).
- Multiagency collaboration is critical because emergency incidents usually require the capabilities of agencies and specialists working together effectively to achieve optimal results. Effective multiagency collaboration is achieved only though developing and practicing high-level trust, communicating directly and clearly, leading, creating a positive climate, and proposing a win–win teamwork environment.
- Leadership is vital in security management, emergency preparedness, prevention, response, and recovery efforts. The lack of it may result in loss of life, property, and public confidence.
- The situational leadership model helps leaders select the most appropriate leadership behavior given certain situations and the followers' developmental and maturity levels. Leaders can select from three styles of behaviors: directing (or telling), participating (or selling), and delegating.
- The benefits of creating a high-level trust environment include commitment and loyalty to the organization, program, or project and willingness to take actions to achieve goals and accept change if necessary.
- The event command group must be able to make sound, timely decisions during an emergency incident. Good problem-solving and decision-making skills can prevent the occurrence of catastrophic situations and enhance recovery processes.

- Regardless of the type of decision (daily versus critical, time sensitive), a standard problem-solving model should be followed: (1) identify the problem, (2) explore alternatives, (3) select the alternative, (4) implement the solution, and (5) evaluate the situation.

- Effective communication requires active listening, understanding of different communication styles, and creating a positive communication climate.

- The most effective communication tool is one that reaches the intended target audience in a timely manner, delivers the message reliably, enhances comprehension of the message content, and can be accessed within resource limitations.

Application Questions

1. Discuss the role of the event command group and the importance of multi-agency collaboration.

2. How does leadership and trust affect collaborative efforts in security planning?

3. How would a leader build a high-level trust environment?

4. Discuss the problem-solving and decision-making process.

Activity

Complete the worksheet (U.S. Department of Homeland Security, 2009c) for a person whom you trust in your work environment. When you are done, reflect on how that level of trust is established and reinforced.

Personal Worksheet: Determining the Profile of a High-Level Trust Person in Your Work Environment

Someone whom I really trust at a high level is _____.

Name

Characteristics and behaviors

I trust this person because he or she is

_____

_____

_____

_____

_____

He or she behaves toward me in the following manner:

_____

_____

_____

_____

_____

From S. Hall, W. Cooper, L. Marciani, and J. McGee, 2012, *Security management for sports and special events* (Champaign, IL: Human Kinetics).

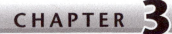

CHAPTER 3

Incident Management Systems

CHAPTER GOALS

- Examine the U.S. Department of Homeland Security and its major strategic goals.
- Discuss the National Incident Management System and National Response Framework.
- Understand the importance of coordinated response activities by multiple agencies.
- Examine the Incident Command System and Unified Command Structure.
- Understand the development of an incident command post (stadium command center).

Building on principles discussed in chapter 2, the multiagency sport or event security command group must be familiar with standard incident management strategies. This chapter provides information on the U.S. Department of Homeland Security and its policies directed toward prevention, preparedness, response, and recovery efforts from all-hazard emergency incidents. In particular, the National Incident Management System (NIMS), Incident Command System (ICS), and National Response Framework (NRF) provide a foundation of common principles for government agencies, nongovernmental agencies, private sector, and emergency responders in their crisis preparations.

Safety and security concerns are not unique to the United States. Countries across all continents have created, developed, and maintained safety and security organizations, policies, and procedures to address security issues and enhance the safety of their citizens. A section on international policies and procedures is provided in this chapter. Although specific laws and procedures vary from country to country, the principles of coordination between venue security staff and other responders, such as law enforcement, emergency medical services, and fire departments are important to all sport and special event venues. The need to coordinate among various jurisdictions and the involvement of different levels of response and resources, depending on the severity of the incident, are also principles that are applicable both in and outside the United States.

United States Department of Homeland Security

On November 25, 2002, President George W. Bush signed the Homeland Security Act of 2002 in an effort to defeat terrorism after the tragic events of 9/11. The act established the country's 15th cabinet-level department, the Department of Homeland Security (DHS), which consolidated 22 existing entities with homeland security missions (U.S. Department of Homeland Security, 2002). For the first time a single federal department had as its primary mission protecting the United States from all hazards, natural and manmade. The vital mission to secure the nation from many threats resulted in five main areas of responsibility: (1) guard against terrorism, (2) secure borders, (3) enforce immigration laws, (4) improve readiness for, response to, and recovery from disasters, and (5) mature and unify the department (U.S. Department of Homeland Security, 2009a). The department's strategic goals include the following (U.S. Department of Homeland Security, 2004):

1. **Awareness**: Identify and understand threats, assess vulnerabilities, determine potential impacts, and disseminate timely information to our homeland security partners and American public.
2. **Prevention**: Detect, deter, and mitigate threats to our homeland.
3. **Protection**: Safeguard our people and their freedoms, critical infrastructure, property, and the economy of our nation from acts of terrorism, natural disasters, or other emergencies.
4. **Response**: Lead, manage, and coordinate the national response to acts of terrorism, natural disasters, or other emergencies.
5. **Recovery**: Lead national, state, local, and private sector efforts to restore services and rebuild communities after acts of terrorism, natural disasters, or other emergencies.
6. **Service**: Serve the public effectively by facilitating lawful trade, travel, and immigration.
7. **Organizational excellence**: Value our most important resource, our people. Create a culture that promotes a common identity, innovation, mutual respect, accountability, and teamwork to achieve efficiencies, effectiveness, and operational synergies.

The 9/11 attacks illustrated the need for government agencies, nongovernmental agencies, and private sector entities to prepare for, respond to, and recover from all-hazard emergencies that may exceed the capabilities of a single entity (Federal Emergency Management Agency, 2005e). Catastrophic events may require a unified and coordinated national approach to planning. To address this need, President George W. Bush issued a series of Homeland Security Presidential Directives (HSPDs) that established a common approach to preparedness and response. Two HSPDs of particular interest to sport and event organizations provide guidance to security command groups in their crisis preparation (U.S. Department of Homeland Security, 2009b):

- **HSPD-5—Management of Domestic Incidents**: Enhances the ability of the United States to manage domestic incidents by establishing a single, comprehensive National Incident Management System (NIMS). NIMS is a template for emergency response operations that can be applied to a wide variety of incidents. The goal is to ensure that all levels of government have the capability to work efficiently together to prevent, prepare for, and respond to all-hazard incidents. The National Response Framework (NRF), also a part of HSPD-5, prescribes roles and structures for various levels of government and nongovernmental organizations when responding to an incident.

- **HSPD-8—National Preparedness**: Identifies steps for improved coordination in response to terrorist incidents, major disasters, and other emergencies by establishing mechanisms for improved delivery of federal assistance to local governments and outlining actions to strengthen capabilities.

HSPDs provide a common approach to national incident management. To provide for the safety of people, facilities, and programs, sport and event programs must be involved in crisis response planning, and this effort must be coordinated with local, regional, state, and federal officials. Effective emergency response requires that personnel perform roles and responsibilities designed to address specific functions during a crisis (U.S. Department of Homeland Security, 2009c).

National Incident Management System Overview

On February 28, 2003, the president issued HSPD-5, which directs the secretary of homeland security to develop and administer the National Incident Management System (NIMS). According to HSPD-5 (U.S. Department of Homeland Security, 2008b, p. 1):

> The National Incident Management System (NIMS) provides a systematic, proactive approach to guide departments and agencies at all levels of government, nongovernmental organizations, and the private sector to work seamlessly to prevent, protect against, respond to, recover from, and mitigate the effects of incidents, regardless of cause, size, location, or complexity, in order to reduce the loss of life and property and harm to the environment. NIMS works hand in hand with the National Response Framework (NRF). NIMS provides the template for the management of incidents, whereas the NRF provides the structure and mechanisms for national-level policy for incident management.

The NIMS provides the nation's first responders and agencies with the same foundation for a variety of domestic incident management activities regardless of cause, size, or complexity. Incidents may include terrorist attacks, natural disasters, or other emergencies. Five major components make up this systems approach (see figure 3.1 on page 46).

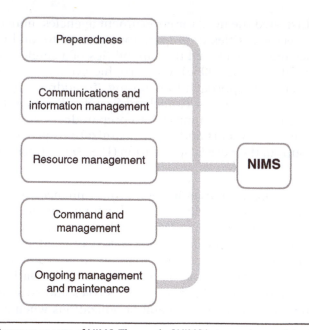

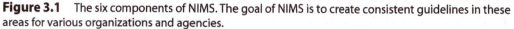

Figure 3.1   The six components of NIMS. The goal of NIMS is to create consistent guidelines in these areas for various organizations and agencies.

The components of NIMS are adaptable to any situation, from routine, local incidents to incidents requiring the activation of interstate mutual aid to those requiring a coordinated Federal response, whether planned (e.g., major sporting or community events), notice (e.g., hurricane) or no-notice (e.g., earthquake). (U.S. Department of Homeland Security, 2008b, p. 6)

NIMS is a complex system and a work in progress for law enforcement, emergency management, and other responding government agencies. In case of a major incident at a sport or other event, these agencies will likely take control of the incident. Even so, sport and event facility managers should be familiar with the overall components of NIMS. The command group (CG) specific to a sport event or venue (described in chapter 2) must understand the systems approach so that they can plan, respond, and communicate during an incident. The following excerpt from the NIMS 2008 guideline (p. 7) provides a synopsis of each major component. A detailed review of each component is provided in the NIMS guideline and can be accessed at www.fema.gov/pdf/emergency/nims/NIMS_core.pdf.

Preparedness: Effective emergency management and incident response activities begin with a host of preparedness activities conducted on an ongoing basis, in advance of any potential incident. Preparedness involves an integrated combination of assessment; planning; procedures and protocols; training and exercises; personnel qualifications, licensure, and certification; equipment certification; and evaluation and revision.

Communications and Information Management: Emergency management and incident response activities rely on communications and information systems that provide a common operating picture to all command and coordination sites. NIMS describes the requirements necessary for a standardized framework for communications and emphasizes the need for a common operating picture. This component is based on the concepts of interoperability, reliability, scalability, and portability, as well as the resiliency and redundancy of communications and information systems.

Resource Management: Resources (such as personnel, equipment, or supplies) are needed to support critical incident objectives. The flow of resources must be fluid and adaptable to the requirements of the incident. NIMS defines standardized mechanisms and establishes the resource management process to identify requirements, order and acquire, mobilize, track and report, recover and demobilize, reimburse, and inventory resources.

Command and Management: The Command and Management component of NIMS is designed to enable effective and efficient incident management and coordination by providing a flexible, standardized incident management structure. The structure is based on three key organizational constructs: the Incident Command System, Multiagency Coordination Systems, and Public Information.

Ongoing Management and Maintenance: Within the auspices of Ongoing Management and Maintenance, there are two components: the NIC and Supporting Technologies.

(1) National Integration Center: Homeland Security Presidential Directive 5 required the secretary of homeland security to establish a mechanism for ensuring the ongoing management and maintenance of NIMS, including regular consultation with other federal departments and agencies; state, tribal, and local stakeholders; and NGOs and the private sector. The NIC provides strategic direction, oversight, and coordination of NIMS and supports both routine maintenance and the continuous refinement of NIMS and its components. The NIC oversees the program and coordinates with federal, state, tribal, and local partners in the development of compliance criteria and implementation activities. It provides guidance and support to jurisdictions and emergency management and response personnel and their affiliated organizations as they adopt or, consistent with their status, are encouraged to adopt the system. The NIC also oversees and coordinates the publication of NIMS and its related products. This oversight includes the review and certification of training courses and exercise information.

(2) Supporting Technologies: As NIMS and its related emergency management and incident response systems evolve, emergency management/response personnel will increasingly rely on technology and systems to implement and continuously refine NIMS. The NIC, in partnership with the Department of Homeland Security Science and Technology Directorate, oversees and coordinates the ongoing development of incident management-related technology, including strategic research and development.

For an example of the way in which NIMS systems and training made a difference in a crisis situation, see appendix 3.1, a case study of efforts to shelter displaced people in Houston, Texas, following Hurricane Katrina.

Incident Command Structure

One important aspect of the command and management component of the NIMS framework is the recognized value of the Incident Command System (ICS) as a more efficient way to manage disaster events. The Incident Command System (ICS) of NIMS is a management system designed to integrate resources from numerous organizations into a single response structure using common terminology and processes. ICS aids domestic incident management activities for small to complex natural and human-made incidents. ICS is the combination of facilities, equipment, personnel, procedures, and communications operating within a common organizational structure. All levels of government in the United States use ICS including local, state, federal, and tribal, and many private sector and nongovernmental organizations use it as well. ICS has five major functional areas: command, operations, planning, logistics, and finance (U.S. Department of Homeland Security, 2008b). These are shown in table 3.1.

Table 3.1   Five Major Functional Areas of ICS

ICS area	Functions
Incident command	Sets the incident objectives, strategies, and priorities and has overall responsibility for the incident.
Operations	Conducts operations to reach the incident objectives. Establishes tactics and directs all operational resources.
Planning	Supports the incident action planning process by tracking resources, collecting and analyzing information, and maintaining documentation.
Logistics	Arranges for resources and needed services to support achievement of the incident objectives.
Finance and administration	Monitors costs related to the incident. Provides accounting, procurement, time recording, and cost analyses.

Reference: Federal Emergency Management Agency, Emergency Management Institute. (2010). *Special events contingency planning for public safety agencies.*

The command element is composed of the incident commander and support staff including a public information officer (PIO), safety officer (SO), and liaison officer (LO). These positions are shown in the top part of figure 3.2. Various other positions can be assigned by the incident command. Figure 3.2 shows an example ICS command structure. Knowledge of ICS and the roles of various departments and agencies are important for all event security personnel. An effective response requires that all staff members understand their roles and perform their specific functions in an emergency response.

When developing the initial ICS organization, the type, location, size, and expected duration of the event are key factors. The number of agencies and jurisdictions involved, facility and logistical support needs, communications resources available, and limitations or restrictions on local resources are also important to consider. Answering these questions will help event planners develop an organizational structure to meet the management needs of the event. See appendix 3.2 for a form that can be used to help identify the organizational structure needs for a sport or other special event.

Most incidents are managed locally, but under certain circumstances the incident spans beyond the control of a single entity or jurisdiction. When this occurs, a Unified Command (UC) Structure is used. "Unified command is an important element in multijurisdictional or multiagency domestic incident management. It provides guidelines to enable agencies with different legal, geographic, and functional responsibilities to coordinate, plan, and interact effectively" (U.S. Department of Homeland

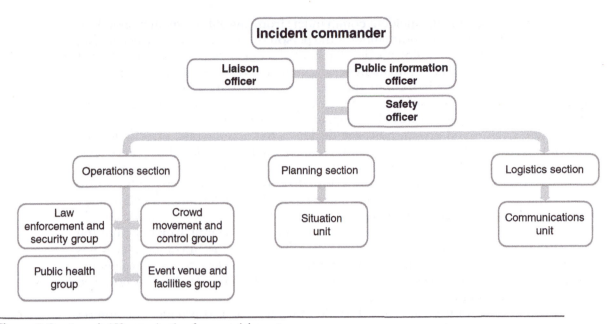

Figure 3.2   Sample ICS organization for a special event.

Reprinted from Federal Emergency Management Agency, 2010, *Special events contingency planning for public safety agencies.* IS-15. B.

Security, 2008b, p. 14). The UC structure coordinates local, state, federal, tribal, and nongovernmental entities with overlapping jurisdiction and incident management responsibilities. Agencies with different responsibilities follow this management structure to coordinate and collaborate effectively. Local response agencies use this system when lacking the resources to implement a full response.

The ICS structure may develop into a Unified Command Structure when dealing with larger incidents that cover wider geographical areas over longer periods. For example, early in the season a postgame civil disturbance erupts in the parking lot of the football stadium after a victory against a long-time rival, which results in multiple personal injuries and culminates with two car fires. This incident would necessitate a response that includes decision makers from local law enforcement agencies, the fire department, and emergency medical services.

The violence then spreads to other private and public parking lot areas and eventually off campus and into the town's business district. Reports indicate malicious activity in the immediate stadium area as well as in other areas of town as the violent activity spreads. This scenario requires multiple agencies and entities to respond from several jurisdictional levels of government (U.S. Department of Homeland Security, 2009c). To represent the interests of every responsible entity, the ICS structure expands to a unified command, in which senior officials from all responsible agencies manage an incident together and establish a common set of incident objectives and strategies. Besides representatives from law enforcement, fire, and emergency services, other agencies that may join the Unified Command Structure include the state police and the Federal Bureau of Investigation. Unified command coordinates the efforts of many jurisdictions and provides for and assures joint decisions on objectives, strategies, plans, priorities, and public communications. During this scenario the incident commander, in coordination with the unified command, would make numerous decisions. These include, but are not limited to, where perimeters should be established, where riot control assets should be staged, what procedures should be used for booking and incarcerating persons arrested, whether affected areas need to be evacuated, and when the environment is safe enough to allow other emergency services, such as fire and emergency medical personnel and resources, to respond.

In this case, only one IC (incident commander) from law enforcement responds to the scenario. The incident commander is the person responsible for all aspects of an emergency response, including the development of incident objectives, management of all incident operations, deployment of resources, and responsibility for all persons involved. The role of incident commander may be assumed by senior or more highly qualified agency representatives upon their arrival or as the situation dictates. The incident commander will always be designated or assumed.

A unified command group, however, decides what actions take priority for the IC's mitigation efforts instead of appointing one person to develop those objectives. The IC directs available personnel to complete the necessary tasks to accomplish the established unified command priorities. Visualize the Unified Command Structure as a company board of directors that meet regularly to determine the company's direction. The chief executive officer, a member of the board, carries out the board's directions on a daily basis. Unified command operates in a similar manner, but the decision-making process in this structure takes a few hours instead of months. Roles change as incidents evolve, and command transitions to the lead agency (designated as the agency with the most significant involvement at the time). At all times, however, there is one incident commander (IC).

Unified command uses a joint information center (JIC) to produce a common media message from all involved organizations. A public information officer (PIO) assists the incident commander with disseminating information. A public information officer (PIO) is designated from the lead agency and assists the incident commander with disseminating information. The necessity of conducting routine press conferences cannot be overemphasized. Efforts must be taken to ensure that all agencies represented in the unified command are releasing a single coordinated message to the media. During this scenario press releases could include emergency notification information regarding areas that the public should avoid because of ongoing public disobedience and riots. Incident command in this particular scenario covers two geographical areas: (1) the stadium and (2) the town's business district. During this scenario the incident commander addresses emergency operations for both locations.

ICS can be adapted to meet the unique needs of a critical incident. Although law enforcement would take the lead in the case of a civil disturbance, for another incident, law enforcement may play a minor role and emergency medical services may play the lead agency role under the incident commander. During the incident, responding agencies adjust their level of involvement based on the need of their services. Incident management is a fluid situation that constantly evolves through the appropriate first responder classifications to meet the situation's needs. ICS expands and contracts as needed to mitigate the objectives developed by the unified command group. As an incident begins to resolve and the demand for resources lessens, the ICS command structure changes accordingly. When the incident commander determines that the area is safe and at the direction of the unified command, assets are released to the respective organizations and property control returns to the appropriate owners (U.S. Department of Homeland Security, 2009c).

Incident Command Locations

Several kinds and types of facilities may be established in and around the incident area. The requirements of the incident and the desires of the incident commander will determine the specific kinds of facilities used and their locations. An incident command post (ICP) and emergency operations center (EOC) may be established and activated. The ICP signifies the location of the tactical level, on-scene incident command and management organization. Typically, the ICP is located at or in the immediate vicinity of the incident site and comprises the incident command and immediate staff (sport or event security command group) and may include other

Stadium Command Centers

Most stadiums built today include a command center (command post) with communication capabilities for security forces to monitor activities inside and outside the stadium perimeter. The command center controls the security functions of the event. The center is normally staffed with the security director, facility management (operations and security), fire, police, emergency medical services, private security, and media representatives.

Copies of security plans, phone directories, and backup technology systems are normally located at this facility. The center has reliable communications and the capability to access the facility public announcement system, fire alarm system, voice activation system, turnstile system, and door access control system.

Command Center Capabilities

- Coordinate internal response to all minor incidents
- Refer support requests to external agencies for major incidents
- Manage all event communications
- Document venue incidents
- Manage event timeline
- Maintain a safe, orderly environment
- Direct and manage venue evacuation
- Expand or contract based on the incident

designated incident management officials and responders from federal, state, local, tribal, private sector, and nongovernmental organizations (see the sidebar). Incident planning is also conducted at the ICP. An incident communication center would also be established at this location.

The emergency operations center (EOC) is the physical location where the coordination of information and resources to support incident management activities normally takes place. For small-scale incidents, or during the initial phase of the response to larger, more complex events, the ICP located at or in the immediate vicinity of an incident site may perform an EOC-like function. But standing EOCs, or those activated to support larger, more complex events, are typically established in a more central or permanently established facility, at a higher level of organization within a jurisdiction. EOCs may be permanent organizations and facilities or may be established to meet temporary, short-term needs. EOCs are organized by major functional discipline (fire, law enforcement, medical services, and so on), by jurisdiction (city, county, region, and so on), or by some combination thereof. For complex incidents, personnel representing multiple jurisdictions and functional disciplines and a variety of resources may staff EOCs. The physical size, staffing, and equipping of an EOC will depend on the size of the jurisdiction, resources available, and the anticipated incident management workload. EOCs may also support multiagency coordination and joint information activities and may be organized and staffed in a variety of ways (U.S. Department of Homeland Security, 2008b). Regardless of the organizational structure used, EOCs should include the following core functions:

- Coordination
- Communications
- Resource dispatch and tracking
- Information collection, analysis, and dissemination

As the postgame rioting scenario continues, an incident command post (ICP) is established in close proximity to the incident. A mobile command post, in the form of a travel trailer, is moved into position to facilitate the needs of the ICP. The mobile command post is equipped with communication capabilities and staffed with representatives from the law enforcement community, as well as fire services, emergency management, and emergency medical. Representatives from the state police and FBI are also on scene.

The county EOC has also been activated and is monitoring the incident. The EOC is located in a permanent building several miles from the incident. Each responding agency has a representative in the EOC. The county emergency management coordinator is in charge of the EOC and will facilitate all requests from the ICP for resource and personnel needs.

On activation of a local EOC, communications and coordination must be established between the incident command post and EOC. EOCs at all levels of government and across functional agencies must be capable of communicating appropriately with other EOCs during incidents, including those maintained by private organizations. Communications between EOCs must be reliable and contain built-in redundancies. The efficient functioning of EOCs most frequently depends on the existence of mutual aid agreements and joint communication protocols among participating agencies. When creating security plans and procedures, the sport or event security command group should address the following questions:

- Where would a command post be established? Will this location provide enough space for multiagency personnel?
- What other government officials, if any, should be notified? Will they be in the incident command post? The EOC?
- What is the availability of additional emergency resources? How soon can they be on scene?
- What is the sport or event organization's policy regarding media affairs?

National Response Framework (NRF) Overview

HSPD-5 also required the secretary of homeland security to develop the National Response Framework (NRF) as a guide to how the United States conducts all-hazards response. The NRF was released in January 2008 after several drafts in response to nationally declared disasters and lessons learned in the response efforts. The NRF provides a framework to facilitate federal response to catastrophes in the United States, its territories, and other jurisdictions. The NRF is an all-hazards plan, an approach that coordinates prevention of, preparedness for, response to, and recovery from terrorism, major natural disasters, and other emergencies. The plan attempts to reduce vulnerability to terrorism and other disasters, minimize damage incurred, emphasize prevention and preparedness, and guide effective response and recovery efforts. It also describes special circumstances in which the federal government plays a larger role in incidents, such as when federal interests are involved or when catastrophic incidents require significant support beyond state resources. The NRF directs the DHS to become involved in all incidents of national significance such as the following:

- Credible threats, indications, or acts of terrorism within the United States
- Major disasters or emergencies
- Catastrophic incidents
- Unique situations that may require the DHS to assist in coordination of incident management

The Federal Emergency Management Agency (FEMA) described the NRF as "a guide to how the nation conducts all-hazards response" (Bullock, Haddow, Coppola, & Yeletaysi, 2009, p. 426). The NRF was built on NIMS to provide a consistent template for managing incidents. It defines basic response roles and responsibilities of government agencies, nongovernmental agencies, and the private sector. These roles and responsibilities are based on five key principles: engaged partnership; tiered response; scalable, flexible, and adaptable operational capabilities; unity of effort through unified command; and readiness to act. Additional information about NRF can be found at www.fema.gov/emergency/nrf/.

Responder Roles

Response represents the actions taken when a crisis actually occurs. The type of response depends on the nature of the crisis. Response includes putting into action many different decisions, including whether to shelter in place or evacuate, which agencies at which level are in charge, and what actions to take to minimize the chaos and damage caused by the crisis. When a crisis occurs at a sport venue, sport venue emergency response personnel and assets may be responsible for the initial response. The initial response includes planning before the incident, establishing a crisis management strategy, setting up interoperable communications at the scene, and notifying the appropriate local, state, and federal agencies of the incident. Organizational, local, state, and federal agencies all have key response roles (U.S. Department of Homeland Security, 2009c).

Sport Organizational Roles

When an incident occurs at a sport venue, the venue's command group immediately plays an integral role. Venue security personnel may command the initial response, which includes venue security, stadium management, a crisis management team, and first responders present on site. Venue security personnel may be responsible for the initial response until local agencies arrive on scene to assist. In addition, venue security personnel are typically responsible for reporting at the scene and notifying the appropriate local, state, and federal agencies. Venue security personnel must understand how their role fits in with those of responding agencies.

For example, consider a scenario where, during pregame preparations, a security guard locates an abandoned backpack inside the stadium. Upon closer visual examination, the security guard notices wires protruding from the top of the backpack. Relying on the protocols included in the stadium emergency operations plan, the security guard contacts the stadium command post and then secures the area around the abandoned backpack. The stadium command post in turn notifies the local law enforcement agency about the backpack and requests assistance.

Sport and event organizations should create all-hazard response plans to prepare for all types of emergency incidents including terrorism and natural disasters. Plans must address prevention, response, and continuity (security planning is covered in chapters 5 and 6). Venue security personnel must be knowledgeable about their venue and experienced in developing and implementing plans that help the program meet challenges. Planning for terrorism acts and other disasters require the same type of knowledge and experience. An all-hazard emergency response plan provides the basis for addressing preparedness needs and develops relationships with local, state, and federal emergency response agencies.

Local Roles

Local response teams are often first to arrive at the incident site and may be already on scene, before a crisis, in support of sport or event security personnel. Local agencies may perform the bulk of major response functions. Mutual aid agreements between the sporting or event entity and local agencies will determine response roles. Key local roles include

- local law enforcement,
- local fire and HAZMAT,
- local emergency medical,
- local public health,
- local emergency management, and
- other first responder assets.

Local response agencies, including the sporting or event entity, must plan and prepare to respond to all types of incidents. As first responders, local agencies may perform emergency rescue and victim recovery operations, provide emergency medical treatment, provide on-site security, establish and maintain a perimeter at the scene, establish interoperable communications, notify the appropriate state and federal agencies, and perform initial investigative functions (crime scene preservation). The NRF indicates that entities must be prepared to manage operations for a minimum of 72 hours before additional resources reach the scene (U.S. Department of Homeland Security, 2009c).

Given the abandoned backpack scenario, after being notified, local law enforcement advise the stadium command post that a law enforcement officer, who is a certified bomb technician, is on scene at the stadium and will inspect the abandoned backpack. Upon inspection the bomb technician confirms that the wires protruding from the backpack are consistent with the characteristics of a possible explosive device. The bomb technician decides that the backpack will need to be rendered safe to mitigate the chance of a detonation. Concurrent to these activities a second abandoned backpack is located in the tailgate area of the stadium. The stadium command post is notified, and a second bomb technician is requested to inspect the second backpack. The local law enforcement agency has only one bomb technician, so a request is made for the state police to provide a second bomb technician.

State and Regional Roles

State and regional agencies provide resources to supplement those provided by local governments. State responsibilities include providing support personnel, equipment, supplies, specialized resources, National Guard or civil support team assistance, and field assessment capabilities to determine additional resource needs; issuing declarations of emergency; and requesting federal support. State and regional response teams may take command of incidents under one or more of the following conditions (U.S. Department of Homeland Security, 2009c):

- Local authorities lack the resources or capabilities to respond or continue an effective response.
- Local authorities request assistance.
- State law prescribes state level control through participation in the Incident Command System (ICS).
- Incident sites are state-owned facilities.

In the potential bomb scenario described earlier, local law enforcement contacted the state police to request additional personnel. Based on the request for a second bomb technician, the state police advises that they have a bomb technician in close proximity to the stadium who can respond and assist. The state police bomb technician arrives on scene.

Federal Roles

Emergency management personnel generally handle incidents at the base organizational and jurisdictional level. When events reach a level of national significance, the federal government provides support and operational coordination to local and state agencies, including resources from a broad range of departments and agencies. Federal responsibilities include

- terrorism investigation,
- recovery assistance,
- support and specialized resources, and
- military support.

The federal government has assumed a lead role in planning for and preventing terrorist attacks. The NRF and NIMS provide a coordinated response structure for campus, local, state, regional, and federal agencies. Preparedness by agencies at levels of government involves training in response tactics and procedures, knowledge of NIMS, and the roles and responsibilities of each agency (U.S. Department of Homeland Security, 2009c).

In our example, the local law enforcement agency bomb technician conducts render safe procedures on the abandoned backpack located inside the stadium. The technician determined that the backpack did contain the components of an explosive device and was maliciously placed inside the stadium to cause injury and death to persons in the area. As a result the stadium command post notifies the FBI that a potential act of terrorism had been committed. The FBI arrives on scene and assumes command of the terrorism investigation. Stadium security, local and state law enforcement, and the FBI work together to secure the stadium and attempt to locate the person or persons responsible for placing the backpack bomb inside the stadium.

Deployment of Resources

A response plan can be viewed as concentric rings that each represent the resources of the sport or event venue and local, state, regional, and federal agencies (see figure 3.3). As more agencies become involved, additional assets assist with the response, which adds complexity to coordinating the operation. Response usually occurs at the base level, and local, regional, state and federal agencies become involved as needed, when resources are exhausted or become ineffective. Additional resources may be more readily available when they are prestaged for large events at sport or event venues.

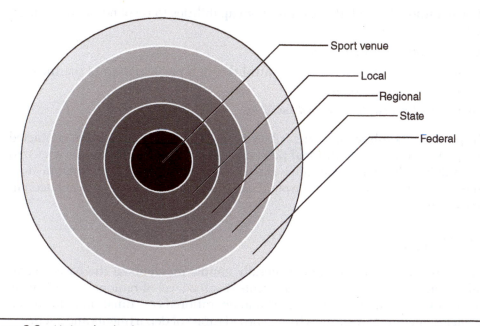

Figure 3.3   Various levels of agencies can be thought of as concentric rings. As more and higher levels of agencies become involved, more resources become available.

An important task is to identify the resources available at the venue level and determine the point at which those resources will be insufficient to address emergency incidents. This process provides sport or event organization executives, the command group, and public safety personnel with guidance for rapid location and mobilization of other necessary resources. The sport or event venue should also be aware of the community's resources. Prior knowledge of the capabilities of community agencies will help coordinate an efficient response. This type of planning must include an all-hazards approach to ensure that responders do not overlook important resources (U.S. Department of Homeland Security, 2009c).

International and National Safety and Security Agencies

National and local sporting events require the collaboration of many domestic agencies. The coordination and structure of these safety and security agencies will vary depending on the country and the type of event. According to Stevens (2007), common national agencies include the following:

- **National event security agencies**: These agencies are formed to coordinate intelligence gathering, risk assessment, and subject matter expertise for major events.

- **National intelligence departments**: These agencies may include secret service, foreign intelligence, and counterintelligence responsible for combating terrorism.
- **Law enforcement and emergency services**: These bodies are normally the domestic agencies that are the first point of contact for event organizers to develop and implement safety and security measures. They may include
  - military forces;
  - national, state, and regional police;
  - specialist police departments (e.g., transport);
  - fire departments;
  - emergency medical services (ambulance and paramedics);
  - first aid provision (e.g., Red Cross);
  - highway patrol agencies;
  - Coast Guard services;
  - customs control; and
  - border guards and immigration control.

In the United States, the level of involvement from national or local law enforcement, intelligence, and emergency services depends on the size and status of the event. Events that draw less than 20,000 spectators and college sporting events, which may attract more than 100,000 spectators, are usually managed by state, county, and city officials. Events of national significance such as the Super Bowl have greater involvement from federal agencies (Stevens, 2007). In 1998 President Bill Clinton issued a presidential directive to address national special security events (NSSE), which are high-profile events of national and international significance (having historical, political, or symbolic significance), attract national and international media coverage, have thousands of spectators in attendance, and are considered a high security risk. When an event receives a NSSE designation, the Secret Service becomes the lead agency and works with state and local authorities to implement security strategies. The Federal Bureau of Investigation has the lead role for intelligence and law enforcement operations (State of Missouri Emergency Management Agency, 2009). Agencies regularly involved in the safety and security management of major sporting events in the United States include representatives from the Central Intelligence Agency (CIA); Federal Emergency Management Agency (FEMA); Transportation Security Administration (TSA); Federal Bureau of Investigation (FBI); Bureau of Alcohol, Tobacco, Firearms, and Explosives (ATF); U.S. Department of State; U.S. Department of Defense; U.S. Environmental Protection Agency (EPA); and Centers for Disease Control and Prevention (CDC) (Stevens, 2007).

In the United Kingdom, major events are planned in coordination with the National Security Advice Centre (NSAC), which provides expert security advice on physical and personnel protective security. The NSAC administers a nonpublic assessment and briefing for the event holder. The NSAC and event holder may also liaise with the National Criminal Intelligence Service (NCIS) (similar to the FBI), which works with all U.K. law enforcement agencies to prevent criminal activity. Sport organizations also work with MI5 and MI6 to counter terrorist threats. MI5 is responsible for internal security within the United Kingdom and issues guidance on terrorist alert levels. MI6 is responsible for foreign intelligence and counterintelligence (Stevens, 2007).

Security needs for major events can require involvement of international organizations as well. Many sporting events are global in nature and require the collaboration and coordination of multinational security agencies. According to Stevens (2007), the most active multinational agencies are the International Police Agency (Interpol), European Police Office (Europol), United Nations Interregional Crime and Justice Research

Institute (UNICRI), and the International Permanent Observatory (IPO). Interpol, founded in 1923, facilitates international cooperation between national police and law enforcement. Based in Lyon, France, the organization consists of 186 member nations and claims to be the world's largest international police organization (Stevens, 2007).

Europol coordinates law enforcement agencies among the European Union (EU). Based in the Netherlands, Europol collects, analyzes, and disseminates information to law enforcement agencies within the EU related to threats, terrorism, and criminal activity. The UNICRI works to provide solutions to major problems of criminal policy, including terrorism. Based in Italy, its projects include analytical and operational components in support of other police, government, and nongovernmental agencies. In 2003 UNICRI created the IPO in Security Measures During Major Events, in cooperation with Europol. This group conducts research to identify best practices in security and provides technical assistance to countries where a major event is located (Stevens, 2007).

CASE STUDY

Georgia Dome

Some areas of the United States are susceptible to severe weather that can occur with little or no advance notice. Many events attract large crowds to open venues or arenas that may not be constructed to withstand the effect of severe weather or to facilitate efficient evacuations. Therefore, those responsible for safety and security must have policies and procedures in place and trained staff who have exercised emergency response plans. The U.S. Department of Homeland Security has developed the National Incident Management System, including Incident Command System (ICS) training, in an attempt to create consistency in emergency response to disaster incidents.

On March 14, 2008, the annual Southeastern Conference (SEC) basketball tournament was in full swing at the Georgia Dome in Atlanta, Georgia. Early in the evening, a close semifinal game between the University of Alabama and Mississippi State University was into the final minutes of the second half. A large crowd was in attendance, and the game was being televised. Suddenly, the ceiling of the dome began shaking, and pieces of debris began falling on the court. It was not immediately clear whether an explosion had occurred, whether severe weather was the cause, or whether some structural collapse was occurring. Fans, players, and officials were confused about what to do.

A command center was in operation and correctly staffed with multiagency emergency response personnel. The command group decided to suspend the game immediately and to implement shelter-in-place procedures because weather reports indicated that a powerful tornado had hit downtown Atlanta. Players, coaches, and officials were informed of the situation and ordered to the locker rooms until further notice. Public service announcements were used to inform, calm, and assist fans during the shelter-in-place process. Event staff manned all exits and strongly suggested that everyone stay inside. In fact, some people from outside the venue were allowed to enter the Georgia Dome for their safety. After the weather calmed and it was surmised that no severe structural damage had occurred, the game was completed. But the following day, because the extent of damage was unknown, the remaining games were moved to the Georgia Tech. University arena.

LESSONS LEARNED

- The command center was in operation and appropriately staffed, which allowed for a quick and clear decision on the best course of action. The command group decided the best type of evacuation was shelter in place because the weather was too severe to allow spectators to leave the venue and be safe.

- In retrospect, lacking a detailed analysis of structural damage to the venue, the game should not have continued.
- Continuity planning is important to ensure that the event can continue at another venue if an incident occurs that renders the current venue unsafe. This goal can be accomplished by establishing mutual aid agreements with nearby venues.

QUESTIONS TO CONSIDER

1. Under what conditions would the decision have been made to evacuate the venue fully or partially rather than implement shelter in place?
2. What were the first priorities of the command group after the incident and why?

Key Chapter Points

- The National Incident Management System (NIMS) is a core set of concepts, principals and terminology for incident command and multiagency coordination.
- The Incident Command System (ICS), a component of NIMS, is a management system designed to integrate resources from numerous organizations into a single response structure using common terminology and processes.
- The Unified Command (UC) Structure coordinates local, state, federal, tribal, and nongovernmental entities that have overlapping jurisdiction and incident management responsibilities.
- The incident command post (ICP) signifies the location of the tactical level, on-scene incident command and management organization.
- The emergency operations center (EOC) represents the physical location where the coordination of information and resources to support incident management activities normally takes place.
- The National Response Framework (NRF) provides a guide to facilitate federal response to catastrophes in the United States, its territories, and other jurisdictions.

Application Questions

1. Discuss the importance of having a National Incident Management System and National Response Framework.
2. Describe the major components of NIMS and the value of ICS.
3. What key personnel should be present in the stadium command post or EOC?
4. What are the roles of the sport or event organization and local, state, and federal agencies in responding to a major incident?

Activity

Visit a local sport or event organization that uses ICS and observe their command post operations during an event. Request information as needed and report on the following three questions:

1. Who is in charge?
2. What is their plan?
3. How do they initiate, communicate, and organize command functions?

Risk Assessment for Sport and Event Venues

CHAPTER GOALS

- Define risk and categorize the different types of risk.
- Examine the risk assessment process.
- Identify the sport or event security command group.
- Evaluate threats, vulnerabilities, and consequences of an incident.
- Develop countermeasure improvements.

This chapter concentrates on the sport or event venue risk assessment process, which includes establishing a command group, identifying assets, assessing threats, assessing vulnerability, analyzing consequences, analyzing risk, and developing countermeasure proposals. Risk is the possibility of loss from a hazard such as personal injury, property damage, death, economic loss, or environmental damage (Kaiser & Robinson, 2005). The three main types of risk for sport and event venues are (1) mission (function) risks, (2) asset risks, and (3) security risks. Mission risks can prevent a sport or event organization from accomplishing its primary mission. Asset risks may harm the organization's physical assets (i.e., stadium structure), and security risks have the potential to harm informational data and people (U.S. Department of Homeland Security, 2003b). The concept of risk is best understood as the product of the consequence (or severity) of an incident and the probability (or frequency) that the incident will occur, also represented as risk = probability × consequence severity. The level of risk increases as the probability and consequence severity of an incident increase. This concept is discussed later in the chapter.

An all-hazard risk management approach is critical for sport and event organizations to protect physical and human assets against potential threats, including terrorism, natural disasters, and crowd control issues (Hall, 2006). According to Decker (2001), "Risk management is a systematic and analytical process to consider the likelihood that a threat will endanger an asset, individual, or function and to identify actions to reduce the risk and mitigate the consequences of an attack." (p. 1). To determine threats and vulnerabilities, an organization must conduct a risk assessment. The U.S. Department of Homeland Security (DHS) (2003b) issued a 10-step risk assessment methodology criterion:

1. Identify the infrastructure sector being assessed
2. Specify type of security discipline addressed (i.e., physical, information)
3. Collect data pertaining to each asset
4. Identify critical assets to be protected
5. Determine the mission impact of the loss or damage of that asset
6. Conduct a threat analysis and perform assessment for specific assets
7. Perform a vulnerability analysis and assessment of specific threats
8. Conduct analytical risk assessment and determine priorities for each asset
9. Identify countermeasures that are relatively low cost to implement and train staff in
10. Make specific recommendations concerning countermeasures

The DHS criterion is general in nature and may be adapted to meet the needs of a specific industry or organization. Sandia National Laboratories has pioneered security risk assessment methodologies. Since the 1970s Sandia has applied performance-based risk methods to high-consequence United States government facilities (Sandia National Laboratories, 2008). In the last several years, this approach has been modified, tested, and applied to other critical infrastructures, such as biological facilities, communities, chemical facilities, dams, energy infrastructure, prisons, and water utilities. Regardless of the type of facility, the approach is the same. Each specific risk assessment methodology (RAM) is composed of the following major components: planning, threat assessment, site characterization, consequence assessment, system effectiveness, risk analysis, risk management, and reduction (Sandia National Laboratories 2008).

Risk Assessment Process

Sport and event facility managers must embrace risk management processes. Sport stadiums are considered critical infrastructure by the U.S. DHS, and sport and special events represent scenarios vulnerable to a variety of risks. Conducting an assessment offers many benefits. The risk assessment will indicate the current security profile of the facility and highlight areas in which greater security is needed. It will also help to develop a justification of cost-effective countermeasures and increase security awareness by reporting strengths and weaknesses in security processes to all staff members, including management (Broder, 2006). The National Center for Spectator Sports Safety and Security Management (NCS[4]) at the University of Southern Mississippi developed a sport-specific risk assessment model based on the DHS risk assessment principles discussed earlier (see figure 4.1). A sample application of all seven steps is shown in the sidebar on pages 74-76. The model was piloted at seven college stadiums in the United States (Hall et al., 2007).

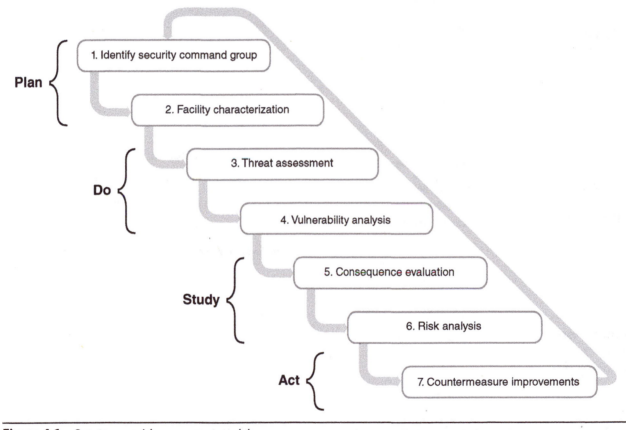

Figure 4.1   Sport venue risk assessment model.

Step 1: Identify Sport or Event Security Command Group

The command group (CG) is responsible for providing information about the event facility and the surrounding area. As previously highlighted in chapter 2, group members may include the facility manager, facility security director, local law enforcement, local emergency management director, emergency medical services, fire and hazardous materials (HAZMAT), public health, and public relations representatives.

Establishing a multidiscipline team to ensure collaborative planning and response efforts is important. The group should be established before the sport or event season and meet regularly, especially after events for debriefing discussions and making future recommendations. Input from the command group during the risk assessment process is critical to ensure that all available information and intelligence about threats and vulnerabilities inside and outside the organization is shared during the risk assessment process. The facility manager and security director provide insight into daily operations and event management. Local law enforcement and emergency management provide information on community situations and threats. The command group must define essential functions of the facility, undesired security events that would interrupt facility operations, the consequences of such events, targets to be protected, and the potential liabilities incurred. Additionally, they must focus on potential threats and the facility's vulnerabilities that compromise security (Biringer, Matalucci, & O'Connor, 2007). Decisions for the command group are presented in figure 4.2.

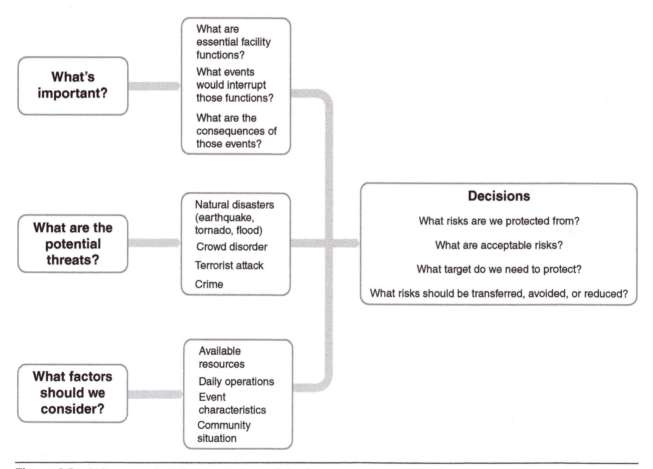

Figure 4.2   Risk management decisions to be made by the command group (CG). The command group must evaluate potential threats and vulnerabilities and decide on the best course of action given available resources.

Step 2: Describe Facility

This step involves a complete characterization of the facility and serves as the foundation of the risk assessment process. Facility characterization includes

1. a complete physical description of the facility,
2. identification of undesired events, and
3. identification of critical assets.

A complete description of the facility is necessary. Data can be collected by the command group through security audits, site visits, and interviews with staff members. Information needed to describe the facility adequately includes physical details, facility operations, security protection systems, and workforce description (Biringer, Mattalucci, & O'Connor, 2007). Physical details should provide information on construction details such as vehicle parking; entrances and exits; utilities; location of heating, ventilation, and air conditioning (HVAC) systems; and location of hazardous materials. Facility operational information such as operating hours and processes during an emergency should be noted. Finally, security protection systems (or physical protection systems [PPS]) must be described. The PPS consists of features that support detection (alarms, entry controls, metal and explosive detectors), delay (barriers), and response functions (actions taken by law enforcement and timely communication and response). The workforce description entails a listing of the types of positions and the authorization afforded to each staff member, including managers, operators, security personnel, custodians, maintenance, contractors, vendors, and visitors. Background screening information should also be described (Biringer, Mattalucci, & O'Connor, 2007).

Undesired events are facility specific and are associated with the loss of mission or threats to public health and safety. Such events can range from catastrophes to minor nuisances (Biringer, Mattalucci, & O'Connor, 2007). For example, undesired events for a sport or event organization may include disruption of event operations, theft of equipment or vandalism of property, crowd crushing, destruction of the venue, compromised data systems, or loss of public confidence. After the facility description has been completed and the undesired events have been identified, the next step is to identify critical assets to be protected. *General Security Risk Assessment Guideline* (ASIS International, 2003) defines an asset as a person, place, or thing that can be assigned a monetary value. Sport and entertainment facility managers must assess both facility assets and surrounding area assets (within a 1-mile [1.6 km] radius). Assets to be protected include human assets, physical assets, and critical information and processes (National Counterterrorism Security Office, 2006). Human assets may include athletes or entertainers, spectators, event staff, and local community residents. Physical assets may include the venue, surrounding facility buildings, municipal police department, fire department, local hospitals, and public utilities (e.g., water, gas). Information and processes, such as electronic data and supply chains, must also be assessed and protected (see the sidebar on page 66).

Step 3: Assess Threats

According to the U.S. Department of Homeland Security, "A threat is a product of intention and capability of an adversary, both manmade and natural, to undertake an action which would be detrimental to an asset" (2003b, p. 11). Sport leagues, teams, and venues must prepare for a wide range of possible threats at their facilities (Hurst, Zoubek, & Pratsinakis, 2003). Sport and entertainment facility managers can obtain threat information from various local, state, and federal sources. Local sources of threat information are obtained from the facility security director, local law enforcement, and state or regional law enforcement.

In the United States, many states have threat and investigation working groups, such as the Joint Terrorism Task Force (JTTF) (Biringer, Mattalucci, & O'Connor, 2007). Pre-9/11 sources of threat information were limited to Internet searches and intelligence and information sharing among professional organizations. More timely and complete information is available today, provided by the Federal Bureau of Investigation (FBI) and the Department of Homeland Security (DHS). The DHS provides information on current threat levels through the Homeland Security Advisory system (covered in chapter 6), including Homeland Security Bulletins. The FBI operates the National Threat Center and maintains the National Security Threat List (NSTL) (Biringer, Mattalucci, & O'Connor, 2007).

List of Critical Assets for a Sport Facility

On Site

- Stadium or arena
- Fans
- Building
- Stadium or arena communications
- Medical services
- In-house security
- Command post
- Electric supply
- Water supply
- Gas supply
- Physical plant
- Vendors and contractors
- Surrounding neighborhoods

Off Site

- Municipal police
- Fire department
- Local hospitals
- Sheriff's office
- Public utilities
- Medical regional response team
- Ambulance operations

Other techniques used to gather information relevant to specific threats include brainstorming and tabletop exercises, modeling and simulation, walk-throughs of the facility before and during the event, knowledge transfer from industry peers, and security surveys (Stevens, 2007) (see appendix 4.1). The threat data collected assists the command group in determining who or what the threats are, their capabilities, and the potential and severity of the threat. Sport and entertainment facility threats include terrorism, natural catastrophes, crowd control, vandalism, theft, fire, fraud, personal assault, traffic incidents, facility intrusion, and technological problems (Stevens, 2007). The sidebar provides a list of all-hazard risks.

Terrorism has been cited as one of the most common threats to sport and entertainment venues, and the U.S. DHS has issued warnings indicating that sport stadiums, as critical infrastructure, are vulnerable targets. International, domestic, and lone wolf terrorists have considered stadiums as targets because such facilities present open access and opportunity to achieve objectives of mass casualties, economic damage, and social and psychological impact. Scenarios of particular concern to the DHS and FBI are explosive devices and the use of aircraft and chemical weapons to attack stadiums and arenas (Federal Bureau of Investigation and U.S. Department of Homeland Security, 2009). An attack on an occupied stadium using improvised explosive devices (IEDs) or vehicle-borne improvised explosive devices (VBIEDs) could cause immediate casualties and facility destruction, create fear and panic among the public, disrupt local businesses, and generate extensive media coverage. A helicopter or small aircraft could potentially blend in with media or advertising banner planes often present over stadiums during major events (Federal Bureau of Investigation and U.S. Department of Homeland Security, 2009). These scenarios are also plausible outside the United States and are evident from recent incidents such as the 2004 Madrid soccer bomb threat that caused the evacuation of 70,000 people, the 2007 and 2008 suicide bombings at Iraqi soccer stadiums, and at the 2000

1. **Bomb threat**: Example scenario—During pregame warm-ups, the stadium switchboard receives a call from an anonymous person who threatens to detonate an explosive device inside the stadium. The call is reported to law enforcement authorities, who determine that the origin of the call is a number associated with a known terrorist organization that has used explosives during previous terrorism incidents. Suspected members of the terrorist organization have recently posted messages on the Internet boasting about "blowing up a stadium." Security personnel inside the stadium have located an unidentified package.

2. **WMD** (**biological**): Example scenario—Numerous spectators have reported being nauseous and vomiting. Symptoms include stomach cramps, dizziness, and weakness. Most of the victims say that they had consumed food from stadium vendors within the past four hours. The symptoms are consistent with the pathogenic botulinum toxin.

3. **Weather threat**: Example scenario—The Weather Service reports localized violent thunderstorms with significant lightning in the area near the stadium. Funnel clouds have also been reported. The Weather Service recommends that all those in the affected area take cover.

4. **Cyber threat**: Example scenario—A cyber terrorist group known as the Computer Commandos has hacked into the stadium mainframe and sabotaged all computer-controlled operations during a scheduled night event. Stadium lighting, the scoreboard, and computer-generated messaging capabilities have all been disrupted.

5. **Industrial accident** (**chemical**): Example scenario—A train derailment has occurred close to the stadium. Several of the derailed tanker cars are carrying liquid chlorine. At least one of the tanker cars has been breached, and a rupture may occur. The resulting chlorine gas plume would be upwind from the stadium. The plume would potentially reach the stadium within four to six hours.

6. **Event cancellation** (**no show**): Example scenario—Members of a rock band scheduled for a concert in the campus auditorium have been delayed at the airport and will not be available to perform. The crowd is informed of the situation, and the concert is cancelled. Some of those in attendance are agitated, and fights are breaking out. Seats are being thrown onto the stage, and other forms of property damage are occurring.

7. **Civil disturbance** (**riot**): Example scenario—Spectators at a sport event, upset with a call made by the officials, have begun to fight and throw objects on the playing field. Law enforcement has responded by launching tear gas canisters into the crowd. The smoke from the gas grenades has panicked the spectators, resulting in mass hysteria. The game has been discontinued.

8. **Bomb threat** (**VBIED**): Example scenario—A person driving a passenger van has crashed through security checkpoints, and the van has come to rest close to the stadium. The person driving the van has been apprehended. On examination, the van is found to contain a large amount of explosives. Closer examination of the cargo and statements from the driver reveal that the explosives are attached to a timing mechanism. Unless rendered safe, the explosives could detonate within minutes.

9. **WMD** (**chemical**): Example scenario—A known terrorist organization contacts the local media and states that the nerve agent sarin has been released into the ventilation system at the stadium. Inspection of the ventilation intakes at the stadium reveals discarded plastic bottles containing a clear liquid residue adjacent to the intake vents.

(continued)

10. **Active shooter:** Example scenario—Shots have been fired in the concessions area of the stadium during halftime. Initial reports identify at least two gunmen and several casualties. The gunmen are moving through the crowd and shooting randomly.

11. **Natural disaster (earthquake):** Example scenario—An earthquake of significant magnitude has caused one section of the stadium to collapse. Numerous casualties have occurred, and debris has blocked various exits.

12. **Airplane crash:** Example scenario—A small fixed-wing aircraft that had been circling the stadium struck one of the stadium light structures and crashed into the stands. Numerous casualties have occurred, and falling burning debris has caused several fires throughout the facility.

Reprinted from U.S. Department of Homeland Security, 2009, *Sport event risk management.*

Australian Olympic Games when New Zealand police thwarted an extremist plot to target a nuclear reactor during the Olympic Games.

The command group is responsible for identifying potential terrorist activities and assessing the following terrorist factors:

1. The existence of a group or individual operating close to the venue
2. Past terrorist activity or a recorded violent criminal history of the group or individual
3. Credible intentions of force or violence, or plans to commit an act of terrorism
4. Capabilities to act such as possessing skills, financial resources, equipment, and transportation to initiate an attack
5. Specific targeting of the sport venue (obtaining floor plans, taking pictures, testing security) (Texas Engineering Extension Service, 2005)

The threat potential or likelihood of an attack occurring can be classified as low, medium, or high:

- **High:** high probability that a threat will occur and cause a loss
- **Medium:** medium probability that a threat will occur and cause a loss
- **Low:** low probability that a threat will occur and result in a loss

Step 4: Analyze Vulnerabilities

Vulnerabilities expose the asset to a threat and eventual loss. The *General Security Risk Assessment Guideline* (ASIS International, 2003) defines vulnerability as "an exploitable capability; an exploitable security weakness or deficiency at a facility, entity, venue, or of a person" (p. 5). The National Center for Spectator Sports Safety and Security identified vulnerabilities at major sport venues relative to emergency preparedness, perimeter control, physical protection systems, access control, credentialing, training, and communication (Hall et al., 2007). The following are common vulnerabilities at sport facilities:

- Lack of emergency response and evacuation plans specific to the facility
- Inadequate searching of the facility before an event
- Inadequate lock-down procedures

- Inadequate searches of fans and their belongings
- Unsecure concession areas
- Inadequate signage concerning searches and restricted items
- Lack of CCTV coverage of the sport facility or surrounding areas
- Storage of dangerous chemicals inside the sport facility
- Lack of accountability for vendors and their vehicles
- Lack of security notification system for fans, players, staff, and so on
- Inadequate training of staff members
- Inadequate communication capabilities among responding agencies

Facility managers need to ask themselves whether their stadium, staff, or upcoming events attract disorder or whether the event or facility is associated with high-profile people or organizations ("Security and Policing," 2005). Events such as political rallies, conferences, and meetings of associations that support political, religious, or government causes can attract the opposition of extremists who want to do harm. For example, the 1999 World Trade Organization Conference generated protest activity in Seattle in support of the antiglobalization movement. Events that attract a large gathering for any purpose are attractive to terrorists and criminals because detecting adversaries in large crowds is difficult and escape is easy because of proximity to transport infrastructure.

Appendix 4.2 provides a checklist of facility conditions to consider when assessing vulnerabilities. These items include emergency preparedness, perimeter control, access control, physical protection systems, and personnel (Hall, Marciani, & Cooper, 2008).

Step 5: Evaluate Consequences

In the consequence evaluation phase, the command group reviews all potential threats (undesired events) and estimates consequence values and potential effects on the facility and its key stakeholders. The command group should establish a standard to discuss consequences by developing a reference table of consequences. The first components of the reference table are the criteria for describing consequences, and these are usually facility specific. Measureable criteria should be used. Common criteria of consequences include deaths, economic loss (to owner), economic loss (to customer), loss of operations, loss of public confidence, loss of assets, and downtime (Biringer, Mattalucci, & O'Connor, 2007). Consequences or severity of loss differs at each facility. The greater the potential for loss or damage to human and physical assets is, the higher the impact of loss is. The U.S. Department of Defense established qualitative values for consequences, which are noted in the DOD Military Standard 882D. Consequence evaluation can be classified as catastrophic, critical, marginal, or negligible (Biringer, Mattalucci, & O'Connor, 2007, p. 77):

Catastrophic: could result in death, permanent total disability, loss exceeding $1 million, or irreversible severe environmental damage that violates law or regulation.

Critical: could result in permanent partial disability, injuries, or occupational illness that may result in hospitalization of at least three personnel, loss exceeding $200,000 but less than $1 million, or irreversible environmental damage causing a violation of law or regulation.

Marginal: could result in injury or occupational illness resulting in one or more lost workdays, loss exceeding $10,000 but less than $200,000, or mitigatible environmental damage without violation of law or regulation, where restoration activities can be accomplished.

Negligible: could result in injury or illness not resulting in a lost workday, loss exceeding $2,000 but less than $10,000, or minimal environmental damage not violating law or regulation.

The DOD standard is a good starting point for facility managers to develop their own reference table of consequences. All types of incidents will have consequences. For example, a slip-and-fall accident may result in one personal injury and a single lawsuit. Alternatively, a major crowd-crushing incident could cause hundreds of casualties, a huge financial loss, and a social stigma to the venue, sport team, league, or governing body (Schwarz, Hall, & Shibli, 2010). Biringer, Mattalucci, & O'Connor (2007) presented a hypothetical reference table of consequences that may be applicable to the sport environment with consequence levels of high, medium, or low (see table 4.1).

Table 4.1   Reference Table of Consequences

Measure of consequence	Low	Medium	High
Economic loss (property loss and revenue)	<$1M	$1–5M	>$5M
Deaths	0	1–3	>3
Downtime	<1 year	1–2 years	>2 years
Geographic impact	Local	Regional	National
Public confidence	<6 months	6 months–1 year	>1 year

Adapted by permission from B.E. Biringer, R.V. Matalucci, and S.L. O'Connor, 2007, *Security risk assessment and management* (Hoboken, NJ: Wiley).

After developing the table, facility managers analyze each threat for the consequence severity that would result if the undesired event occurred. Consequences are estimated by the command group with input from technical experts. The consequence severity of a threat and eventual loss must also be evaluated. The manager must consider both the severity and the financial and nonfinancial effect on the sport program. Financial losses for a sport venue may include ticketing, hospitality, sponsorship, parking, and concession revenues associated with the sporting event. Nonfinancial losses incurred, such as the value and reputation of the sport organization's brand, can damage the long-term viability and sustainability of a venue, event, or team (Stevens, 2007). Each threat must be evaluated individually along with the effect that it will have on the ability of the facility or organization to perform its mission. When more than one criterion is used to evaluate the consequence, the highest consequence criterion value is selected to estimate the consequences of the undesired event. Figure 4.3 shows an example of estimating consequences for undesired events at a sport facility resulting in high, medium, and low consequences.

Step 6: Analyze Risks

Evaluating risk and potential of loss helps the facility manager decide whether to accept, reduce, transfer, or avoid identified threats and risks (U.S. Department of Homeland Security, 2003b). Figure 4.4 illustrates the risk decision matrix. Threats are evaluated based on probability (likelihood) and consequence (severity). Threats that have a high probability of occurring and that would cause a high degree of loss (consequence) should be avoided (Ammon, Southall, & Blair, 2004). Avoidance is practical in extreme circumstances, such as the postponement of the Ryder Cup in 2001 after the 9/11 events, the relocation of the New Orleans Saints organization following Hurricane Katrina in

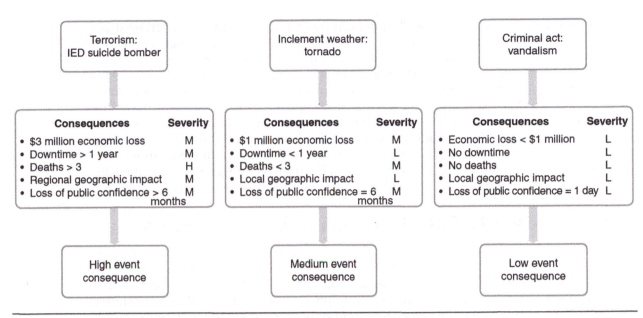

Terrorism: IED suicide bomber		Inclement weather: tornado		Criminal act: vandalism	
Consequences	**Severity**	**Consequences**	**Severity**	**Consequences**	**Severity**
• $3 million economic loss	M	• $1 million economic loss	M	• Economic loss < $1 million	L
• Downtime > 1 year	M	• Downtime < 1 year	L	• No downtime	L
• Deaths > 3	H	• Deaths < 3	M	• No deaths	L
• Regional geographic impact	M	• Local geographic impact	L	• Local geographic impact	L
• Loss of public confidence > 6 months	M	• Loss of public confidence = 6 months	M	• Loss of public confidence = 1 day	L

High event consequence	Medium event consequence	Low event consequence

Figure 4.3 Estimation of consequences for three possible events at a sport facility.

2005, and the cancellation of the 31st National Games in Pakistan because of heightened security concerns within the country. Avoidance is deciding to cancel an event that could be an additional target in a heightened security environment or relocate an event because a major disaster makes it impossible to continue at the initial location because of various risks (damage or increased crime in the surrounding area). This decision is made in the best interests of the participants, staff, spectators, and local community.

Threats of average frequency and moderate severity can be transferred to a third party. For example, theft and venue damage because of vandalism can be transferred to an insurance company. Sport and entertainment facility operators can transfer risk in the form of waivers, independent contractors, indemnification clauses, leasing agreements, or through insurance methods. Insurance is the most commonly used method to transfer risk. Insurance coverage is critical for all sport and special events,

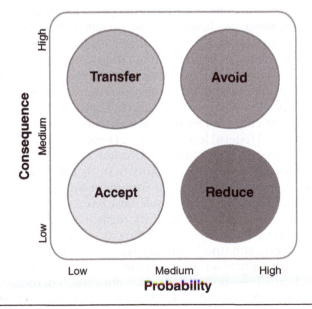

Figure 4.4 The risk decision matrix provides a framework for deciding whether to transfer, avoid, reduce, or accept risks.

especially in the event of cancellation because of a security threat or terrorist act (Stevens, 2007). According to Stevens (2007), the three key forms of insurance are (1) liability coverage, including public, personal, employer, and general (i.e., fire, theft); (2) asset protection, including damage to buildings, vehicles, or equipment; and (3) cancellation or abandonment by the venue operator, rights holder, or participants.

Some facility managers may decide to accept the risk and assume financial responsibility. Threats such as vandalism, theft, and crowd management issues can be accepted and reduced. Facility managers can reduce risk through risk reduction strategies, such as reducing the likelihood of an incident through implementing deterrence strategies, improving security system effectiveness, mitigating consequences, or a combination thereof. These strategies are discussed in the following section.

Step 7: Identify Countermeasure Improvements

Countermeasure improvements are also referred to as risk reduction strategies; these recommendations are provided to management based on venue assessments to address security weaknesses and enhance emergency planning and recovery efforts. Countermeasures are any actions involving physical, technical, and administrative measures taken to reduce the probability and severity of risks (Long & Renfroe, 1999). They are provided to management to enhance decision-making abilities. After the risk assessment is complete, a list of countermeasures is developed related to the threats and vulnerabilities identified. Management then decides which measures (if not all) will be implemented, considering need and available resources. Countermeasures may be recommended in levels of priority, an approach that would help management decide which measures should be implemented first if they do not have the resources available to implement all recommendations immediately.

Possible security measures that can be used to reduce the likelihood of an undesired event include increasing security protection system effectiveness through physical upgrades, good personnel practices, information security, staff training, preventative facility maintenance, and development of a risk management plan (covered in chapter 5) to be included in the standard operating procedure (SOP) (Ammon, Southall, & Blair, 2004). Physical upgrades include detection, delay, and response strategies. For example, detection methods can include intrusion sensing (perimeter penetration), access control (identity check), alarm communication, and closed-circuit television (CCTV). Delay mechanisms may include the use of locks and security personnel stationed at restricted access areas of the facility. Response functions may include communication response time to deployment of resources postincident (Biringer, Mattalucci, & O'Connor, 2007).

Some measures are designed to be implemented on a permanent basis to serve as routine protection for a facility; these actions are referred to as baseline countermeasures. Additional measures can be implemented or increased in their application during times of heightened alert (Protective Measures Guide for U.S. Sports Leagues, 2008). Responding to threat elements requires the sharing of intelligence and information at the local, state, and federal level. The U.S. Department of Homeland Security created a National Terrorism Advisory Alert System (NTAS) which replaced the previous color-coded Homeland Security Advisory System. NTAS uses alerts that list specific information in response to a threat or imminent threat (see figure 4.5; U.S. Department of Homeland Security, 2010). Each alert has a sunset date after which it is no longer active. Specific protective security measures are covered in chapter 6. Britain also has a five-tiered alert system starting at low and continuing through moderate, substantial, severe, and finally critical (Hui, 2010). The National Terrorism Public Alert System for Australia has four levels that guide national preparation and planning. The four levels are low—terrorist attack is not expected; medium—terrorist attack could occur; high—terrorist attack is likely; and extreme—terrorist attack is imminent or has occurred (Australian National Security, 2010).

National Terrorism Advisory System

Alert

www.dhs.gov/alerts

DATE & TIME ISSUED: XXXX

SUMMARY

The Secretary of Homeland Security informs the public and relevant government and private sector partners about a potential or actual threat with this alert, indicating whether there is an "imminent" or "elevated" threat.

DURATION

An individual threat alert is issued for a specific time period and then automatically expires. It may be extended if new information becomes available or the threat evolves.

DETAILS

• This section provides more detail about the threat and what the public and sectors need to know.

• It may include specific information, if available, about the nature and credibility of the threat, including the critical infrastructure sector(s) or location(s) that may be affected.

• It includes as much information as can be released publicly about actions being taken or planned by authorities to ensure public safety, such as increased protective actions and what the public may expect to see.

AFFECTED AREAS

■ This section includes visual depictions (such as maps or other graphics) showing the affected location(s), sector(s), or other illustrative detail about the threat itself.

HOW YOU CAN HELP

• This section provides information on ways the public can help authorities (e.g. camera phone pictures taken at the site of an explosion), and reinforces the importance of reporting suspicious activity.

• It may ask the public or certain sectors to be alert for a particular item, situation, person, activity or developing trend.

STAY PREPARED

• This section emphasizes the importance of the public planning and preparing for emergencies before they happen, including specific steps individuals, families and businesses can take to ready themselves and their communities.

• It provides additional preparedness information that may be relevant based on this threat.

STAY INFORMED

• This section notifies the public about where to get more information.

• It encourages citizens to stay informed about updates from local public safety and community leaders.

• It includes a link to the DHS NTAS website http://www.dhs.gov/alerts and http://twitter.com/NTASAlerts

If You See Something, Say Something™. Report suspicious activity to local law enforcement or call 911.

The National Terrorism Advisory System provides Americans with alert information on homeland security threats. It is distributed by the Department of Homeland Security. More information is available at: **www.dhs.gov/alerts.** To receive mobile updates: **www.twitter.com/NTASAlerts**

If You See Something Say Something™ used with permission of the NY Metropolitan Transportation Authority.

Figure 4.5 The format for alerts issued under the National Terrorism Advisory System (NTAS).

Several strategies are used to mitigate consequences of incidents at major sport or special events related to people (loss of life), facilities (loss of stadium), revenues (loss of mission), or community (loss of services or public confidence) (Hall et al., 2007):

- **Implement a vendor program**: Facility managers should require vendors and contractors to meet minimum standards when accessing the venue, including identification, background checks, and uniforms.
- **Participate in an information sharing and analysis center (ISAC)**: Facility managers should consider participation in a security information sharing and analysis center. Shared information would include suspicious behavior, threats, and upcoming events. In the United States, state offices of homeland security have fusion centers, DHS has a lessons-learned information-sharing site (www.llis.gov), and the NCS⁴ has a membership data center that distributes sport-specific safety and security information (www.ncs4.com).
- **Improve access control**: Facility managers should conduct regular safety and security meetings to address past security issues as well as upcoming events. Additionally, facility credentialing needs to be evaluated and concern should be given to identification, record keeping, authorization areas, gate access, sign-in procedures, and stadium lock-down before an event.
- **Develop and test emergency and evacuation plans**: The sport or event organization should develop and exercise its event emergency and evacuation plans, including testing its crisis communication network.
- **Improve physical protection systems**: The organization should install security cameras, adequate lighting, and interoperable communication networks.

These countermeasures serve an all-hazard purpose because by planning for a terrorist incident they are also ensuring that measures are in place for other incidents such as crowd control issues and inclement weather. For example, managers must develop and test an evacuation plan that can be implemented for reasons such as an explosion, an imminent tornado or lightning strike, or a credible bomb threat. Plans should also be in place for access control, information sharing, and physical protection systems. Efficient access control can alleviate crowd crushes during ingress and egress of a venue. Venue- or event-specific intelligence and information sharing can help law enforcement prevent or plan for potential scenarios and ensure an effective response from responding agencies with adequate communication capabilities. The addition of physical protection systems such as CCTV aids in the detection of criminal behavior and illegal activity inside and outside the venue perimeter.

Complete Risk-Assessment Process for a Sport and Event Venue

The following sections describe what the seven risk-assessment stages would look like for a hypothetical sport and event facility, the Sportsplex stadium.

Step 1: Identify Sport Security Command Group

The Sportsplex organization decided to review its safety and security measures to ensure a safe environment for patrons. The Sportsplex owner appoints the facility manager as the lead in identifying key stakeholders in the safety and security management of events held at the Sportsplex. These key stakeholders will form a command group (CG). The CG will serve as the core functional group for all safety and security efforts, including assessing risk; conducting training and exercises; implementing protective measures;

and coordinating response, recovery, and continuity capabilities. In addition to the core CG, the facility manager invites the following entities and individuals who play a role in the security operations of the Sportsplex: state Department of Homeland security representative, state public health and safety representative, local media and public relations representative, public utilities representatives, outsourced private security contractor, and vendor representatives.

Step 2: Facility Characterization

The Sportsplex stadium was built in 2002 and is located in a small city that has a population of about 100,000. The venue is an outdoor facility and is located just off a major highway. It is home to a local college football team and hosts other events including intramural games, concerts, and graduations. Bleacher seating for more than 35,000 is available. The stadium is surrounded by residential and business properties. The CG gathers all the necessary facility maps, diagrams, and personnel records pertaining to the physical description and operations of the stadium.

The CG identifies several undesired events:

1. **Inclement weather**: The location is susceptible to hurricanes and tornadoes that may cause the delay or cancellation of an event. In some instances an evacuation of stadium spectators may be necessary.
2. **Cyber attack**: The stadium press box and command post houses video and communication capabilities that may be disrupted during an event.
3. **Criminal acts**: Fan and player violence, vandalism, and theft all pose a concern to stadium operations.
4. **Terrorism**: Terrorist acts such as a suicide bomber, VBIED, or release of a biological agent could cause mass destruction or casualties.

The CG also described the stadium and surrounding community assets:

- Stadium spectators, participants, and staff
- Stadium structure
- Communications
- Campus police
- Public works (water, power)
- Local police and fire
- Local emergency medical services
- Surrounding neighborhoods and businesses

Step 3: Assess Threats

The CG identified the following potential threat elements and determined the likelihood that the incident would occur as high, medium, or low:

- Severe tornado (high)
- Active shooter (medium)
- Vandalism (low)
- Crowd violence (medium)

Step 4: Analyze Vulnerabilities

The CG identified the following vulnerabilities:

- Screening of spectators entering the facility is inconsistent.
- Evacuation procedures have not been established.
- Facility break-ins have occurred in the past year, resulting in theft of property and vandalism.
- The security staff lacks training, and a volunteer recruitment plan is not in place.
- An emergency response plan for incidents has not been exercised or tested.
- Lighting at entry gates and in parking areas is inadequate.
- A credentialing system for athletes, officials, and security staff is not in place.
- Incidents of crowd violence have occurred previously.
- A control system for vendor and concessionaire delivery is not in place.

(continued)

Complete Risk-Assessment Process for a Sport and Event Venue   *(continued)*

Step 5: Evaluate Consequences

The CG assessed potential consequences for several incidents. For example, see the potential consequences for a tornado incident in figure 4.3 on page 71. For this incident, the economic loss is estimated as being medium ($1 million), the potential for deaths medium (<3), the impact on public confidence medium, and the downtime and geographic impact low.

Step 6: Analyze Risks

The CG made the following analysis pertaining to the example of a tornado incident:

Tornado—high probability and medium consequence severity will be countered by transfer and reduce. The risk involved requires facility management to seek insurance through a third party. In addition, management needs to establish an evacuation plan and exercise the plan to ensure an effective response if such an event occurs while spectators are inside the venue.

Step 7: Identify Countermeasure Improvements

The CG identified the following countermeasure improvements:

- Utilize security technologies, that is, a text messaging system, to curb fan violence.
- Develop emergency response and evacuation plans.
- Practice evacuation drills to test operations and assess capabilities.
- Train staff in terrorism and security awareness.
- Ensure that proper and consistent screening procedures are used. Train staff in screening procedures.
- Establish a vendor control system and schedule concession deliveries when security officials are present.

U.S. Department of Homeland Security Risk Self-Assessment Tool

The mission of the Department of Homeland Security's (DHS) Office of Infrastructure Protection is to prevent the catastrophic loss of life and manage disruptive impacts to commercial facilities from manmade and natural threats. DHS developed the online Risk Self Assessment Tool (RSAT) to assist facility managers with managing and reducing their most serious risks. The RSAT application uses facility input in combination with DHS threat and consequence estimates to assist facility managers in identifying and understanding their security preparedness and to provide them with information on methods of increasing protection for the greatest risks facing their facilities. The RSAT develops risk information by collecting data in the following three areas:

- **Venue characterization**: gathers information about the facility, including its major uses, size, and capacity.
- **Threat ratings**: gathers information on manmade (e.g., IED) and natural threats (e.g., tornados).
- **Vulnerability assessment**: gathers information from the user about the general security posture of the facility, including emergency planning, training, personnel access, and security forces information.

Sport and entertainment facility managers should consider using the DHS online risk assessment tool. Available at no cost and easily accessible, this tool provides a

CASE STUDY

Louisiana Superdome, New Orleans, Louisiana

The September 11, 2001, terrorist attacks targeted symbolic venues within the United States. Included within the list of future potential targets are venues of mass gatherings, specifically sport venues. After the 9/11 terrorist attacks in the United States, security concerns were elevated nationwide for sport venues that attract mass gatherings of people. This concern continues to prevail. A United States Department of Homeland Security (USDHS) assessment, released on January 26, 2009, referenced a posting on a jihadist message board in February 2006. Titled "How You Can Kill Thousands of Americans With a Few Hundred Dollars and Three Men," the message advocated targeting U.S. sporting venues and other public facilities during events (U.S. Department of Homeland Security, 2009e). A recent release, on September 21, 2009, of a joint FBI–DHS bulletin warned that terrorist groups continue to view popular sport and entertainment venues as potential targets. The bulletin references the Al-Qaeda training manual that specifically lists "blasting and destroying the places of amusement, immorality, and sin . . . and attacking vital economic centers" as a key objective (Federal Bureau of Investigation and U.S. Department of Homeland Security, 2009).

Immediately following the 9/11 terrorist attacks, counterterrorism concerns were elevated in terms of security preparations for upcoming major sporting events. On the near horizon was the 2002 Winter Olympic Games, to be hosted in Salt Lake City, Utah. Security preparations for this event had been ongoing since 1997.

Even sooner to occur was the 2002 Super Bowl, scheduled to be held in the Louisiana Superdome in New Orleans, Louisiana, on February 2, 2002. To determine whether any gaps existed in the Superdome security apparatus, a thorough risk assessment needed to be completed before the 2002 Super Bowl. Several factors contributed to the need for heightened security:

- The recent terrorist attacks on the United States on September 11, 2001
- The weeklong NFL Experience that precedes the Super Bowl and attracts large crowds
- The concurrent Mardi Gras celebrations that would be ongoing in New Orleans
- Law enforcement threat assessments that suggested the Super Bowl as a possible target for terrorist attack
- The expectation that 130,000 spectators and support personnel would be inside the Superdome for the 2002 Super Bowl

The Louisiana Superdome is the largest steel-constructed room, unobstructed by posts, in the world. The stadium itself covers 13 acres (5.2 ha), and is situated on a 52-acre (21 ha) expanse of land located in the heart of New Orleans' central business district, approximately 1.5 miles (2.4 km) from the Mississippi River. The Superdome is 273 feet (83 m) high, and the area of the dome roof is 9.7 acres (3.9 ha). All components of the Superdome's structure are designed to contribute to the overall stability of the building. The system of columns, braces, domed roof, and tension ring combine to assure the structural integrity of the building.

Super Bowl XXXVI was the ninth time that the Louisiana Superdome had hosted the National Football League (NFL) championship game, more than any other venue. The last time before 2002 was the 1997 Super Bowl. In preparation for the 1997 game, a detailed risk assessment was conducted by a multiagency team consisting of the Federal

(continued)

Case Study   (continued)

Bureau of Investigation (FBI), the New Orleans Police Department (NOPD), the New Orleans Fire Department (NOFD), and the Louisiana State Police (LSP). In preparation for the 2002 Super Bowl, the same team of agencies was convened to update the previous risk assessment.

Using the 1997 risk assessment as a baseline as well as a risk assessment methodology developed by the FBI Special Events Management Unit, the multiagency risk assessment team reexamined the Superdome facility and discovered that numerous changes had been made, including new internal construction, reconfigured fan seating and room layouts, and the addition of the 20,000-seat-capacity New Orleans Arena, adjacent to the Superdome, that would simulcast Super Bowl XXXVI. These changes directly affected various considerations that would be included during a tactical resolution. The addition of the New Orleans Arena provided a relocation option for spectators in the event that a portion of the Superdome would need to be evacuated. The facility crisis response plan was updated to include all the noted changes.

The risk assessment was completed and provided to event planners. The results of the risk assessment were used to prioritize noted security gaps and subsequently dedicate funding for corrective actions.

LESSONS LEARNED

- Consider current threat assessment information when conducting risk assessments of the sport venue.
- Use a reliable risk assessment methodology.
- Include multiagency representation on the risk assessment team.
- Do not rely on previous risk assessments. Changes occur frequently within sport and entertainment venues.
- Identify security gaps and recommend corrective actions.

QUESTIONS TO CONSIDER

1. How often should a risk assessment be conducted for a sport or entertainment venue?
2. Is information developed during a risk assessment confidential to the facility and security personnel?
3. Should the media be involved in the risk assessment process? Why or why not?

REFERENCES

U.S. Department of Homeland Security, Office of Intelligence and Analysis. (2009e, January 26). *Threats to College Sports and Entertainment Venues and Surrounding Areas.*

Federal Bureau of Investigation and U.S. Department of Homeland Security. (2009, September 21). *Potential Threats to Popular Sport and Entertainment Venues.* Intelligence Bulletin No. 326 Joint FBI–DHS Bulletin.

self-assessment report and a benchmark report to assist the facility manager with security preparedness. The self-assessment report provides facility management with information regarding its existing security strengths and its most vulnerable areas. Explanations, options for enhancements, and references to more information are provided as part of this report. The benchmark report compares the user's facility to similar facilities that have completed the RSAT process.

Key Chapter Points

- Risk is the possibility of loss from a hazard such as personal injury, property damage, death, economic loss, or environmental damage. The three main types of risk are (1) mission (function) risks, (2) asset risks, and (3) security risks.

- An all-hazard risk management approach is critical for sport and entertainment organizations to protect physical and human assets against potential threats, including terrorism, natural disasters, and crowd control issues.

- Sport and entertainment facility managers must embrace risk management processes by conducting risk assessments of their facilities and operations. By conducting an assessment, a manager can (1) obtain a current security profile of the facility and highlight areas in which greater security is needed, (2) help develop a justification of cost-effective countermeasures, and (3) increase security awareness by reporting strengths and weaknesses in security processes to staff members.

- The risk assessment process involves seven key steps: (1) identification of a security command group, (2) facility characterization, (3) threat assessment, (4) vulnerability analysis, (5) consequence evaluation, (6) risk analysis, and (7) countermeasure improvements.

- The security command group should include several agencies that offer multiple-discipline perspectives in security planning, response, and recovery operations at a sporting or special event.

- Facility characterization includes (1) a complete physical description of the facility, (2) identification of undesired events, and (3) identification of critical assets.

- The consequence evaluation phase allows the command group to review all potential threats (undesired events) and estimate consequence values and potential impact on the facility and its key stakeholders.

- Evaluating risk and the potential of loss assists the facility manager's decision-making process to accept, reduce, transfer, or avoid identified threats and risks (U.S. Department of Homeland Security, 2003b).

- Countermeasure improvements are also referred to as risk reduction strategies; these recommendations are provided to management based on venue assessments to enhance decision-making ability.

Application Questions

1. Discuss the importance of conducting a risk assessment.

2. You have been tasked with creating a security command group. What representatives would you request to serve on this important team and why would you select them?

3. Describe potential threats and vulnerabilities at sport and entertainment stadiums and arenas.

4. What general countermeasure improvements (risk reduction strategies) would you suggest to strengthen facility security systems?

Activity

This activity is an exercise in applying risk assessment principles. Choose a sport and event facility and conduct a site visit to obtain information on facility assets, threats, vulnerabilities, and consequences. Prepare a report and conduct a presentation on your findings, using the following outline:

- Gather facility site information
- Identify and list key personnel responsible for security at the facility
- Identify facility assets at venue and in the surrounding area (within 1 mile [1.6 km])
- Identify and describe potential threats to the facility, including any past activities
- Identify facility security strengths
- Identify facility security vulnerabilities (gaps)
- Estimate consequences of undesired events
- Provide recommendations (risk reduction strategies) to improve security operations

CHAPTER 5

Security Planning, Policies, and Protective Measures

CHAPTER GOALS

- Define planning and understand the importance of planning in the sport and special event security system.
- Examine the problem-solving process.
- Develop, implement, and evaluate a risk management program.
- Develop a game-day or event-day operations plan.
- Develop a facility emergency action plan.
- Develop venue policies, procedures, and protective measures.

The guiding principle of effective security management is to assure that all key functions pertaining to the mitigation of potential disaster incidents at sport and other events are addressed and that plans are in place to respond efficiently and effectively. In the security realm, a lack of planning could have devastating consequences and most certainly increases the chances of error should a disaster occur. The purpose of this chapter is to emphasize the importance of planning for all-hazard emergencies and to discuss the development and implementation of plans, policies, and protective measures to combat potential incidents.

Planning is the process of proactively preparing before an event to develop and implement critical plans for prevention, response, and recovery from all-hazard emergencies. The security command group (CG) and other key stakeholders (as deemed necessary given the unique organizational and political structures which govern sport and event venue ownership) responsible for the security management system should envision desired results and develop the necessary procedures and operations to achieve those results. As previously highlighted in this book, the security command group consists of (but is not limited to) representatives from the following key areas: facility management, law enforcement, emergency management, fire and hazardous materials (HAZMAT), and emergency medical services (EMS). Sport governing bodies, leagues, and teams vary widely in their approach to security management. Some organizations maintain in-house security operations, whereas others contract with an outside firm to provide security services. Regardless of the method of delivery of security functions, those responsible for implementation must get to know one another, build trust, and work closely with those they depend on during an incident crisis.

Planning is required to ensure that an effective event security management system is in operation that defines assets, assesses risks, analyzes threats, and develops appropriate plans, policies, and protective measures. A standard planning process may include the following steps (U.S. Department of Homeland Security, 2009c):

1. **Clarify the problem**: For example, the problem may be lack of a defined security system for sport or special events, such as a facility emergency action plan (EAP) that addresses all-hazard incidents.

2. **Canvas resources**: Determine who is most competent or has the specialized capabilities needed to address the specific problem area.

3. **Explore alternatives**: Brainstorm the many concerns relative to potential disaster incidents that could affect sport or other events.

4. **Provide solutions**: Identify needs, such as an upgraded lighting or camera system, a clear signage policy, or updated access control and credentialing processes.

5. **Define priorities**: What is most important? For example, most university athletic departments function as auxiliaries and must generate some, if not all, of their revenue. Funds for optimal security systems are most likely not readily available, so decisions have to be made regarding which security item to address first.

6. **Develop action plans**: The question now becomes what items are committed to and what actions are going to be implemented, by whom, and when. These actions first require that the right people get on the bus and take the right seats (Collins, 2001).

7. **Follow up**: The final stage of the process involves assessing the action plans implemented and determining whether they are achieving the desired results. This step ensures continuous refinement and quality improvement.

Poor planning or planning without purpose or direction will not result in a highly effective security management system for sport or other events. Effective planning is based on a defined process and incorporates documented best practices. A major principle of Stephen Covey's *Seven Habits of Highly Effective People* (1989) is "Begin with the end in mind." Effective planning for event security management is produced by a knowledgeable and skilled command group that meets regularly, participates in training (see chapter 7), and continually reviews and exercises plans (see chapter 8) to find ways to improve. The security command group should be committed to the continuous improvement cycle of plan → do → study → act (see figure 5.1).

Developing a game plan and then exercising or practicing that plan should be standard protocol. Anyone connected with sport knows that, to be successful, coaches must develop a game plan and players must correctly practice that game plan if the intent is to win. If the game plan is well conceived and based on exploiting the vulnerabilities of the opponent, the chances of winning are enhanced. The ultimate goal is to have well-documented security management plans in place and to exercise them regularly. A sport or event organization may depend on multiple agencies for safety and security operations and must coordinate planning efforts with these agencies (identified in chapter 2). The security command group should consider developing and implementing a risk management plan, inclusive of a game-day or event operations plan and facility emergency action plan. Business continuity and recovery planning is also critical and is covered in chapter 6.

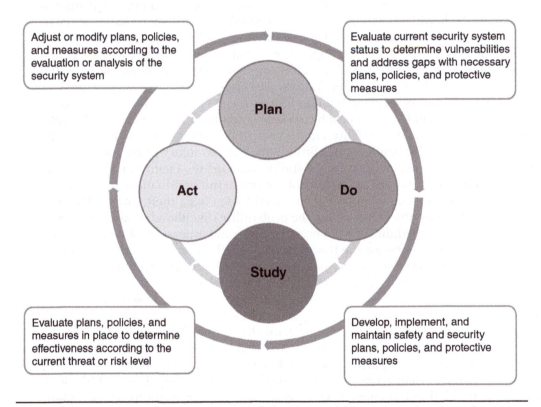

Figure 5.1 Plan–do–study–act process. As with the SESA model, these stages interact to form a cycle of continuous improvement.

Creating Plans for Risk Management

A risk management program adds value to a sport or event operation in four dimensions. It can enhance participant experience through safety protocols and lessening the fear of risk. It can provide good stewardship of assets because good risk management practices protect financial, physical, and human resources. Risk management also forestalls problems, including legal actions from undue liability exposure. Finally, risk management encourages professional practices, resulting in more efficient operations (Kaiser & Robinson, 2005).

According to Kaiser & Robinson (2005), "All organizations, regardless of size or type, should have a current risk management plan" (p. 714). The risk management plan can identify, monitor, and mitigate facility risks on a continuous basis. Mitigation strategies reduce the likelihood that a threat will occur or limit the extent of damage caused by and after an incident (Lindell, Prater, & Perry, 2007). Sport and event managers have a legal duty to provide a safe environment for patrons. Failure to recognize and treat risks may result in injury to patrons, participants, and employees and provide the basis for legal action. The DIM risk management process—developing, implementing, and managing—is a tool to help facility managers establish an effective risk management program. This process involves three key steps: (1) developing the risk management plan, (2) implementing the risk management plan, and (3) managing the risk management plan (Ammon, Southall, & Nagel, 2010).

Step 1: Develop the Plan

Developing the risk management plan consists of three stages, including (1) identification of risks, (2) classification of risks, and (3) method of treatment for identified risks (Ammon, Southall, & Nagel, 2010). These three stages were addressed in chapter 4. The identification of risks can be completed by conducting a risk assessment, which allows the manager to identify specific facility or event risks and evaluate the potential effect that they may have on event operations (i.e., catastrophic, critical, marginal, or negligible). Risks can be categorized into four areas: (1) property loss or damage to facilities or equipment (from natural hazards or vandalism); (2) non-negligent public liability such as contractual liability, employee actions, and invasion of privacy (e.g., pat-down searches); (3) negligent public liability, such as injury resulting from negligence of the venue owner, operator, or staff to manage the facility in a reasonably prudent manner (e.g., failure to implement terrorism mitigation measures); and (4) business operations, such as potential financial losses (e.g., theft, embezzlement). Classifying risk is possible by assessing the probability (likelihood) and frequency of occurrence (i.e., low, medium, high). The recognition and evaluation of potential risks allows the manager to choose the best treatment method (accept, reduce, transfer, or avoid) depending on the severity of impact on facility assets. Treating the risk is imperative because negligence can be the cause of legal action.

Regardless of the size of the organization there should be an assigned risk manager, a risk management team or committee, and supportive administrators. Risk management tasks should be assigned specifically to one person who can lead the effort to reduce risk (Kaiser & Robinson, 2005). Larger sport or event organizations may be able to devote one person just to risk management tasks, but in some cases the facility manager may act as the risk manager. After risks are identified (through the process highlighted in chapter 4) the risk manager can begin to develop plans to monitor facility activities and address areas that need improvement. Facility protective measures are addressed later in this chapter. Generic components of a risk management plan are highlighted in appendix 5.1.

Step 2: Implement the Plan

According to Busowsky (n.d.), the implementation of a risk management plan first includes doing the things that need to be done only once, such as installing extra perimeter controls (bollards), relocating hazardous materials, or developing signs for spectator awareness. These tasks typically require additional funds and someone to complete the work. The second action is acquiring additional safety equipment for OSHA (in the United States) or other legal safety compliance. This could apply to the risk of fires starting inside the venue. Although little can be done to prevent some risky events from occurring, when they do occur the organization can respond efficiently if the correct equipment is in place. New documented procedures can be included in manuals for personnel training, and manuals can be consulted when an incident occurs.

The facility manager (risk manager) may form a risk management committee to monitor the risk management program. The risk management committee should consist of facility employees who provide assistance and suggestions to the manager. Communication is critical during the implementation stage. The risk management plan must be communicated to all employees to ensure their commitment to risk planning tasks and enforce the concept of shared responsibility. Methods of communicating the risk management plan and its importance to employees must begin at the initial hiring orientation to the organization, and the employee handbook should include an excerpt of risk reduction guidelines. Guidelines would cover the facility layout, operations, rules and regulations, organizational structure, responsibilities of employees determined by job title, methods of record keeping, and emergency response actions. The employee handbook should be reviewed annually and when changes are made to the plan. Methods of communicating and training employees are covered in chapter 7. The risk manager can request that the risk committee review operational safety manuals, promote a safe attitude among the workforce, provide risk management training, review accident claims, and conduct periodic facility inspections (Kaiser & Robinson, 2005). The success of the risk management plan depends on management's financial commitment to risk management processes (Ammon, Southall, & Nagel, 2010; Kaiser & Robinson, 2005).

Step 3: Manage the Plan

After the plan is in place, it should be assessed annually to measure progress toward procedural goals and objectives and results-related goals and objectives (Kaiser & Robinson, 2005). Procedural goals and objectives are measures of action. For example, facility managers may inspect facility equipment quarterly to reduce risk of injury from defective equipment. Results-related goals and objectives focus on decreasing the consequence severity or frequency of incidents. For example, the number of slip-and-fall incidents may decrease from three per year to one per year and subsequently to zero per year. Using both sets of goals helps the risk manager assess progress and define specific improvement achievements. Goals that are measurable can be evaluated easily, modified if needed, and used as standards for the granting of rewards when the goals are met. Goals and objectives should be reviewed systematically to understand shortcomings and to adjust accordingly to ensure continuous improvement. The risk management plan is not a static document. The risk environment is constantly changing, so the designated risk manager and risk management committee must review and update the plan at least annually (Kaiser & Robinson, 2005).

To review the plan, key personnel should meet to discuss additions to the plan based on facility inspections, event observations, current trends, and new policies. The updates would then be made within the document itself. For example, the staff may have figured out that a huge surge of traffic hits one of the entrance points at a football stadium 15 minutes before kickoff. Knowing this, management may decide to place extra staff at this choke point to assist ticket takers and security personnel. Management would then adjust the plan pertaining to staff requirements and location of staff within the venue.

David has been recently appointed to a large multipurpose outdoor facility that hosts soccer, rugby, and track and field events. The facility also occasionally hosts major rock concerts. The facility was built in 1999, is located in a major city, and has easy access to public transportation systems. The facility is surrounded by residential and business properties. It has 70,000 club seats, 500 box seats, 30 corporate suites, 11 main entrances with turnstiles, and a parking area within 100 feet (30 m) of the facility. The press box has a command post and CCTV capabilities. Event security is outsourced to a local security provider, but local police, fire, and emergency medical services are available on event day.

David decides to implement a risk management program with the help of his command group. The team analyzes operational policies and procedures, speaks with facility employees and supervisors, and reviews past facility reports and records. David and his team discussed the following issues:

- The facility was built in 1999 (prior to 9/11) and designed with little focus on security features.
- The multipurpose facility hosts soccer, rugby, athletic events, and concerts. Fan demographics are different for each type of event.
- There has been a history of fan violence during soccer matches.
- Procedures used to screen spectators entering the facility have been inconsistent.

- The facility sells alcohol.
- Evacuation procedures (full, partial, or shelter in place) have not been established.
- Management is concerned with the training requirements for security staff and volunteers.
- Facility break-ins have occurred in the past year, resulting in theft of property and vandalism.
- Restricted areas of the facility are not properly controlled during events, allowing patrons access to secure areas.
- Facility lighting at entry gates and in parking areas is inadequate.
- A credentialing system is not in place for athletes, officials, and security staff.
- Storage for facility equipment and maintenance items, which include chemicals that may be used for terrorist purposes, is unsecured.
- Militant political and religious groups are active in the metropolitan area.
- A potential surge of casualties following a major incident would overwhelm current emergency medical resources in the city.

David identified the following risks (in no particular order), assigned levels of probability, consequence, treatment method, and suggested recommendations to mitigate risks.

Risk	Probability	Consequence	Treatment	Recommendations
Vandalism or property damage	Medium	Negligible	Reduce	Ensure that all restricted areas (e.g., press room, storage space) are secured at all times.
Improvised explosive device (IED) or vehicle-borne IED	Low	Catastrophic	Avoid or transfer	Conduct a structural assessment of the facility and reevaluate or redesign security features within the facility. Schedule concession deliveries when security officials are present. Transfer liability to a third party.

Risk	Probability	Consequence	Treatment	Recommendations
Theft or embezzlement	Low	Marginal	Reduce	Obtain insurance.
Fan or player injury	High	Either (depending on extent)	Reduce or transfer	Obtain insurance. Enforce waivers. Abandon activities that present continuous problems and excessive potential loss.
Political demonstrations (i.e., civil disturbance)	Low	Negligible	Accept	Ensure that staff are trained in crowd management techniques.
Biological agent release in facility	Low	Catastrophic	Transfer	Obtain insurance. Ensure that restricted areas (e.g., HVAC systems, hazardous materials storage space) are secured at all times.
Active shooter inside facility	Medium	Catastrophic	Reduce or transfer	Ensure that proper and consistent screening procedures are used.
Suicide bomber inside facility	Medium	Catastrophic	Reduce or transfer	Ensure that proper and consistent screening procedures are used.
Fan or player violence	Medium	Critical or marginal	Reduce or transfer (or avoid, depending on history of event)	Evaluate threats and risks for each event because they may differ. Use security technologies (e.g., text messaging system) to identify troublemakers. Abandon events that present continuous problems and excessive potential loss.
Negligence because of inadequate emergency and evacuation plans	Medium	Critical	Reduce	Develop emergency response and evacuation plans. Practice evacuation drills to test operations.
Crowd crushing at concert event	Medium	Catastrophic	Reduce or transfer (or avoid)	Use leasing agreements and indemnification clauses. Abandon events that present continuous problems and excessive potential loss.
Negligence because of untrained staff	Low	Critical	Reduce or transfer	Use certified independent contractors. Require all staff to complete security training (i.e., terrorism awareness training, crowd management, search policies, and so on). Exercise plans to test operations.
Inclement weather (e.g., hurricane)	Medium	Either (depending on extent and time of event)	Reduce or transfer	Establish mutual aid agreements with response agencies and ensure that alternative playing sites are available for continuity of operations.

Venue Policies

Eliminating risk altogether is impossible, so managers should identify the policies and measures that can reduce risk to a level as low as reasonably practical. The goal is to protect the critical aspects of the sport and event business. Achieving this goal involves instituting policies and procedures, establishing physical security measures, and training and managing security staff (U.S. Department of Homeland Security, 2008c). There is little point investing in costly physical security measures and training security staff if spectators can easily undermine venue policies and procedures. The enforcement of venue policies and procedures is therefore essential to a successful security and safety program. The following key areas should serve as a guide for the development of policies, procedures, and protective measures (U.S. Department of Homeland Security, 2009c):

- **ADA** (e.g., ensuring accessibility to stadium seating for the special needs population): The venue must comply with U.S. federal law, and all spectators must be able to access the venue and their seats.

- **Alcohol** (e.g., preventing access and consumption of alcohol within the venue): For example, the sale of alcohol is not allowed at U.S. college sporting events. Many college campuses are alcohol-free zones. The sale of alcohol is permitted at professional sport events, although league policy and venue management can restrict the number of servings per individual and stop sales after a certain time (e.g., third quarter of an NFL game).

- **Communications** (e.g., establishing an interoperable communication system among first responders): All responding agencies should be able to access the same network to communicate in a time of crisis. Radios and cell phones may be used for communication purposes.

- **Credentialing** (e.g., establishing a credentialing system for event staff, players, team officials, media, and so on): Management may decide to conduct a background check on employees and issue photo credentials to all event-day staff. Credentials may be color coded to indicate stadium zone access (e.g., VIP, field access).

- **Emergency medical services** (e.g., partner with local EMS and hospitals to provide emergency care at stadium): Management should collaborate with emergency response agencies to ensure that adequate medical personnel and supplies are provided at the event and in the case of an incident.

- **Evacuation** (e.g., developing and exercising evacuation procedures): An evacuation plan is critical to ensuring a safe and efficient evacuation, whether partial, full, or shelter in place. After a plan is developed, management should practice the plan to ensure that it works and to identify problem areas before an incident occurs.

- **Fan conduct** (e.g., establishing policy to curb unruly behavior and abusive language): See sidebar.

- **Media and communications** (e.g., identify a public information officer to address the media and the public after an incident): A trained public relations officer should address the media's questions and prevent the public from creating rumors and unnecessary panic.

- **Missing child or person** (e.g., implement a missing child alert system): Management should have procedures in place to notify staff, responding agencies, and local authorities when a person is reported missing. This procedure may include radio notification, public address announcements, or electronic video display announcements.

- **Parking** (e.g., designate restricted parking areas and guard parking areas to prevent illegal entry): Parking staff should be trained and aware of their roles and

NFL Fan Code of Conduct

The National Football League and its teams are committed to creating a safe, comfortable, and enjoyable experience for all fans, both in the stadium and in the parking lot. We want all fans attending our games to enjoy the experience in a responsible fashion. When attending a game, you are required to refrain from the following behaviors:

- Behavior that is unruly, disruptive, or illegal in nature.
- Intoxication or other signs of alcohol impairment that results in irresponsible behavior.
- Foul or abusive language or obscene gestures.
- Interference with the progress of the game (including throwing objects onto the field).
- Failing to follow instructions of stadium personnel.
- Verbal or physical harassment of opposing team fans.

Event patrons are responsible for their conduct as well as the conduct of their guests or persons occupying their seats. Stadium staff will promptly intervene to support an environment where event patrons, their guests, and other fans can enjoy the event free from the above behavior. Event patrons and guests who violate these provisions will be subject to ejection without refund and loss of ticket privileges for future games.

responsibilities for their designated areas. Only vehicles possessing the correct pass information for that particular zone should be allowed access.

- **Prohibited items** (e.g., establish signage to inform the public of prohibited items): Venues vary in their policies concerning prohibited items. Some venues allow backpacks, whereas others have a zero-tolerance bag policy. Regardless of the policy, the prohibited item list should be well communicated inside and outside the venue to inform patrons. This task can be accomplished by stating the policy on the sport league or team website, locating signage outside the venue where spectators can see it before they arrive at the gate entry, and printing the policy in season ticket packages and on the reverse sides of ticket stubs.

- **Protecting critical system controls** (e.g., guard utility systems, such as HVAC, gas, and electrical): Plans and procedures should be in place to prevent unauthorized access to critical systems in the event of sabotage. A terrorist act, such as releasing a biological agent in the air-filtering system of a venue, could cause mass casualties.

- **Search policy** (e.g., implement stadium entry pat-downs): Some sport venues, such as NFL stadiums, have implemented a mandatory pat-down search policy. Spectators are aware that they are subject to such conditions when they purchase a ticket.

- **Tailgate** (e.g., designate tailgating areas and patrol with security staff): Tailgate areas should be properly monitored with adequate security personnel before, during, and after the event. Normally, alcohol is consumed in tailgating areas, and crowd control issues may arise.

- **Ticket taking** (e.g., establish an electronic system): An electronic ticketing system can help prevent the use counterfeit tickets and provide management the capability of knowing who is in the venue and where they are seated.

Protective Measures

In trying to manage risk, managers need to develop protective measures that change, reduce, or eliminate the probability or consequences of a harmful action. "Protective measures include equipment, personnel, training, and procedures designed to protect a facility against threats and mitigate effects of an attack" (Department of Homeland Security, 2008c, p. 4). Protective measures are employed to increase awareness among facility managers, reduce vulnerabilities of sporting and other events and their critical assets (physical or human), enhance the defense mechanism against an incident, and enhance preparedness among security stakeholders to respond to and resolve incidents (Department of Homeland Security, 2008c). Protective measures should meet four key objectives:

1. Devalue: lower the value of a facility to terrorists, that is, make the facility less interesting as a target.
2. Detect: spot the presence of adversaries or dangerous materials and provide responders with information needed to mount an effective response.
3. Deter: make the facility more difficult to attack successfully.
4. Defend: respond to an attack to defeat adversaries, protect the facility, and mitigate any effects of an attack (Department of Homeland Security, 2008c, p. 4).

The first essential administrative action step in identifying the protective measures baseline is assessing the specific venue vulnerabilities and practicing prudent risk management and mitigation measures (as discussed in chapter 4). Some protective measures are applicable to a wide range of facilities and against various threat streams, whereas others are designed to address specific needs or threat streams for a designated venue. The implementation of protective measures involves the commitment of many resources, such as personnel, equipment, time, and financial support. Sport and event organizations need to coordinate and cooperate with local and state agencies and emergency responders to determine what measures should be implemented, how extensive they should be, and how long they should be kept in force to maximize security (Department of Homeland Security, 2008c).

Many sport governing bodies, leagues, and teams have developed best practices in security as a guideline for league members. After the tragic events of September 11, 2001, the National Football League (NFL), National Basketball Association (NBA), and National Hockey League (NHL) developed a best practices guideline of protective security measures to assist league members in their security efforts (Schwarz, Hall, & Shibli, 2010). Security management was enhanced at the intercollegiate level as well. The National Collegiate Athletic Association (NCAA) issued a security-planning options guideline for university athletic events (Schwarz, Hall, & Shibli, 2010). Several other checklists, guidelines, and best practices have been published to assist the sport and event security manager. Pantera et al. (2005) developed a security measures checklist that addressed concerns before and after a sport event (see appendix 5.2). Appendix 5.3 provides a checklist for routine nonevent security measures proposed by the U.S. Department of Homeland Security. According to Hall et al. (2010), sport programs should also consider implementing protective security measures in the following key areas.

Physical Security

- Establish security zones and perimeters.
- Provide law enforcement presence before, during, and after the event.
- Secure buildings surrounding the stadium.
- Secure all HVAC systems.

Technical Security

- Secure utility areas with alarms.
- Use closed-circuit television for monitoring at the stadium.
- Ensure adequate facility lighting.
- Implement interoperable communication system.
- Consider cyber security.
- Use telephone trap and trace.

Access Control

- Use designated entry checkpoints and conduct searches for prohibited items.
- Search all staff (media, VIPs, and so on).
- Scan tickets electronically.
- Have law enforcement present at each entry point.
- Schedule delivery times for vendors.
- Lock down the stadium before the event.
- Conduct staff background checks.
- Issue staff photo credentials.

Emergency Management

- Develop an emergency action plan.
- Establish a command post.
- Establish mutual aid agreements with response agencies.
- Conduct briefing and debriefing event meetings.
- Conduct a risk assessment.

Training and Exercise

- Use licensed and certified security providers.
- Conduct emergency response and evacuation exercises.
- Orient game- and event-day staff to their specific job responsibilities.
- Train all game- and event-day staff in security awareness and evacuation procedures.

These procedures are effective in the case of a wide range of incidents and can all be applied to nonsport event venues as well. Some events have unique needs and may require additional protective measures. At concerts, crowd energy and emotion often run high. The sidebar on page 92 lists some strategies for preventing violence and crowd disorder at concerts. See appendix 5.4, Planning Considerations for Special Events, for a discussion of the needs of other types of events.

Game- and Event-Day Plans

As previously mentioned, planning is a critical step in the overall process of ensuring a safe and secure environment. Game- or event-day plans ensure that management has addressed risks and threats, crowd management strategies, personnel needs, staff training, communication capabilities, and emergency response procedures. See appendix 5.5 for a list of additional considerations for a game- or event-day plan.

Concert Violence Risk Reduction Strategies

- **Eliminate general admission**: Prevent dangerous crowd density and the potential for mosh pits. Management should not sell tickets beyond venue capacity.

- **Adhere to schedule**: Advertise times such as when doors will open and when performers will start. Communicate potential delays.

- **Use professional security**: Management should consider using professional security services with sufficient training.

- **Provide onsite medical care**: Management should provide onsite medical care for all major concerts and festivals, besides having staff certified in first aid.

- **Transport**: The venue should coordinate with local law enforcement and emergency management agencies to develop plans and procedures for transporting injured attendees.

- **Limit drug and alcohol use**: Given the documented association of alcohol and drugs with aggressive behavior, venues should implement strict policies of denying admittance to or not serving intoxicated people, as well as removing intoxicated people at the first indication of violent behavior.

- **Limit projectiles**: Thrown projectiles are a major risk factor and can be addressed by limiting promotional giveaways and serving drinks in small, lightweight cups.

- **Lower volumes**: Given the research on the association of volume and aggressive behavior, venue management should consider reducing volume levels.

- **Create safer environment**: If moshing and crowd surfing cannot be banned or policies are not enforced, management can have artists address the risks of moshing during shows.

Reference: *Concert violence: A brief history of concert violence.* (2010). Retrieved from http://blog.lib.umn.edu/morga364/myblog2/.

Reviewing Historical Files

Records should be kept of all emergency and medical incidents that occur during an event. At the end of each event security personnel should prepare an after-action report that summarizes the event and describes its successes, failures, and problem areas. These documents should be retained on file for inquires, lawsuits, and historical documentation. They will contain useful information that can be used as a guide or reference for future events at the facility.

Conducting a General Survey

A general survey is the collection of information regarding the specifics of a facility. Key security personnel may use this information, which should contain detailed information regarding capacity, structures, installations, and various other components such as mechanical and electrical systems. These surveys allow managers to plan for events and control crowd movements. When considering crowd movements managers should consider circulation, direction, and movements. Physical elements include standing areas, ingress, egress, stairways, ramps, concourses, vomitories, and fire and emergency routes. Proper safety and security management should include the entire venue rather than focus on a particular area of concern.

The general survey will help establish site post assignments, instructions, and a site post diagram that shows all staff locations. Post assignments refer to the positioning of event staff throughout the venue before an event. The facility manager assigns personnel to each event. A post diagram ensures that staff are placed in strategic positions throughout the venue and allows them to be moved to different locations as needed during an event. Post assignments facilitate communication and enable issues to be directed efficiently to designated personnel.

All facility staff should understand their designated post assignments. The facility manager must be certain to staff the event properly. Responsibilities will vary according to the event and various postings that staff will be attending to during an event. Facility supervisors will be responsible for ensuring several aspects of staffing:

- Attendance of personnel
- Staff compliance with policies and procedures
- Attendance at a pregame or preevent briefing
- Proper positioning of personnel
- Proper communication
- Proper response to problems, questions, and concerns
- Completion of postevent reports
- Ready availability to staff

All facility staff should be required to wear facility-issued laminated cards before, during, and after all events. These cards should contain a step-by-step response for medical emergencies, fire emergencies, and evacuations. This approach will limit confusion and reduce response time. The cards should include several items:

- Supervisor and general contact numbers
- Emergency, medical, and fire contact numbers
- Responsibilities and duties in a medical emergency
- Responsibilities and duties in an evacuation

The facility manager should develop a site post diagram before each event so that she or he and other security and safety personnel have an immediate visual reference of all staff locations. The manager should assign available personnel strategically throughout the venue as needed. A site post diagram should also include all transportation routes so that the safety and security staff have a visual reference of police and medical vehicle locations throughout the surrounding area. In an emergency these diagrams will help police and medical personnel make decisions on movement of emergency vehicles.

Site Walk-Through

A site walk-through before the day of the game or event should be arranged by the facility manager. The walk-through should include lead representatives from police, fire, medical, facility supervisors, communications, and physical plant. Its purpose is to discuss the event schedule, team or entertainers' movements, crowds, and other related safety and security issues. The various personnel can address event details and solve any issues that would impede a safe and secure event.

Staff Briefing and Review

Staff briefings are a necessary component of effective safety and security management. The facility manager should address the issues, concerns, or problems with the staff before any event. Concerns or issues may vary depending on the event or facility.

The issues that staff should be briefed on include the following:

• **Nature of the event**: Events are an organized occasion that may vary from sporting events, to entertainment events, to political rallies. Understanding the complexity and nature of the event will help the facility manager develop and enhance safety and security procedures as well as emergency response capabilities. By evaluating potential threats and vulnerabilities the manager will better recognize which threats are dangerous, how they can be mitigated, and how resources should be allocated. The variables that will change the nature of the event include

  • type of event (sports, entertainment, political),
  • sequence of the program, and
  • special effects.

• **Access control**: Among the most important functions of safety and security are access control, screening systems, and monitoring systems. These practices provide orderly movement of spectators into and through the appropriate areas as well as securing spectators, buildings, and venues. Access control limits who can enter a facility and where they have access, screening systems limit what items are allowed into the venue, and monitoring systems observe spectators in and around the venue.

• **Environment**: Facility managers must understand the environment in which an event will be conducted, both the permanent elements of the facility and the temporary structures. Site control measures can safely and securely manipulate, control, and direct the movement and location of spectators, staff, and vehicles.

• **Policies and procedures**: Policies and procedures are established methods of accomplishing an orderly and safe event. Facilities should have a standard set of established policies and procedures that provide basic guidelines for facility staff to follow. Although certain policies and procedures are appropriate for particular venues, all policies and procedures should follow a basic set of guidelines.

• **Media concerns**: Many sporting and nonsporting events attract large public attention and media coverage. A facility manager should coordinate press movements with facility personnel and assign specific facility staff to coordinate press issues with media representatives. For very large events at least two staff members should be assigned to aid with media relations. Note that facility staff acting as press coordinators are facility employees and do not work for the media.

Understanding Site Dynamics

Facility managers should be familiar with the site dynamics of each facility. They should have a complete understanding of movements and locations of everyone at the site from the time when they park to the time when they leave. This knowledge allows facility managers to manipulate the movements or maneuver personnel, teams, or entertainers.

As the lead representative at the venue on game day or event day, the facility manager will be in contact with many people during an event. When he or she identifies a problem, issue, or concern, the manager needs to determine which contact will best help in solving the issues. A list of important contacts should be kept on hand on the day of the event (see appendix 5.5).

Site Control

After site dynamics are identified, strategies need to be in place for controlling movement of people and vehicles. Some aspects to consider are site control rooms, control areas, and control measures.

• **Site control rooms** are used to direct movement and location of people and vehicles. These rooms will be designated for security and safety operations or will house teams, entertainers, or high-profile dignitaries. Rooms will need to be selected strategically and have limited access.

- Room selection
- Command post
- Security room
- Staff room
- Holding room (telephone available)
- Bathroom
- Medical emergency room
- Crises room

- **Site control areas** are necessary control measures that should be considered. These areas include ingress and egress routes and other areas that teams, entertainers, or high-profile dignitaries will be moving through. Facility managers should anticipate the movements and plan accordingly.

- Arrival and departure areas
- Room for motorcade
- Routes (hallways, stairs, elevators)
- Covered, tented, and private areas
- Press and public containment
- Event areas
- Holding room
- Suites
- Stage

- **Site control measures**, which provide the ability to control and manipulate movements of spectators and vehicles, are necessary when planning a safe and secure environment. The facility manager should coordinate with lead safety and security representatives, appropriate sport or event organization personnel, physical plant, vendors, and other event-related organizers when selecting proper crowd control measures (see appendix 5.5). A strong event-day operations plan with good control over movements of spectators is essential, regardless of the type of venue. The sidebar on page 96 describes a tragic example of this need, one that resulted in the deaths of several spectators at an off-road auto-racing event.

Assessing Site Vulnerability

Vulnerability assessments address the security of venue sites. A vulnerability assessment is a validation of the risk assessment that should be completed before athletic seasons or events. The primary purpose for conducting vulnerability assessments is to increase security awareness. Facility managers need to consider the various site variables of a facility to assess its vulnerability. If rival opponents, entertainers, or high-profile dignitaries are headlining an event, they may be subject to greater risk because of various site variables. An adjustment of allocated assets may be necessary because of additional risk. Consideration should be given to local, state, and federal assets. Site variables that may bring additional risk to a facility include the following:

- Above-average public interest
- Site in an area with a high crime rate or history of demonstrations
- Outdoor venue, location, and weather
- Local support entities unable to provide adequate control

Crowd Tragedy at Poorly Planned Off-Road Race in California

Authorities questioned the planning and management of an off-road race in the Mojave Desert in Southern California on August 14, 2010. One of the drivers lost control of his vehicle and plowed into an unsuspecting crowd that had gathered along the road. Many of the spectators were standing so close to the track that they had no time to react to the oncoming vehicle. Eight people died when the modified pick-up truck flipped over and crashed into the crowd at high speed. Many others were injured and traumatized.

The California 200 event was organized by Mojave Desert Racing Productions (MDR). It was suggested that the event organizers knew, or should have known, that a crowd would try to move as close as possible to the excitement of any sporting event, including a road race,

or other events such as political rallies and concerts. Crowd security and barricades are typically positioned between spectators and stages, racetracks, and playing areas to protect spectators and participants.

The event organizers knew from past events that crowds would migrate to the race track, and they stated on their company website that spectators should stay 100 feet (30 m) back from the track. But organizers failed to provide customary protective barriers and crowd management security that would require spectators to stay a safe distance from the race course. Additionally organizers are accused of not providing basic emergency medical services.

Reference: Crowd management strategies. (2010). "Desert Disaster: No Crowd Management + No Barriers = 8 Dead, Scores Injured." Retrieved from www.crowdsafe.com/new.asp?ID=2050.

- Site or event rivalry; politically sensitive or controversial
- High-profile persons, teams, or entertainers
- Known technical, mechanical, or chemical hazards
- Personnel medical concerns because of site considerations

Technical Considerations

Facility managers must be familiar with the technical and mechanical aspects of their facility when preparing for an event. Lead representatives of physical plant, engineering, fire marshal, and law enforcement can provide information about environmental considerations, mechanical considerations, fire safety considerations, and physical security considerations.

Emergency Preparedness

Facility managers are responsible for the safety and security of staff and spectators at all times. They should understand and anticipate any problems that might occur. Emergency preparedness must be coordinated with police, fire, medical, and emergency management agencies before any event. The U.S. Department of Homeland Security (2008c) in its *Protective Measures Guide for U.S. Sports Leagues* presented a facility emergency action plan (EAP) guideline that outlines basic aspects of an emergency plan:

1. Coordinate the plan with local, state, and federal emergency management agencies.
2. Include protocol for event delays, cancellations, incident response (i.e., partial versus full evacuation), communications, and recovery issues.

3. Maintain copies of the EAP in redundant locations and protected from unauthorized disclosure.

4. Identify the chain of command (i.e., decision makers) through the incident command system in coordination with local, state, and federal authorities. For each sporting event, document who has the authority to make decisions relative to manmade or natural disasters.

5. Include contact numbers for personnel identified in the chain of command and provide a sequence of notification. Describe the primary and backup communication systems.

6. Ensure that relocation areas for evacuations are accessible and secure. For shelter-in-place scenarios ensure that the facility is stocked with supplies. For full evacuations make sure that the facility is locked down and safe before reoccupancy.

7. Develop a timeline for conducting training exercises to test the decision-making process and communications.

8. Ensure that employees know the protocol for shutting off utility services (i.e., electricity, gas).

9. Develop an emergency medical plan as part of the EAP to include procedures for catastrophic event requiring primary and secondary triage. Identify triage and transport sites and secure emergency routes in and out of the facility.

10. Develop audio or video scripts for specific emergency announcements (i.e., inclement weather, bomb threat, explosion).

11. Do not release information on internal security measures to the press. Appoint a single person to address the media.

The type of plan and the amount of support will vary among events and sites. Emergency response plans will be discussed in more detail in chapter 6. In addition, a readiness assessment instrument titled *How Prepared Is Your Business for an Emergency* developed by the National Safety Council is provided in appendix 5.6.

In concluding this chapter, it is important to reflect on the planning process. This process includes problem solving; developing, implementing, and managing a risk management plan; and developing and implementing venue policies and protective security measures. The following checklist summarizes items to consider from this chapter:

- The problem-solving process: (1) clarify the problem, (2) canvas resources, (3) explore alternatives, (4) provide solutions, (5) define priorities, (6) develop action plans, and (7) follow up.

- Risk management planning: (1) develop the plan, (2) implement the plan, and (3) manage the plan.

- Game-day or event-day operations plan.

- Facility emergency action plan.

- Venue policies: ADA, alcohol, communications, credentialing, emergency medical services, employee code of conduct, evacuation, fan conduct, media and communications, missing child or person, parking, prohibited items, protecting critical system controls, search policy, staff evaluation, tailgate, ticket taking, and waste management.

- Protective security measures: devalue, detect, deter, and defend.

- Pre- and postevent measures; nonroutine measures; physical security, technical security, access control, emergency management, and training and exercise.

CASE STUDY

Hillsborough Disaster

The Hillsborough disaster was the worst stadium disaster in English football history, resulting in the deaths of 96 people. On April 15, 1989, the FA Cup semifinal match between Liverpool FC and Nottingham Forest at the Hillsborough football stadium was abandoned six minutes into the game because of a human stampede in the Leppings Lane end of the stadium holding Liverpool fans.

• **Prematch**: Opposing fans were segregated in the stadium. The police assigned Nottingham Forest fans to the Spoin Kop end of the stadium, which had a capacity of 21,000. The Liverpool supporters were assigned to the Leppings Lane end of the stadium, which had a capacity of 14,600, even though Liverpool FC would have a larger supporter group than Nottingham Forest. Kickoff was scheduled for 3:00 p.m. Fans were encouraged to be in their seats 15 minutes before kickoff, and those without tickets were advised not to attend. Between 2:30 p.m. and 2:40 p.m., a buildup of fans occurred in the small area outside the turnstile entrance to the Leppings Lane end. The Leppings Lane terrace had three separate areas. The central area filled up quickly, while the side areas remained relatively empty. A bottleneck developed outside the stands.

• **Kickoff**: The match kicked off and fans started to push. An estimated 5,000 fans were trying to get through the turnstiles. To prevent crushing outside the stadium, the police opened a series of gates (intended as exits) that did not have turnstiles. Thousands of fans rushed through the gates and into the central area at the Leppings Land end. In five minutes 2,000 fans passed through, and most made their way to the central areas. A huge crush developed at the front of the terrace where fans were pressed against the fencing (that acted as a barrier between the spectators and football pitch) by the crowd behind them. The fans entering were unaware of the problems at the fencing. Normally, police or stewards would stand at the entrance of the central area to redirect fans to the side areas if capacity was reached, but they were not present at those locations on the day of the match.

• **Six minutes later**: At 3:06 p.m. the referee was advised by police to stop the match as fans tried to climb the fence to escape the crush. A small gate in the fencing was opened for some fans to escape as others were pulled to safety by fellow fans in the stand directly above the Leppings Lane terrace. Fans were packed so tightly in the central area that many died of compressive asphyxia while standing up. The fence finally broke under pressure from the fans. The pitch filled with people. The police, stewards, and emergency medical services were overwhelmed. Fans attempted to help the injured, and advertising billboards were used as makeshift stretchers.

• **Aftermath**: Ninety-six people died and over 400 received hospital treatment. Following the disaster, Lord Justice Taylor was appointed to conduct an inquiry. An interim report on the events of the day stated, "The main reason for the disaster was the failure of police control." A final report known as the *Taylor Report* made general recommendations for football ground safety. This report recommended that major stadiums be converted to all-seated venues and that perimeter fencing be outlawed.

LESSONS LEARNED

• **Police control**: After the disaster attention focused on the decision to open secondary gates. It was also suggested that match kickoff could have been delayed, an action that had been taken at other venues and matches. Furthermore, police or stewards were not present to direct fans away from areas filled to capacity.

- **Stadium design**: The Hillsborough stadium was criticized for having a low number of turnstiles at the Leppings Lane entrance. It was estimated that it would have taken until 3:40 p.m. to get all ticket holders into the Leppings Lane end. The official capacity of the central areas at the Leppings Lane terrace was 2,000, but the health and safety executive later determined that it should have been 1,600 because the crush barriers did not conform to the *Guide to Safety at Sports Grounds* standards. It is estimated that over 3,000 people were in the areas after kickoff. This overcrowding caused the fatal crush.

- **Alcohol consumption**: The consumption of alcohol by fans before the game may have aggravated the situation.

- **Ticketing**: The possibility of fans attempting to gain entry without tickets or with forged tickets could have aggravated the situation.

QUESTIONS TO CONSIDER

1. Discuss lessons learned from this incident. What suggestions would you offer to enhance security management systems?

2. Should all sport venues adhere to a set of safety and security standards? Why or why not?

SOURCES

Hillsborough Disaster, retrieved from http://en.wikipedia.org/wiki/Hillsborough_Disaster

Hillsborough Timeline to Disaster, 2009, April 3, BBC.co.uk, retrieved from www.bbc.co.uk/liverpool/content/articles/2009/04/03/hillsborough_timeline_feature.shtml

The Hillsborough Stadium Disaster, 1989, August, Interim Report, Inquiry by the Rt. Hon. Lord Justice Taylor.

Schwarz, E., Hall, S.A., & Shibli, S., 2010, *Sport Facility Operations: A Global Perspective*, Oxford, UK: Butterworth-Heinz (reprint permission granted).

Reprinted, by permission, from E. Schwarz, S. Hall, and S. Shibli, 2010, *Sport facility operations management* (London: Butterworth-Heinemann).

Key Chapter Points

- Planning is the process of taking proactive steps before an event to develop and implement critical plans for prevention, response, and recovery from all-hazard emergencies.
- A standard problem-solving process may include the following steps: clarify the problem, canvas resources, explore alternatives, provide solutions, define priorities, develop action plans, and follow up.
- The sport or event security command group should consider developing and implementing a risk management plan, inclusive of an event operations plan and facility emergency action plan or response plan.
- The DIM risk management process involves three key steps: (1) developing the risk management plan, (2) implementing the risk management plan, and (3) managing the risk management plan.
- The goal is to protect the critical aspects of the security business. This involves instituting policies and procedures, developing physical security measures, and training and managing security staff.
- Protective measures are employed to increase awareness among facility managers, reduce vulnerabilities of events and their critical assets (physical or

human), enhance the defense mechanism against an incident, and enhance preparedness among sport or event security stakeholders to respond to and resolve incidents.

Application Questions

1. Discuss the importance of planning for effective security management. How can risk management planning add value to sport or event operations?

2. What plans, policies, and protective measures should be considered when planning a major sporting or other event?

Activity

Review the plans, policies, and protective measures of a sport or event venue. Provide the top 10 protective security measures for the venue and an action plan for areas that need improvement.

CHAPTER 6

Emergency Response and Recovery

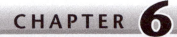

CHAPTER GOALS

- Understand the importance of emergency planning.
- Examine the emergency management cycle—preparedness, response, recovery, and mitigation.
- Develop an emergency response plan (ERP).
- Understand the importance of evacuation planning.
- Develop a business continuity plan (BCP).

This chapter addresses the four key components of emergency management that a sport or event facility manager must consider: preparedness, response, recovery, and mitigation activities, including business continuity and contingency of operations. Many sport venues are multipurpose facilities that host events such as music concerts, graduation ceremonies, disaster triage, and possibly evacuation shelters in an emergency crisis (Hall, Marciani, & Cooper, 2008). These types of mass gatherings require that a comprehensive emergency management system be in place to deal effectively with all-hazard emergencies.

The Center for Venue Management Studies (2002) defined an emergency situation as "any incident, situation, or occurrence that could affect the safety/security of occupants, cause damage to the facility, equipment and its contents, or disrupt activities of the facility" (p. 1). Examples include medical emergencies, fire hazards, bomb threats or explosions, power or equipment failure, natural disasters or inclement weather, crowd control issues or riots, hazardous material release, domestic or international terrorism, and evacuations (partial, full, and shelter in place). Emergency planning is important for several reasons (Center for Venue Management Studies, 2002):

- Adherence to professional standards and expectations provides a safe environment for facility patrons and local community stakeholders.
- Experience has shown that planning, training, and implementation of an emergency plan reduce potential damage and loss associated with emergency incidents.
- Adherence to legal public safety requirements, such as fire safety and ADA requirements, improves the safety and security of occupants.
- Documentation of an emergency plan minimizes liability to facility, owners, and operators when an emergency occurs.
- Good planning practices minimize negative media exposure and enhance the image of the facility in the local community.

Components of Emergency Management

Emergency management practices attempt to avoid or reduce potential losses from all hazards and ensure appropriate assistance to achieve rapid and effective recovery after an emergency (Warfield, 2008). Sport and event managers must focus on all components of this interrelated process. Preparedness is a state of readiness to respond to a disaster, crisis, or any other type of emergency. Response is a unified crisis and consequence management effort that provides effective and efficient interoperability and compatibility among all levels of agencies responding to an incident. Recovery is a process that begins in the initial hours following a disaster and can continue for months and in some cases years. This process includes rebuilding homes, replacing property, resuming employment, restoring businesses, and permanently repairing and rebuilding infrastructure. Mitigation is a sustained action taken to reduce or eliminate risk to people and property from hazards and their effects (Warfield, 2008). The security command group must work closely with external agencies involved in the planning and response operations at events. The four components to all-hazards emergency management cover the spectrum of incident management (see figure 6.1).

Preparedness

Ensuring a risk-free environment and protecting against all potential hazards is impossible. Therefore, preparedness—taking actions before an emergency occurs—is a key way of reducing the impact of an incident. Preparedness involves completing tasks and activities to build, sustain, and improve capabilities to prevent, protect

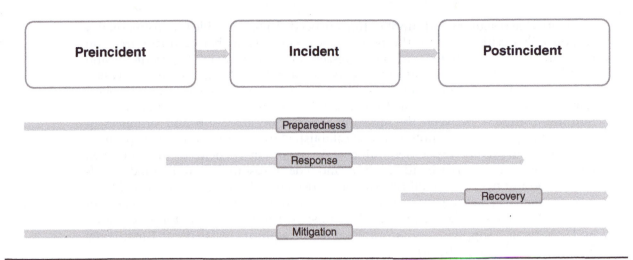

Figure 6.1   The roles of preparedness, response, recovery, and mitigation before, during, and after an incident.

against, respond to, and recover from incidents. Preparedness is a continuous process and involves all key players in the security command group, as well as local, state, and federal agencies as needed. Preparedness activities may include (1) developing an emergency response plan (ERP), (2) recruiting and training staff, (3) identifying resources and supplies, and (4) designating facilities for emergency use (Federal Emergency Management Agency, 2006a).

The ERP describes how the sport or event program will do business in an emergency. The emergency plan documents the steps and actions to be taken by the facility staff and public response agencies to minimize or eliminate potential harm to facility patrons or damage to the facility. The ERP ultimately reduces exposure to risks and results of emergencies through prevention, detection, communication, evacuation, damage control, and recovery efforts (Center for Venue Management Studies, 2002). The security command group becomes the emergency planning team (EPT) responsible for developing the venue emergency response plan in coordination with local and state authorities. The EPT has working knowledge of the facility and its systems, is responsible for resources, makes decisions, and has the ability to implement the plan. The plan should be developed with specific actions and responses to any given emergency. A sport or event emergency response plan outline appears in appendix 6.1.

After an emergency response plan has been developed, key staff and facility personnel responsible for implementation should be trained and tested. Staff training is discussed in detail in chapter 7. The following list highlights some training techniques (Center for Venue Management Studies, 2002):

- Conduct training sessions (seminars).
- Do role playing and practice drills.
- Hold preevent briefings.
- Provide event staff with handheld cards that contain brief notes of information pertaining to emergencies and specific positions and assignment.
- Test the staff's knowledge of the facility ERP.
- Conduct combined training sessions with external public agencies involved in responding to facility emergencies (e.g., police, fire, community utility companies).
- Produce training videos to orient new employees or to use during briefing events.

Identifying resources and supplies that are needed and available for an emergency response is a critical part in the preparedness stage. Gaps between resources on hand and resources needed may be addressed through mutual aid agreements and standby contracts. "Mutual aid agreements are formal, written agreements between jurisdictions that provide conditions under which resource sharing can take place during an emergency" (Federal Emergency Management Agency, 2006a, p. 3.8). Standby contracts between the sporting or event organization and suppliers of critical equipment and supplies can be established to ensure obtaining a specified quantity of an item at a specified unit cost. In major emergencies or disasters (i.e., natural disaster, terrorist incident) state and federal resources will be made available. In addition, certain facilities should be designated for emergency use during a crisis, such as an emergency operations center (or command center, discussed in chapter 3); shelters to house displaced victims; distribution centers for food, water, and emergency supplies; and storage areas for equipment (Federal Emergency Management Agency, 2006a).

Response

Emergency response has three distinct goals: (1) to protect people, (2) to limit damage from primary impacts, and (3) to minimize damage from secondary impacts (Lindell, Prater, & Perry, 2008). Response efforts begin when an emergency is imminent or immediately after an incident occurs. Response includes tasks and activities that address the short-term (direct) effects of an incident to limit loss of life, personal injury, and property damage. Response activities may include (1) executing the ERP and evacuation procedures, (2) applying intelligence to lessen effects and consequences of an incident, (3) increasing security operations, (4) investigating the nature and source of a threat, (5) restoring critical infrastructure, and (6) ensuring continuity of critical services (i.e., public works) (Federal Emergency Management Agency, 2006a). A response operations activity is presented at the end of the chapter.

Evacuation Plan

Planning for an evacuation at sporting and special events requires coordination, communication, and cooperation by the facility operators and all levels of the response community (federal, state, local, and private). Evacuation planning should take into consideration all potential hazards for a particular facility, including weather-related incidents. An evacuation plan should be an essential component of the facility's emergency plan and should be included as an appendix to the facility's emergency plan without being redundant and restating operations and procedures inherent in the emergency plan (U.S. Department of Homeland Security, 2008a). A stadium evacuation plan template is provided in appendix 6.2.

Facility managers must consider several factors when developing an evacuation plan, including immense crowds, ingress and egress from the facility, and location of the facility. A critical element to evacuation planning is determining the necessary control of movement of the stadium spectators, participants, staff, vendors, and general public in response to a hazardous situation (i.e., full evacuation, partial evacuation, sheltering in place, or relocation) (U.S. Department of Homeland Security, 2008a). Whether directing traffic outside the facility, sheltering patrons inside the facility, relocating patrons, or fully evacuating the facility, the principles guiding the execution of an evacuation are the same. These principles include assessing risks, planning a response, informing the public, and implementing the plan. Making the decision to evacuate, shelter in place, or relocate during an incident is complicated and requires input from various entities knowledgeable about the structure of the stadium, the size and distribution of the spectators and participants, the hazard involved, and the anticipated response to that hazard (U.S. Department of Homeland Security, 2008a). The incident commander (i.e., police chief or emergency management director; see chapter 3) determines whether to conduct a full evacuation, partial evacuation, or shelter in place. A full evacuation may be conducted because of explosion, severe storm, plane crash, major structural failure, earthquake, or chemical spill. A partial evacuation may be conducted because of a bomb threat, minor fire, small explosion, minor structural damage, or unruly fan behavior.

An evacuation planning process and procedures guideline is provided in appendix 6.3. To ensure a well-managed and coordinated evacuation, stadium operators must coordinate their evacuation plans with the local, state, and, if appropriate, federal authorities. Coordination is best accomplished through maintaining ongoing communications with local emergency authorities, planning for all-hazard incidents, and training and exercising plans with emergency authorities (U.S. Department of Homeland Security, 2008a).

The International Association of Assembly Managers (IAAM) provides resources and training on development and implementation of such plans (further information

Considerations and Guidelines for Evacuation

The decision to evacuate will be made when an emergency occurs that requires the movement of persons from a dangerous place because of the threat or occurrence of a disastrous event. The evacuation may be either full or partial. The following questions for consideration and statements of supporting actions are useful in performing an evacuation.

Considerations

- What is the reason for evacuating (fire, structural failure, equipment failure, crowd control)?
- What criteria are used when making evacuation decisions?
- How effective is the evacuation in removing the stadium spectators and participants from a dangerous situation?
- How many people can be evacuated in a reasonable amount of time? Does this number meet evacuation needs? How can the evacuation rate be increased?
- Who will make the decision to evacuate? Who will implement the decision and how?
- What steps need to be taken before an event occurs? How will it be determined whether harmful contaminants are in the air?

Supporting Actions

- Develop decision criteria to assist in making the evacuation decision.
- Identify the person who will make the decision to evacuate.
- Develop procedures for implementing evacuation activities.
- Establish roles and responsibilities for the evacuation team to effect evacuation.
- Ensure that air-monitoring teams and equipment are on site and functioning to address any possible chemical or other contaminant situations.
- Be prepared and conduct exercises for the unintended self-evacuation (i.e., flight response) that may result when spectators decide on their own to evacuate the stadium. Be prepared to direct and mitigate the effects of an unintended evacuation, especially if it conflicts with a potential hazard.

Reprinted from the U.S. Department of Homeland Security, 2008, *Evacuation planning guide for stadiums*.

can be retrieved at www.iaam.org). Items to consider when developing evacuation procedures include the following (Center for Venue Management Studies, 2002):

- Facility staff must be present to direct patrons to a safe area. This procedure will greatly help to reduce panic and chaos that may ensue.
- A chain of command should be identified. The person of authority who will make the evacuation decision (normally the incident commander) should also be identified.
- Alternative points of egress from every point in the facility should be determined in advance.
- When the incident is localized, such as in a fire emergency, staying in place or evacuating to another area of the facility may be less risky than evacuating large crowds to the outside.
- The training of supervisory and event staff is important. Instruction should be given through preevent briefings and by issuing handheld information cards about specific positions, locations, and evacuation procedures.
- Prepared evacuation announcements should be played when an evacuation is deemed necessary.
- A plan should include what to do with the patrons after they have been evacuated outside the venue to ensure that they are out of danger and that the emergency is under control.

Shelter in Place

According to *Evacuation Planning Guide for Stadiums* (U.S. Department of Homeland Security, 2008a), sheltering in place requires patrons to take immediate shelter within the facility. Spectators and participants should shelter in place when an incident occurs outside or external to the facility. In some instances sheltering in place may be necessary to keep patrons inside the facility, such as when inclement weather has occurred outside the facility. Exiting the stadium may take too long or expose spectators and participants to more danger than they would be subject to by remaining in the facility (e.g., secondary improvised explosive device). Under these circumstances, facility management with the help of the command group members must consider the following items (Center for Venue Management Studies, 2002):

- Maintain constant communication with patrons by providing updates on the emergency situation. This objective can be achieved through prescripted and prerecorded public address announcements for possible scenarios, scoreboard signage, video screens, or verbal communication between event staff and patrons.
- The facility should obtain cellular phones to allow continued communication in the event that hard-wire phone lines into the facility are rendered out of service. Provide an opportunity for patrons to contact family or friends if communication capabilities exist.
- Complimentary food and beverages may be offered if patrons are required to remain in the facility for a long period. This action can be organized in cooperation with concessionaires and vendors.
- Develop partnerships with local emergency response agencies, such as the Red Cross, to obtain emergency supplies if needed. These partnerships can be established through a mutual aid agreement before the sport season.
- Implement a crisis communication plan that uses local radio and television broadcasters or an organizational website to convey critical information. A public information officer representative should be appointed by the sport or event organization to address the public through local media outlets.

Sheltering in place is a precaution aimed at keeping people safe while they remain indoors or at a location that is somewhat protected from an incident (e.g., underneath the stands, in a restroom, and so on). The following questions for consideration and statements regarding supporting actions are useful in performing sheltering in place.

Considerations

- What is the reason for sheltering (fire, structural failure, equipment failure, crowd control)?

- What criteria are used to select shelter-in-place locations?

- How effective are the shelter-in-place locations for providing protection?

- How many people can be sheltered at each sheltering location?

- Who will make the decision to shelter in place? Who will implement the decision and how?

- What are the kinds of protection (clothing, masks, shelters) needed for the different types of incidents that could result in sheltering in place?

- What steps need to be taken before a shelter-in-place event occurs? What areas should be designated as safe for sheltering? Outside the stadium, in the stands, on the field?

- What types of supplies will be available for the evacuees at the shelter-in-place locations?

- What effect will sheltering in place have on the event? How long can people remain sheltered inside the stadium?

- Determine how to handle stadium spectators and participants who want to leave despite shelter-in-place orders.

- How long can shelter in place be sustained with resources (food, medical care, sanitation, and so forth) on hand in the stadium?

- How will it be determined whether harmful contaminants are in the air?

- By whom and how will the "all clear" be communicated?

Supporting Actions

- Develop decision criteria to assist in making the shelter-in-place decision.

- Identify the person who will make the decision to shelter in place.

- Develop procedures for implementing shelter-in-place activities.

- Develop a plan to inform the patrons of the reason for the sheltering in place and advise them of the potential hazards should they chose to evacuate.

- Establish roles and responsibilities for the evacuation team to effect sheltering in place.

- Consider using a capacity model to determine when, where, and how long patrons can be sheltered inside the stadium.

- Identify shelter-in-place supplies (food, water, blankets, medical supplies, portable sanitation facilities, communication devices, security, and so on).

- Ensure that air-monitoring teams and equipment are on site and functioning to address possible chemical or other contaminant situations.

Reprinted from the U.S. Department of Homeland Security, 2008, *Evacuation planning guide for stadiums*.

Considerations and Guidelines for Relocation

The following questions for consideration and statements regarding supporting actions are useful in performing a relocation.

Considerations

- What is the reason for relocating (fire, structural failure, equipment failure, crowd control)?
- What criteria are used to identify relocation and staging areas?
- What is the effect of the incident on the event? What is the effect of the relocation activity on the event?
- How effective are the relocation and staging areas for providing protection?
- How many people can be relocated at each designated relocation and staging area?
- Who will make the decision to relocate? Who will implement the decision and how?
- What steps need to take place before a relocation event occurs? What areas should be designated as safe for relocation? Are the areas outside the stadium, in the stands, or on the playing field?
- How will it be determined whether harmful contaminants are in the air?
- How long can persons remain safely in the relocation or staging area?
- By whom and how will the "all clear" be communicated?

Supporting Actions

- Develop decision criteria to assist in making the relocation decision.
- Identify the person who will make the decision to relocate.
- Establish relocation areas by purpose and capacity. Identify routes to get to each relocation area and specify capacity.
- Develop procedures for implementing relocation activities.
- Establish roles and responsibilities for the evacuation team to effect relocation activities.
- Ensure that air-monitoring teams and equipment are on site and functioning to address possible chemical or other contaminant situations.

Reprinted from the U.S. Department of Homeland Security, 2008, *Evacuation planning guide for stadiums*.

Relocation

Relocation may occur at a stadium in response to a localized incident that does not require a mass evacuation. During a relocation occurrence, stadium spectators and participants will be moved from the area where a localized incident occurred to another area of the stadium or stadium property. The relocation may be temporary or permanent depending on the incident and the timeframe of the event. Relocations do not usually result in termination of the event occurring at the stadium. Relocation areas will be designated by stadium staff, and the public will be directed to these locations when the situation warrants. See the sidebar for more information on relocation.

Gathering Intelligence

Response involves implementing preparedness plans. Before plans can be appropriately implemented, though, one of the first response tasks is to assess the situation and gather intelligence by conducting an immediate rapid assessment of the local situation.

Rapid assessment includes response activities linked to determining initial lifesaving and life-sustaining needs and to identifying imminent hazards. Local governments need to perform a rapid assessment within the first few hours after an incident to provide an adequate response for life-threatening situations and imminent hazards (Federal Emergency Management Agency, 2010a). Rapid assessments enable local government to prioritize response activities, allocate scarce resources, and request assistance from mutual aid partners (or state or federal agencies depending on level of incident). Critical information, also called essential elements of information (EEI), is collected pertaining to (1) lifesaving needs, such as evacuation and search and rescue; (2) the status of critical infrastructure, such as transportation, utilities, communication systems, and fuel and water supplies; (3) the status of critical facilities, such as police and fire stations, medical providers, water and sewage treatment facilities, and media outlets; (4) the risk of damage to the community (e.g., dams and levees, facilities producing or storing hazardous materials) from imminent hazards; and (5) the number of people who have been displaced because of the event and the estimated extent of damage to their dwellings (Federal Emergency Management Agency, 2010a).

Information about the potential for cascading events is also included in the assessment. Cascading events are events that occur as a direct or indirect result of an initial event (Federal Emergency Management Agency, 2010a):

> For example, if a flash flood disrupts electricity to an area and, as a result of the electrical failure, a serious traffic accident involving a hazardous materials spill occurs, the traffic accident is a cascading event. If, because of the hazardous materials spill, a neighborhood must be evacuated and a local stream is contaminated, these are also cascading events. (p. 3.14)

The same kind of sequence can occur during sport and special events. If a severe storm disrupts electricity to the facility, causing facility lighting to be shut off and resulting in a serious spectator injury (e.g., falling down stairs), the accident is a cascading event.

Recovery

The goal of recovery is to return the operations of the sport or event organization to normal as quickly as possible. Recovery involves the development, coordination, and execution of restoration plans for the affected organization and venue. Recovery from an incident is unique to each emergency and depends on the extent of damage caused and the resources available. The process includes (1) identifying needs and resources, (2) addressing long-term care of affected persons, (3) implementing measures for organizational and venue restoration, (4) evaluating the incident and identifying lessons learned, and (5) incorporating mitigation measures to lessen effects of future incidents (Federal Emergency Management Agency, 2006a). Short-term recovery begins immediately after the incident and is an extension of the response effort to restore basic services and functions. Long-term recovery is the restoration of the personal lives and livelihood of the sport or event organization and the surrounding community. Long-term recovery may take several months or even years. Recovery is primarily the responsibility of local government, but by presidential declaration of a disaster in the United States, a number of assistance programs may be available under the Stafford Act (see sidebar on page 110).

The two major categories of federal aid are public assistance and individual assistance. Public assistance is for repair of infrastructure and public facilities and removal of debris. Individual assistance is for damage to residences and businesses or for personal property losses. Recovery from a disaster is unique to each sport or

Stafford Act: Emergency and Major Disaster Declarations

Types of Incidents

- **Emergency**: Emergencies involve any event for which the president determines that there is a need to supplement state and local efforts to save lives, protect property and public health, and ensure safety. A variety of incidents may qualify as emergencies. The federal assistance available for emergencies is more limited than that available for a major disaster.

An emergency is defined as

any occasion or instance for which, in the determination of the President, federal assistance is needed to supplement State and local efforts and capabilities to save lives and to protect property and public health and safety, or lessen or avert the threat of a catastrophe in any part of the United States.

A presidential declaration of an emergency provides assistance that

- is beyond state and local capabilities,
- serves as supplementary emergency assistance, and
- does not exceed $5 million of federal assistance.

The governor of an affected state must request a presidential declaration for an emergency within five days of the incident.

- **Major disaster**: Major disasters may be caused by natural events such as floods, hurricanes, and earthquakes. Disasters may include fires, floods, or explosions

that the president believes are of sufficient magnitude to warrant federal assistance. Although the types of incidents that may qualify as a major disaster are limited, the federal assistance available for major disasters is broader than that available for emergencies.

A major disaster is defined as

Any natural catastrophe . . . or, regardless of cause, any fire, flood, or explosion, in any part of the United States, which in the determination of the President causes damage of sufficient severity and magnitude to warrant major disaster assistance under this chapter to supplement the efforts and available resources of states, local governments, and disaster relief organizations in alleviating the damage, loss, hardship, or suffering caused thereby.

A presidential disaster declaration provides assistance that

- is beyond state and local capabilities and
- supplements available resources of state and local governments, disaster relief organizations, and insurance.

The governor of an affected state must request a presidential declaration for a major disaster within 30 days of the incident. Additional information on the request process is presented later in this section.

Reprinted from Federal Emergency Management Agency, 2010, *Fundamentals of emergency management: IS-230.A.*

event business and local community depending on the amount and kind of damage caused by the disaster and the resources that the community has available or has access to (Federal Emergency Management Agency, 2010a). The chapter case study provides an example of a sporting business' response and recovery efforts after a natural disaster.

Mitigation

Mitigation activities try to prevent disasters or lessen the damage of unavoidable disasters and emergencies (Hall, Marciani, & Cooper, 2008). Mitigation activities may be implemented before, during, or after an incident and are incorporated from lessons learned from prior incidents. Mitigation measures are identified in conjunction with a threat and risk analysis that helps identify potential hazards in or around the respective sport or event venue, the likelihood that an event will occur, and the potential consequences such as loss of life, destruction of property, disruption of critical services, and economic impact of recovery (covered in chapters 4 and 5). The sport or event organization should develop an overall mitigation strategy to include the following: (1) alternate power sources (e.g., generators), (2) alternate communications (e.g., handheld radios, cell phones), (3) policies and procedures (e.g., chain of command communication protocol), (4) data backup (e.g., hardware backup), and (5) records management (e.g., electronic management) (Broder, 2006). The sport or event business' mitigation strategy must consider ways to reduce risks associated with all hazards and potential losses. According to FEMA's *Fundamentals of Emergency Management* (2010), an effective mitigation strategy is based on several factors:

- **Prevention measures** to prevent existing risks from becoming worse based on new development or other changes within the facility. Prevention measures can be very effective in areas that have not been developed or are in an early phase of development (for example, physical protection security features in building design).

- **Property protection measures** to modify buildings or their surroundings to reduce the risk of damage from a known hazard. Property protection measures may be relatively simple and inexpensive to implement (for example, raising generators to prevent damage from flooding).

- **Emergency services measures** to protect people before and after an incident occurs. These measures may include warning notifications (for example, public address announcements), response tasks, and protective measures for critical facilities. Emergency protective measures should be included in the emergency planning process, exercised, and revised to incorporate lessons learned from both exercises and actual emergencies.

- **Structural projects** to protect people and property through the construction of manmade structures (for example, bollards) to control the damage from a known hazard (for example, VBIED).

- **Public information** to inform and remind people about the hazards that they face and measures that they should take to avoid damage or injury. Public information measures may include outreach projects, technical assistance, or educational programs (for example, safety and security awareness workshops hosted by the sport or event organization).

The mitigation strategy developed must consider the risks faced, the potential damage or impact, and the overall needs of the organization and facility. The mitigation measures must be consistent with the strategy and considered as part of the larger emergency management cycle. A mitigation planning activity is presented at the end of the chapter. Figure 6.2 on page 112 depicts the interrelated components of emergency management and offers potential considerations for sporting or event organizations under each key area (a checklist of considerations is also provided in appendix 6.4).

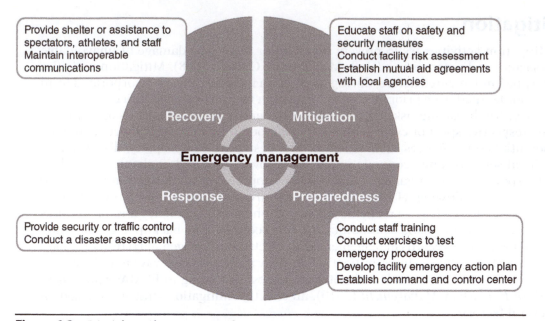

Provide shelter or assistance to spectators, athletes, and staff
Maintain interoperable communications

Educate staff on safety and security measures
Conduct facility risk assessment
Establish mutual aid agreements with local agencies

Recovery | Mitigation

Emergency management

Response | Preparedness

Provide security or traffic control
Conduct a disaster assessment

Conduct staff training
Conduct exercises to test emergency procedures
Develop facility emergency action plan
Establish command and control center

Figure 6.2 Principles and components of emergency management.

Reprinted, by permission, from E. Schwarz, S. Hall, and S. Shibli, 2010, *Sport facility operations management* (London: Butterworth-Heinemann).

Emergency Management Examples

The scenarios that follow, excerpted from the list of all-hazard potential risks presented in chapter 4, represent emergencies that could occur during a sport event or other special event. For each one, the stages of emergency response are briefly described—preparedness, response, recovery, and mitigation.

1. Bomb Threat

Scenario overview: During pregame warm-ups the stadium switchboard receives a telephone call from an anonymous person who threatens to detonate an explosive device inside the stadium. The call is reported to law enforcement authorities, who determine that the origin of the call is a number associated with a known terrorist organization that has used explosives during past terrorism incidents. Suspected members of the terrorist organization have recently posted messages on the Internet, boasting about "blowing up a stadium." Security personnel inside the stadium have located an unidentified package.

Preparedness: Conduct staff awareness training (recognizing suspicious packages and behavior); ensure that telephone operators are trained in the bomb threat reporting protocol (see the bomb threat checklist in appendix 6.5); develop a facility emergency response plan and evacuation plan; exercise plans.

Response: Conduct a threat assessment; contact bomb squad authorities to examine the package; implement an evacuation plan; effectively communicate with facility patrons.

Recovery: Provide shelter and assistance to spectators, participants, and staff; effectively communicate with local authorities and the public.

Mitigation: Train staff in proper search procedures; reevaluate prohibited items list (i.e., no backpack policy).

2. Weather Threat

Scenario overview: The Weather Service reports localized violent thunderstorms with significant lightning in the area of the stadium. Funnel clouds have also been reported. The Weather Service recommends that all those in the affected area take cover.

Preparedness: Develop an emergency response plan for all-hazard incidents including inclement weather; collaborate with local weather authorities and the local county emergency management director to evaluate weather-related hazards; develop public address announcements for emergency incidents.

Response: Assess the current weather situation and implement an evacuation plan (shelter in place or relocation depending on situation and facility design).

Recovery: Maintain interoperable communications.

Mitigation: Establish mutual aid agreements with local and regional partners.

3. Event Cancellation (No Show)

Scenario overview: Members of a rock band, scheduled for a concert in the campus auditorium, have been delayed at the airport and will not be available to perform. The crowd is informed of the situation, and the concert is cancelled. Some of those in attendance are agitated and fights are breaking out. Seats are being thrown onto the stage, and other forms of property damage are occurring.

Preparedness: Develop a facility emergency action plan; exercise the plan; train staff in crowd management procedures; develop public address announcements; establish a ticket refund policy. See appendix 6.6 for some common policies and measures used to prevent spectator violence.

Response: Coordinate with security force and local law enforcement to manage crowd control.

Recovery: Establish triage sites for injured patrons.

Mitigation: Develop a contingency plan (i.e., rescheduling events).

4. Civil Disturbance (Riot)

Scenario overview: Spectators at a sport event, upset with a call made by the officials, begin to fight and throw objects onto the playing field. Law enforcement responds by launching tear gas canisters into the crowd. The smoke from the gas grenades panics the spectators, resulting in mass hysteria. The game is discontinued.

Preparedness: Develop a fan code of conduct; ensure adequate distance between fans and the playing field; develop public address announcements; train staff in crowd management techniques (see appendix 6.6).

Response: Coordinate with security force and local law enforcement to manage crowd control.

Recovery: Partially evacuate stadium; arrest the culprits.

Mitigation: Evaluate response to crowd control issues.

5. Active Shooter

Scenario overview: Shots have been fired in the concessions area of the stadium during halftime. Initial reports identify at least two gunmen and several casualties. The gunmen are moving through the crowd and shooting randomly.

Preparedness: Develop an emergency action plan; exercise the plan; train staff in response procedures to active shooter incidents.

Response: Coordinate with local law enforcement to capture the shooters; implement a crisis communication plan.

Recovery: Establish a triage site for injured patrons.

Mitigation: Enhance entry search procedures.

Business Continuity Planning

"Business continuity involves developing measures and safeguards that will allow an organization to continue to produce or deliver goods and services under adverse conditions" (Sauter & Carafano, 2005, p. 333). After the initial incident response is deemed under control, the focus shifts to business continuity and recovery operations. Continuity planning makes good business sense and is important for numerous reasons, such as reducing the cost of downtime, rebuilding, reconstructing lost critical data, and minimizing loss of revenue. The costs associated with the aftermath of a large-scale incident may severely damage the sport or event organization's operations or even inhibit their ability to recover (Broder, 2006). Sport and event organizations should therefore develop a business continuity plan to ensure that operations are maintained. According to Broder (2006), "A business continuity plan is a comprehensive statement of consistent action taken before, during, and after a disaster or outage." (p. 179). The business continuity planning process is also a training exercise for the security command group because they must think through contingencies and be familiar with actions required to recover from all types of incidents (Broder, 2006).

Examples of issues to consider include relocation of athletes, use of alternative facilities, enrollment of athletes in other institutions, and rescheduling of games or events. All these actions occurred in the aftermath of Hurricane Katrina, although planning was largely absent (see chapter case study on page 116). Hurricane Katrina affected many professional and college sport programs in the Gulf Coast region and New Orleans area. The New Orleans Saints played home games in three different cities during 2005, and the Hornets resided in Oklahoma City for their 2005–2006 schedule (Matheson & Baade, 2006).

Louisiana State University's athletic department lost or paid other schools approximately $3.5 million and spent $400,000 to repair facility damage (Steinbach, 2006). Contracts should be in place for immediate restoration, and secondary locations to hold event bookings should be identified in case an incident occurs. Mutual aid agreements should be included as part of both the ERP and recovery plan. This action ensures that prearranged resources and services are available and provided, if needed. A sample business continuity and recovery plan template can be found in appendix 6.7.

Sauter and Carafano (2005) identified the following key planning steps in developing a business continuity plan (BCP):

1. **Obtain management commitment**: The facility owner or operator must ensure that sufficient time and resources are committed to the planning process. Without adequate support and explicit acknowledgment that continuity planning is a priority, resources and finances may be diverted to other projects.

2. **Establish a planning committee**: The security command group (CG) would serve as the planning committee and would develop and document the plan. Establishment of this group is discussed in chapters 2 and 4. The multiple agencies represented in the group enable a multidisciplinary perspective and recruitment of resources and expertise in various areas of safety and security. These individuals and agencies can provide insight into the needs of an organization after an incident and the community aspects that must be addressed to return the community to its pre-incident state.

3. **Perform a risk assessment**: The most vital task in developing an effective business continuity plan is a risk assessment. This process includes assessing threats, vulnerabilities, and costs so that priorities can be determined for preparedness efforts. The risk assessment process is detailed in chapter 4. For business continuity, the process of risk assessment is the same, but it focuses on risks that would interrupt business and measures that would need to be taken. By identifying specific threats and vulnerabilities the command group can develop countermeasures and strategies to combat potential incidents and develop plans, policies, and strategies to be implemented after an incident.

4. **Establish operational priorities**: The CG must identify critical elements of the sport or event business operations, such as resources or capabilities whose loss would stop or significantly affect essential business activities (such as equipment, personnel, and electronic records). This process ensures that those critical parts of the business are addressed first. The identification of critical assets and critical operational functions is also considered in chapter 4.

5. **Determine continuity and recovery options**: The CG group should collect critical data needed to respond to a disaster, such as personnel listings with telephone numbers, inventories of equipment, list of vendors, storage locations, data backup files, and important contracts. The CG should also assess current capabilities by reviewing existing plans and policies, such as the evacuation plan and mutual aid agreements. Additionally, the CG should review the availability of internal assets available to respond to an incident, such as emergency medical teams, public relation representatives, fire equipment, communication equipment, warning systems, emergency power, and shelter areas. Consultation with external groups will provide insight to availability of external resources or assets available in coordination with agencies such as local emergency management, fire and police departments, ambulance services, public works, hospitals, Red Cross, and so forth.

6. **Develop a contingency plan**: When the CG has decided what measures and procedures will be taken before, during, and after an incident, they will document their efforts in a comprehensive plan. Supporting documents may also be included, such as building and site maps indicating utility and shutoff locations, escape routes, and location of emergency equipment and hazardous materials. These documents may be needed if the facility is completely destroyed and management needs to rebuild. Also, if the facility is not completely destroyed and responders are clearing debris, they need to know where hazardous materials were located because they pose a danger to health.

7. **Implement the plan**: After the plan has been drafted, it should be tested, and procedures should be established to maintain and update the plan as needed. Training and exercising of the plan is critical (these concepts are discussed further in chapters 7 and 8). Employees who participate in training activities tend to respond faster and make better decisions in an emergency. The American Society Industrial Security (ASIS) International developed a business continuity guideline that can be viewed at www.scnus.org/local_includes/downloads/9742.pdf. In addition, the

FEMA Emergency Management Institute (EMI) offers a free course in special events contingency planning, which can be viewed at http://training.fema.gov/EMIWeb/IS/is15.asp.

Continuity plans often have flaws. First, a one-size-fits-all approach to continuity planning is not effective. Each plan should be customized to a specific venue and business, because all entities are unique and offer different resources, capabilities, and planning activities. As previously mentioned, training employees and testing the BCP are important. Deficiencies in testing could result in failure to notice significant gaps in the plan that may be exposed during a crisis. To test the continuity plan, managers can conduct a review or simulation exercise. In a plan review, the facility manager and command group discuss the business continuity plan. The team essentially looks for missing elements and inconsistencies within the plan (Continuity Central, 2009). A simulation exercise is more appropriate to determine whether business continuity management procedures and resources will work in a realistic situation. This type of exercise uses business continuity resources, such as the alternative event site, backup equipment, services from recovery vendors, and transportation. Errors, omissions, missing or insufficient resources, and limited mutual aid capabilities of partners may appear in this exercise. Simulations may also uncover staff issues regarding the nature and the size of their tasks and training needs (Continuity Central, 2009). Training and exercise options are discussed in further detail in chapters 7 and 8.

After a plan has been developed it should be adequately maintained and updated regularly because business regulations or standards may change within the industry. A lack of senior management (facility owner or operator) support could thwart a successful planning process. Finally, the age-old belief that nothing bad will ever happen to me may encourage complacency and reduce the urgency to plan and prepare for all-hazard emergencies.

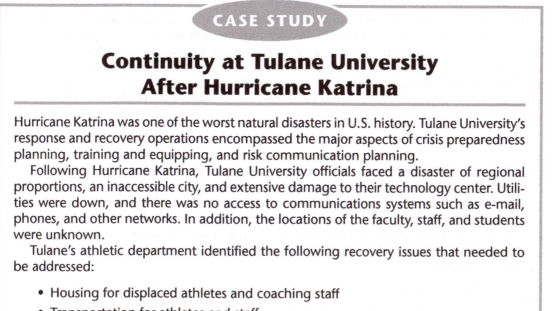

CASE STUDY

Continuity at Tulane University After Hurricane Katrina

Hurricane Katrina was one of the worst natural disasters in U.S. history. Tulane University's response and recovery operations encompassed the major aspects of crisis preparedness planning, training and equipping, and risk communication planning.

Following Hurricane Katrina, Tulane University officials faced a disaster of regional proportions, an inaccessible city, and extensive damage to their technology center. Utilities were down, and there was no access to communications systems such as e-mail, phones, and other networks. In addition, the locations of the faculty, staff, and students were unknown.

Tulane's athletic department identified the following recovery issues that needed to be addressed:

- Housing for displaced athletes and coaching staff
- Transportation for athletes and staff
- Media relations
- Financial issues within the athletic department
- Educational issues for athletes

Tulane University implemented several additional response actions:

- Kept its athletic teams intact to buoy school spirit and help hold the school together.
- Assigned displaced athletes (as well as other students) and staff to unoccupied rooms at residence halls or on one of two cruise ships leased by the university.
- Declared that the school would accept credit for all courses with a passing grade from regionally accredited universities that applied to a student–athlete's course of study.
- Established an online registration form for university employees to regain lost contact information from the disruption of the payroll system.
- Held an extra semester in May 2006 to allow students affected by Hurricane Katrina to stay on track with their degree programs.
- Set up town hall meetings across the country where there were large numbers of students. Campus executives spoke to the groups, and videos were shown of campus restoration progress.
- Monitored blogs to see what concerns were circulating about the university and its athletic program.

Because of these efforts, 90 percent of the university's students returned to the campus by January 2006.

LESSONS LEARNED

- A university athletic administration should develop a business continuity and recovery plan for its athletic program to ensure the recovery of its specific operations aside from the university's recovery issues.
- The plan should incorporate procedures for dealing with all sport programs, athletes, coaching staff, and administrative staff.
- A crisis communication plan should be established to notify staff, athletes, and families.
- Mutual aid agreements need to be established with other universities to host the displaced athletic sport program or accept student–athletes into their programs.

QUESTIONS TO CONSIDER

What additional measures could the Tulane University athletic department have implemented to assist in its recovery and business continuity efforts?

REFERENCE

U.S. Department of Homeland Security, 2009, *Sport event risk management.*

Key Chapter Points

- An emergency situation is defined as any incident, situation, or occurrence that could affect the safety and security of occupants; cause damage to the facility, equipment, and contents; and disrupt activities of the facility.
- Emergency planning is important for several reasons: (1) Adherence to professional standards promotes a safe environment; (2) planning, training, and implementation of an emergency plan reduce potential damage and loss; (3) adherence to legal public safety requirements improves the safety and security

of occupants; (4) documentation of an emergency plan minimizes liability to facility, owners, and operators; (5) good planning practices minimize negative media exposure and enhance the image of the facility.

- The four key components of emergency management are preparedness, response, recovery, and mitigation.
- Preparedness involves completing tasks and activities to build, sustain, and improve capabilities to prevent, protect against, respond to, and recover from incidents.
- An evacuation plan should be an essential component of the facility's emergency plan.
- The goal of recovery is to return the operations of the sport or event organizations to normal as quickly as possible. Recovery involves the development, coordination, and execution of restoration plans for the affected organization and venue.
- Mitigation activities try to prevent disasters or lessen the damage of unavoidable disasters and emergencies.
- Business continuity involves developing measures and safeguards that will allow an organization to continue to produce or deliver goods and services under adverse conditions.

Application Questions

1. Discuss the four key components of emergency management. Why is emergency management planning important for a sport or event facility manager?
2. What measures should management of a sport or event facility consider under each component?
3. Discuss the components of an ERP.
4. What issues must be taken into consideration when conducting an evacuation?
5. Discuss the business continuity planning process and areas of consideration for a professional sport organization and a college sport program.

Activity

Select a venue and meet with the facility manager. Ask the following questions:

1. Think about a recent emergency event at your venue. What types of damages occurred because of the incident?
2. What personnel were directly involved in the response efforts?
3. What do you think worked well with the response?
4. If the situation occurred again, what would you do differently?
5. In what ways did preparedness activities contribute to the response?

Then, for the same venue or a different venue with which you are familiar, answer the following questions:

1. What hazard presents the highest risk to the venue?
2. What type of damage is likely to occur if this hazardous event occurs?
3. What steps can be taken to reduce the damage from this known hazard?
4. How would you evaluate whether the mitigation efforts were successful?

Adapted from Federal Emergency Management Agency, 2006, The spectrum of incident management actions.

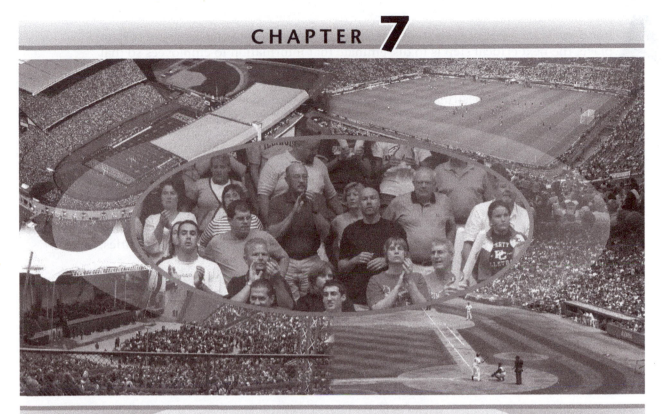

Training and Policy Implementation

After a sport or event organization's plans, policies, and protective measures are in place, the next critical step is to disseminate that information to employees so that they can execute the plans (Academy for Venue Safety and Security, 2006). Plans are effective only if they are implemented correctly. Therefore, a key component in protecting critical infrastructures such as stadiums and arenas is the effective training of staff members. This chapter addresses the training needs of sport and event organizations and the various levels of staff training: multiagency, supervisory, and event (line) staff. Types of training and sources for training are highlighted. The sport or event organization should provide adequate resources for recruitment, training, and evaluation of personnel responsible for the security of sport and event venues. Staff training should center on incident management strategies (chapter 3); risk management practices (chapter 4); safety and security plans, policies, and protective measures (chapter 5); and response and recovery principles (chapter 6). This training will help personnel recognize threats and eliminate or reduce facility vulnerabilities, thus mitigating risk at sporting and other events.

The effective training of staff is essential to transferring management expectations. Sennewald (2003) defined training as "an educational, informative, skill-development process that brings about anticipated performance through a change in comprehension and behavior" (p. 97). Management wants employees to understand three things: (1) what management wants them to do, (2) why management wants them to do it, and (3) how management wants it done (Sennewald, 2003). Before the security manager begins developing a training plan, he or she must consider the basic questions of what, why, who, when, and how.

- What kinds of plans, policies, and measures need to be communicated to employees for them to fulfill their roles and responsibilities?

- Employees should be made aware of the reasons and justification for why specific plans and policies are in place. This awareness will help them understand why they are performing certain security roles and what the intended outcome is of their actions (or inactions). For example, facility staff would need to know why they are implementing a facility entry pat-down policy. The reason may be an increase in the security alert level nationally, a recent threat assessment for the local event, or simply the need to prevent dangerous items from entering the facility and causing harm.

- Management should consider who should be involved in the training program and to what extent. For example, new employees and returning employees may be oriented to general facility policies through an orientation seminar. Employees expected to perform certain key roles or tasks during a crisis may be required to complete specific training exercises. For example, an employee who might need to perform first aid would need to be CPR certified.

- When should management conduct training? Training is an ongoing process, not a one-time event. Training may be conducted annually for extensive in-depth training exercises (covered in chapter 8) or semiannually for refresher training courses. Generally, short seminars and briefs are conducted close to the day of the event (even on an off day). Complex training sessions such as exercises are conducted periodically, sometimes years in advance (such as for the Olympics), and continue until the day of the event.

- Developing and implementing an effective training program begins with an assessment of training needs to determine workforce size and the specialized knowledge and skills required to implement an effective event security management system. The plans, policies, and measures to be implemented dictate the type and level of training required for personnel to perform certain roles and responsibilities. Training can be delivered through various methods, such as an orientation seminar, workshop, or briefings, or more extensively through discussion-based or operational-based exercises (covered in chapter 8).

Planning a Training Program

What

- What plans need to be communicated?
- What policies need to be communicated?
- What security measures need to be communicated?

Why

- What is the reason or justification for specific plans, policies, and measures?
- Do employees understand security roles and intended outcomes?

Who

Who should be involved in the training program?

When

When should management conduct training and how often?

How

How should management implement training given the various delivery methods?

At this stage, training is an ongoing responsibility, and management should have a continuous training and evaluation system in place so that employees maintain or obtain the necessary knowledge, skills, and capabilities needed to complete job functions and tasks successfully. As previously mentioned, training can be conducted annually, semiannually, or as needed if plans, policies, or measures change within the system. When resources are limited, training tends to be the area that suffers first, but it is essential for management to have a training system in place and provide training opportunities to employees.

Identifying Training Needs

According to the National Center for Spectator Sports Safety and Security (NCS[4]), training should be conducted at three main levels (see figure 7.1): command group (multiagency leadership team), supervisory leaders, and event staff (U.S. Department of Homeland Security, 2009c).

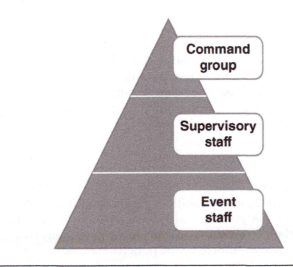

Figure 7.1 Levels of staff for training purposes.

Most of the training will be directed toward effective communication and cooperation among the various agencies represented in the command group (CG). The CG is composed of specialists from five distinct areas as discussed in chapter 2: facility management, police, emergency management, fire and HAZMAT, and emergency medical and health services. This group should be trained in basic concepts relative to multiagency collaboration, risk assessment, planning, and recovery and business continuity. The expectation is that this leadership team will be adequately trained and sufficiently knowledgeable to coordinate the development of an effective event security management system at the venue, including security operations, planning, and implementation (U.S. Department of Homeland Security, 2009c).

The main responsibilities for the supervisory staff are enforcing security policy and procedures, overseeing the training program, evaluating personnel, and coordinating emergency responses. A key aspect for the implementation of the security system is for management to give the supervisory corps the responsibility, authority, and accountability for staff training and evaluation of personnel. For an effective security plan to achieve its objectives, a qualified and trained venue staff is essential. The following sections describe the job duties of various venue staff and their roles in a security plan. In addition, appendix 7.1 provides a detailed list of capabilities, tasks, and key security considerations for each staff position (Contemporary Services Corporation, 2007; U.S. Department of Homeland Security, 2009c; Stevens, 2007).

Parking Attendants

Parking attendants direct ingress and egress from facility parking areas. They generally perform the following duties: vehicle screening, preevent parking lot sweep procedures, traffic flow control, and parking pass and credential control measures. Parking attendants are required to make efficient use of all available space and prevent unauthorized parking. They should be able to provide accurate directions and guard against unsafe or unlawful activity.

Gate Security

Gate security staff protect people and property inside and around the facility by preventing unauthorized entrance to the venue, keeping prohibited items out of the venue, securing perimeters around the venue, conducting security inspections, and verifying tickets and credentials.

Ticket Takers

Ticket takers verify tickets and credentials and prevent unauthorized entrance to the facility. Ticket takers are required to tear or scan tickets depending on whether turnstiles are in use. They also verify credentials, such as whether someone has an all-access pass or field pass. Ticket takers are also responsible for reporting suspicious behavior and packages and enforcing ticket policy regarding lost tickets, duplicate tickets, relocations, and will call and special tickets.

Ushers

Ushers maintain a safe, orderly environment and guide spectators to their seats. Ushers prevent unauthorized access to facility areas and seating without a proper ticket or credential. They answer guest questions and assist with guest problems. An important component to their job is the safe evacuation of patrons from the facility in case of an incident. Ushers also enforce venue policies such as fan code of conduct, eviction policy, and smoking policy.

Concessions and Maintenance

Concession and maintenance staff maintain a clean and safe venue; sell food, beverages, and merchandise; and respond to spills and incidents. They also assist guests with problems and guard against unsafe and unsanitary practices. Concession workers must be able to operate cash registers and check identification of customers who want to buy alcohol. Maintenance people are responsible for securing critical assets during an emergency. They also implement facility policy for HAZMAT storage, service area access, lost keys, and mutual aid agreements.

Field, Playing Area, or Stage Staff

These staff maintain a safe and orderly environment and prevent unauthorized entrance to the playing area. They normally observe and report problems in the crowd, protect the field, resolve problems for teams, and evacuate the playing area if necessary. They are responsible for facility policies concerning teams and officials, credential verification, preevent and postevent activities, and media relations.

Security Force

The security force consists of police officers or security guards employed to protect physical (facility) and human (people) assets. Their primary responsibilities are keeping the crowd under control, protecting the athletes or performers, and providing protective escorts when needed. The security forces are leaders in the coordination of response efforts to all-hazard incidents. They manage event communications, document incidents, and direct evacuation procedures.

Meeting Staffing Needs

Management must ensure that they have sufficient staff with the appropriate skills. They do not want to be understaffed (which may present a legal concern) or overstaffed (which may be a financial concern to the venue owner or operator). When determining the number of staff required for an event, several factors need to be considered, including (1) size of the event (expected attendance); (2) number of events (for example, is it a multidiscipline event like the Olympics or a one-time sport event like the Super Bowl); (3) level of knowledge and expertise required for each specific role; (4) scheduling of shifts for personnel; (5) staff composition, that is, full-time, temporary, and volunteer; (6) potential threats, and (7) staff allocations, that is, male and female personnel or specific assignments associated with cultural sensitivities (Stevens, 2007). The National Fire Protection Association (NFPA) industry standards for fire prevention and safety also apply to crowd management principles and indicate that one trained crowd management professional should be present for every 250 spectators in any facility with a capacity over 250 people (Fried, 2005).

Major sporting events such as the FIFA World Cup and Olympics require the recruitment and training of thousands of staff members. For example, the 2006 FIFA World Cup required 52,000 security staff, including 30,000 federal police officers, 15,000 private security professionals, and 7,000 armed forces personnel (Stevens, 2007).

When management determines staff roles and numbers for a specific event, they need to consider a recruitment strategy and subsequent training techniques. Organizations can choose to use outsourcing services through an independent contractor or operate using in-house safety and security personnel. Some organizations may outsource because of the difficulty of recruiting (and training) part-time, temporary staff and volunteers or because low unemployment rates and relatively low wages make it difficult to recruit event security personnel. A significant increase has occurred in the market for outsourcing security personnel at sporting events since the 1990s because of the growth of the sport industry (Stevens, 2007). Using an outsourcing company for security personnel has several advantages (Stevens, 2007):

1. **Cost reduction**: The sport or event organization does not need to invest time and money in recruiting staff, training, and paying salaries. The outsourcing company is responsible for providing trained staff and compensating them.

2. **Focus**: Specific agencies provide expertise on event personnel, resulting in a specialized staff with sufficient training in certain roles and functions.

3. **Efficiency**: The outsourcing company can provide staff with adequate experience to fulfill roles as needed.

4. **Resourceful**: The outsourcing company may have access to infrastructure and processes that can assist the venue command group in emergency response and evacuation situations.

5. **Flexible**: The outsourcing company can be contracted to provide staff for one-time events or multiple events with specific requirements. The company will have access to the required number of staff.

6. **Consistent**: The company may have developed standard operating procedures for their staff and response efforts that ensure a workforce with consistent capabilities and training.

7. **International capability**: The company may have an international pool of workers and be able to provide multilingual personnel for global events.

At the same time, however, several disadvantages to outsourcing security must be weighed against the benefits. Management ultimately loses control of security staff and subsequent training of the staff. They rely on the independent contractor to provide the necessary workforce with sufficient training. Staff recruited through an outsourcing program may be unfamiliar with the venue and not understand the venue layout and emergency procedures as an in-house security workforce would. Among the disadvantages to outsourcing are the following (Stevens, 2007):

1. **Perception**: The sport or event organization may have to deal with complaints about the behavior of outsourced personnel who are not directly under their control.

2. **Knowledge**: The sport or event organization must ensure that personnel receive adequate training to perform their duties.

3. **Experience**: A high turnover of staff may result in recruitment of personnel with limited experience at live events and in the specific venue.

4. **Responsibility**: Staff not employed directly by the organization may not share the organization's values or act in an inappropriate manner.

5. **Control**: The sport or event organization does not manage the staff on a day-to-day basis.

Sport or event organizations that choose to operate using in-house human resources must develop their own recruitment and training policies. Larger organizations may have their own human resources officer or department, but smaller organizations may not have this luxury and may seek expertise through a consulting agency. Regardless of the method, certain steps should be taken to ensure that best practices are being followed (Stevens, 2007). The organization should consider

Sample Job Description

Company name:	Security company
Job title:	Event staff
Job type:	Seasonal part-time
Hours:	Varies
Pay rate:	Hourly
Location:	Dallas, Texas

The primary responsibilities of event staff are guest relations and the safety and security of the facility. Event staff must enforce all facility rules, regulations, and policies. Responsibilities include (but are not limited to) the following:

- Wear assigned uniform at all times
- Greet guests in a friendly manner
- Attend your assigned position during the event
- Secure entrances, exits, and restricted areas
- Implement facility rules and regulations
- Have knowledge of the facility or event credentialing system
- Monitor guests
- Assist with crowd management issues
- Notify supervisor of problems in your designated area
- Respond in a timely and professional manner to incidents

Additional Information:

- Must have a flexible schedule
- Subject to a criminal background check
- Must complete a four-hour preassignment training certificate
- Must complete an eight-hour on-the-job training program

developing a formal job description to help the applicant understand duties and responsibilities on event days. A typical job description will include several elements (Stevens, 2007):

- **Identification data**: job title, department, pay grade, and location of position
- **Organization data**: often presented as an organization chart that indicates the working relationship (responsible to and responsible for) for each position
- **Job summary**: outline of the basic requirements of the employee
- **Job content**: explanation of main duties, responsibilities, and expected outcomes

The sidebar shows an example of a well-written job description.

Working With Volunteers

"A volunteer is an individual who, beyond the confines of paid employment and normal responsibilities, contributes time and service to assist in the accomplishment of a mission." (Federal Emergency Management Agency, 2006b, p. 2.1). People volunteer for a number of reasons. For example, they want to give back, share their skills and experiences, develop new skills, be part of a sport team or entity, or network with others. Volunteers are an essential addition to event staff for major sporting events, typically representing over 50 percent of all event personnel. For example, 61,000 volunteers were enrolled for the 2000 Sydney Olympic Games, and it is projected that 71,000 volunteers will be recruited for the 2012 London Olympics (Stevens, 2007). Volunteers, however, represent a significant security challenge for event management. People of all ages and all types of skills apply for volunteer positions. In addition, without a sufficient employee screening process, management runs the risk of hiring a potential terrorist or someone with goals of doing harm. The volunteer position allows access to the facility, restricted areas, and event-specific intelligence that adversaries can use. A background check should be conducted, and volunteers should be registered well in advance of the event (Stevens, 2007). The integration of full-time staff, part-time staff, temporary workers, and volunteers is critical to the success of events. All those involved must understand roles and responsibilities.

Volunteers do not receive financial compensation for their time; therefore, they are motivated by other factors. Proven nonfinancial motivators are uniforms and official event merchandise, travel, accommodation, meals, social events and activities, and rewards and incentives (i.e., promotional gifts and experiences) (Stevens, 2007). Recruiting volunteers is sometimes difficult when they are requested to commit to long-term positions or when the roles are routine or mundane. Volunteer roles should be aligned with personal skills and experiences so that volunteers can feel successful in their jobs. This approach prevents turnover and therefore saves training resources that would be needed for new personnel.

Most important, event management must ensure that volunteers who lack sufficient training and knowledge do not compromise the security system (Stevens, 2007). Volunteers might lack knowledge of the facility layout and be unfamiliar with emergency procedures and communication protocol, which could be dangerous in an emergency. Poorly trained volunteers could also expose the facility to risk in various ways, such as by inadequately checking bags entering the stadium or serving alcohol to underage patrons.

But working with volunteers offers some benefits, especially for existing facility staff, such as the following:

- Staff who supervise volunteers can demonstrate managerial ability.
- Staff who supervise volunteers and are seeking promotion to managerial positions can gain on-the-job experience.
- Volunteers can reduce the overall workload for everyone.
- Volunteers can do tasks that staff does not have time to do.

The sidebar lists some additional benefits and challenges involved in working with volunteers. In addition, appendixes 7.2 and 7.3 list common concerns of volunteers and staff and provide a checklist for evaluating the volunteer–staff climate. More information on developing and managing volunteers can be found in FEMA's independent study guide to developing and managing volunteers (2006) available at http://training.fema.gov/emiweb/downloads/IS244.pdf.

Involving Volunteers—Benefits and Challenges

Benefits

- Provide services more cost effectively.
- Provide access to a broad range of expertise and experience.
- Increase effectiveness of paid staff members by enabling them to focus their efforts where they are most needed or provide additional services.
- Provide resources for accomplishing maintenance tasks or upgrading what would otherwise be put on the back burner while immediate needs are met.
- Enable the agency to launch programs in areas in which paid staff lacks expertise.
- Act as liaisons with the community to gain support for programs.
- Provide a direct line to private resources in the community.
- Facilitate networking.
- Increase public awareness and program visibility.

Challenges

- Training and supervision of volunteers take a lot of time.
- Volunteers do not stay, so the time spent training them is wasted.
- Technically competent people do not volunteer.
- Volunteers threaten paid staff by competing with them.
- Volunteers lower professional standards.
- Volunteers become territorial or attempt to take over.
- Insurance rates increase.
- Volunteers are not available during business hours.
- Using volunteers interferes with the ability to negotiate for additional funding or new paid staff positions.

Reprinted from Federal Emergency Management Agency, 2006, *Developing and managing volunteers: Independent study.*

Training Techniques

After employees are recruited, they must receive appropriate training. According to Bob Stiles, USA vice president of operations for the 1999 FIFA Women's World Cup and 1994 FIFA World Cup, "Humans can make more complex judgments than machines. You've got to train them and you've got to keep them" (Stevens, 2007, p. 93). There are many methods and styles of training, but the ultimate goal is to train staff to confront and handle multiple threats facing sporting or other events. Training allows staff to practice emergency scenarios proactively before an incident occurs, thereby ensuring that future response efforts are most effective.

Many opportunities are available to train event staff, and training must be an ongoing process (Academy for Venue Safety and Security, 2006). According to Sennewald (2003), the two basic strategies for training are on-the-job training and formal classroom training (off the job). On-the-job (OTJ) training takes place under normal working conditions with the actual tools, equipment, and materials that trainees will use. For example, management wants all bag checkers to learn the correct method of searching bags. First, a trainer provides a demonstration of the task, encourages questions, and verifies the learner's understanding. The new employee then has an opportunity to perform the newly acquired skill on site with guidance and reinforcement from the trainer. Feedback is provided immediately to prevent the new employee from developing bad habits.

Off-the job training takes place away from the work environment so that trainees can focus on the training itself. Formal structured training can take place in a classroom setting and can include expert lectures, role playing, training videos, or virtual interactive software training programs. This type of training should include pre- and posttesting of trainees' knowledge and understanding of curriculum presented. A minimum score should be required for successful completion (Sennewald, 2003).

The following training techniques, promoted by the Academy for Venue Safety and Security (2006) and the International Association of Assembly Managers (more information available at www.iaam.org), are useful in presenting basic foundational functions and tasks to new employees (higher-level exercises are used to test specific skills and planning capabilities; these are discussed in greater detail in chapter 8):

- **Orientation**: Orientation is the foundation of most training programs. After employees are hired they must learn administrative fundamentals—organizational structure, facility details, job functions, uniform policy, parking, break times, check-in and check-out procedures, required equipment, emergency evacuation procedures, and instructions for responding to various situations.

- **Mentoring program**: After the orientation meeting, management can assign supervisors to work with staff as mentors. Supervisors should be responsible for a reasonable number of staff to ensure that each member receives adequate training in job functions. New employees can learn organizational security and emergency procedures first hand and receive immediate feedback that encourages positive behaviors.

- **Event briefing**: Briefings before an event are important for two reasons: (1) each event is unique and may involve a different type of risk or threat that should be assessed, and (2) staff meetings are an opportunity to reinforce skills and discuss possible hazards and scenarios. Briefings may include (Academy for Venue Safety and Security, 2006, p.5) the following:
  - Event time and timeline
  - Event type
  - Expected attendance
  - Ingress and egress
  - Person in charge
  - Alcohol management
  - Event staff positions in the facility
  - Event security requirements
  - Staged incidents during an event, such as fireworks
  - Identified risk or threat and the plan to address the risk or threat
  - National threat level
  - Dignitaries or VIPs in attendance
  - Restricted zones or areas inside and outside the facility
  - Access badges

- **General training**: All event staff should receive training on response strategies to all-hazard emergencies that may occur any time during an event or during the workday, such as emergency contacts, workplace injury or violence, workplace harassment, use of protective devices, emergency communication process, fire safety and evacuation, and various event threats (e.g., weather, crowd crush, biological release). All employees should know what to do in an emergency, whether minor or catastrophic. They should know who to call, what information to communicate, and where emergency personnel are located for assistance and pick up. In addition, employees should know how to operate specialized equipment such as magneto-meters. Training in other areas such as conflict resolution or handling a bomb threat is also advised for all event staff.

Training should be ongoing and conducted preseason, during the season, and postseason. Training will help build relationships, trust, and a commitment to the security plan among trainees. The organization can use training resources available to plan and manage event security training. Federal and state agencies provide free training, including the FEMA's Emergency Management Institute (EMI) and Department of Homeland Security. The National Center for Spectator Sports Safety and Security (NCS[4]) recommends that all members of the command group consider completing the following courses:

- **IS-100, Introduction to Incident Command System (ICS)**: This course describes the history, features, principles, and organizational structure of the Incident Command System. It also explains the relationship between ICS and the National Incident Management System (NIMS). The primary audience for this course is persons involved with emergency planning and response or recovery efforts (http://training.fema.gov).

- **IS-200, ICS for Single Resources and Initial Action Incidents**: This course is designed to enable personnel to operate efficiently during an incident or event within the Incident Command System (ICS). It provides training and resources for personnel who are likely to assume a supervisory position within the ICS. The primary audience for this course is persons involved with emergency planning, response or recovery efforts (http://training.fema.gov).

- **IS-700, National Incident Management System (NIMS), an Introduction**: This course introduces and overviews the National Incident Management System (NIMS). NIMS provides a consistent nationwide template to enable all government, private sector, and nongovernmental organizations to work together during domestic incidents. The primary audience for this course is people with emergency management responsibilities including prevention, preparedness, response, recovery, and mitigation (http://training.fema.gov).

- **IS-800B, National Response Framework, an Introduction**: The course introduces participants to the concepts and principles of the National Response Framework. This course is intended for government executives, private sector and nongovernmental organization (NGO) leaders, and emergency management practitioners (http://training.fema.gov).

- **AWR 167, Sport Event Risk Management**: The National Center for Spectator Sports Safety and Security (NCS[4]) in conjunction with the Department of Homeland Security and with cooperation from the National Association of Collegiate Directors of Athletics (NACDA) developed a sport event risk management workshop to be delivered to NCAA institutions. The workshop focuses on building multiagency collaboration capabilities among university sport security command groups (www.ncs4.com/workshop.php).

- **Sports Venue Safety and Security Training for Event Staff (for ushers, gate security, ticket takers, and parking attendants)**: NCS[4] developed training courses to enhance safety and security efforts by building security awareness and improving capabilities for planning, emergency response, and evacuations. The Sport Venue Safety and Security Staff Training program can serve as a primary training program, as a supplemental training program that complements existing training, and as a screening device for potential venue staff (www.ncs4.com/training.php).

CASE STUDY

ABC Security Company

USA University hired ABC Security Company to manage event security for their entire athletic department. The athletic department is classified as an NCAA Division I institution. The football stadium has a capacity of 76,000, the basketball facility holds 19,000, and the baseball stadium has a capacity of 7,000. As part of their contract with the university, the security company was responsible for the management, training, and evaluation of security operations. During the third year of the three-year contract, the athletic department staff noticed a change in the preparation and operation of game-day security, causing the athletic director to become concerned.

After the second home football game of the season, the director of operations and security for the athletic department reported that he had several concerns about the inconsistent oversight of the ABC Security employees. His report indicated a lack of proper staff training. He observed the pregame and postgame staff sessions and the records of staff training. What brought all these training issues to the table was inconsistency in inspection procedures and identification of suspicious items. Spectators began to joke about which gate was the easiest to enter without an inspection. This finding firmed up the idea that security supervision and oversight of the ABC employees was unsatisfactory.

Three home football games remained, as did the entire basketball season and baseball season. In the past, the athletic department did not attend the security company's training sessions or review the credentials of the company's staff. The athletic director needed to make a critical security decision with three football games remaining and other athletic events on the schedule later in the year.

The athletic director and the director of operations and security met with the supervisor of ABC Security Company the following week. The security agreement called for extensive staff training, oversight, and evaluation. The ABC Security supervisor indicated that he was having difficulty recruiting staff and that his turnover rate was above normal. He admitted that his supervisors were not training staff properly because of the large turnover. Based on the findings and the interview, the athletic director fired ABC Security because of lack of staff oversight. He immediately began hiring security staff by using money previously spent on external security. By building an in-house workforce that are trained properly, compensated fairly and committed to the organization, the athletic director hoped to ensure a lower turnover rate.

LESSONS LEARNED

- There is the potential for inconsistency of security operations when using an outsourcing firm.
- Good communications and accountability are critical components of an agreement. Open dialogue between the agency and the vendor is crucial.
- Lack of training could be detrimental to the safety and security of spectators.
- Consistency of operation is essential.
- In this case, the agency should have maintained better oversight of the vendor prior to discovery of not fulfilling contract obligations.
- A background check should have been done to investigate the vendor's capabilities more thoroughly.

QUESTIONS TO CONSIDER
1. What are the advantages of outsourcing security operations?
2. What are the advantages of keeping the security operations in house?
3. What critical elements should be incorporated in the bidding contracts for security services?
4. What strategies can a selection committee use to pick an outsourcing security firm?
5. What is the significance of a partner philosophy between the athletic department and the security firm?

Key Chapter Points

- A key component in protecting sport and special event facilities is the effective training of staff members.
- Management wants employees to understand three things from a training program: (1) what management wants them to do, (2) why management wants them to do it, and (3) how management wants it done.
- According to the National Center for Spectator Sports Safety and Security (NCS[4]), training should be conducted at three main levels: command group (multiagency leadership team), supervisory leaders, and event security staff.
- When determining the number of staff required for an event, several factors need to be considered, including (1) size of event, (2) number of events, (3) level of knowledge and expertise required for each specific role, (4) scheduling of shifts for personnel, (5) staff composition (i.e., full time, temporary, and volunteer), (6) potential threats, and (7) staff allocations.
- Sport and event organizations can choose to operate using an in-house safety and security program or using outsourcing services through an independent contractor.
- The two basic strategies to training are on-the-job training and formal classroom training (off the job).
- Possible training components include orientation, mentoring program, event briefing, and general training.

Application Questions

1. Discuss the capabilities, tasks, and key considerations for each event staff position (ushers, ticket takers, and so on).
2. Discuss the advantages and disadvantages of using an outsourcing company for security personnel.
3. Discuss possible strategies that management can use to recruit volunteers and motivate them to perform an effective role in a security system.
4. Compare and contrast the following training techniques: (1) orientation, (2) mentoring program, (3) event briefing, and (4) general training.

Activity

Review the courses offered by FEMA's Emergency Management Institute (http://training. fema.gov/) and complete at least one course offering pertaining to your area of interest.

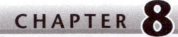

CHAPTER 8

Exercises: Testing Your Plans

CHAPTER GOALS

- Define exercise and discuss the importance of exercising plans.
- Examine the two types of exercises: discussion based and operations based.
- Identify exercise personnel.
- Discuss exercise design and development, including conducting an exercise and developing an after-action report.

One must learn by doing the thing, for though you think you know it, you have no certainty until you try.

Sophocles, 5th century BC

Sport and event organizations should conduct exercises to test plans and promote awareness of staff roles and responsibilities during an incident scenario. "An exercise is a focused practice activity that places the participants in a simulated situation requiring them to function in the capacity that would be expected of them in a real event" (Federal Emergency Management Agency, 2008a, p. 2). After sport or event facility managers have assessed risks, developed necessary plans and policies, and trained their staff members, they should consider testing their operational plans to assess their level of preparedness. Exercises improve readiness by evaluating operations and plans and reinforcing the concept of teamwork. Exercises help facility managers to (Federal Emergency Management Agency, 2009b)

- clarify roles and responsibilities,
- improve interagency coordination and communication,
- reveal resource gaps,
- develop individual performance,
- identify opportunities for improvement, and
- gain program recognition and support of administration.

This chapter outlines the Homeland Security Exercise and Evaluation Program (HSEEP) of the U.S. Department of Homeland Security. The importance of exercising plans and the types of exercises available to the sport or event manager are presented. These include discussion-based exercises (i.e., seminars, workshops, and tabletop exercises) and operations-based exercises (i.e., drills and full-scale exercises).

Successful responses to emergencies in the past have demonstrated the value of exercising and its positive effect on response efforts when an incident occurs. For example, in 2000, Urban Search and Rescue (US&R) Task Forces participated in two major exercises: an earthquake scenario in California and a building collapse scenario through a planned demolition of a Denver sport arena. In 2001 some of these same US&R Task Forces were sent to New York to search for victims after the collapse of the World Trade Center towers during the 9/11 terrorist attacks (Federal Emergency Management Agency, 2008a). Responders typically respond to incidents in the way in which they have been trained. Similar to sport teams, responders practice their plans and schemes to ensure effective implementation on game day. Exercises are an opportunity to observe operations, test capabilities, identify gaps, and address issues before the emergency incident occurs.

> Exercises are the only practical, efficient and proven method by which management and safety personnel can test and validate planned arrangements and procedures. As the inquiries into various disasters have repeatedly confirmed, untested plans are likely to fail at the crucial moment. (Football Licensing Authority, 2007, p. 3)

Exercises are not a one-time event; they must be conducted on a continuous basis to address the changing elements of the industry—evolving threats, new plans and procedures, new equipment, training new personnel, and so on (see figure 8.1).

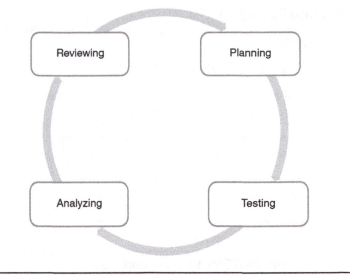

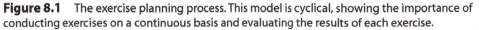

Figure 8.1 The exercise planning process. This model is cyclical, showing the importance of conducting exercises on a continuous basis and evaluating the results of each exercise.

Because the financial impact and potential loss of life from disasters are significant, many industry governing bodies have mandated preparedness training and exercising requirements. In the United States, nuclear power plants must exercise their plans annually and conduct a full-scale exercise (FSE) every two years that is evaluated by the Nuclear Regulatory Commission (NRC). Airports, hospitals, and health care facilities must conduct an FSE every two years to maintain a license to operate. Additionally, the Occupational Safety and Health Administration (OSHA) requires many employers to develop an emergency action plan (EAP) and exercise it at least annually (Federal Emergency Management Agency, 2008a). In the sport and event industry, however, no government mandates require organizations to conduct specific training and exercises. After 9/11, most sport governing bodies enhanced security efforts by developing best practices for their league members that often includes having adequately trained and exercised staff.

Types of Exercises

The Exercise and Evaluation Program (HSEEP) of the U.S. Department of Homeland Security (2007a) defined seven types of exercises that are considered either discussion based or operations based (see table 8.1 on page 136).

Discussion-Based Exercises

Discussion-based exercises familiarize participants with current plans and policies, or they may be used to develop new plans and policies. Facilitators or presenters usually lead the discussion, keeping participants on track toward meeting exercise objectives. Discussion-based exercises are normally used as a starting point in the building-block approach of escalating exercise complexity. Types of discussion-based exercises include seminars, workshops, tabletop exercises, and game simulations (U.S. Department of Homeland Security, 2007a):

• **Seminars** use a number of instructional strategies such as lecture, panel discussions, case studies, and multimedia presentations. Seminars are informal and productive for small and large groups and are usually used for orientation to

Table 8.1 Exercise Types and Examples

Exercise	Example
DISCUSSION-BASED EXERCISES	
Seminar	New staff attend a lecture and PowerPoint presentation on the general security procedures of the sport or event venue.
Workshop	The command group attends a multiagency management and leadership workshop to develop an all-hazard emergency response plan.
Tabletop exercise (TTX)	The command group tests the emergency response plan by working through an incident scenario, such as an active shooter in the stadium.
Game simulation	The command group attends a virtual learning laboratory to participate in a decision-making exercise.
OPERATIONS-BASED EXERCISES	
Drill	Stadium management tests the stadium alert and notification system before the day of the game or event.
Functional exercise (FE)	The command group and local responding authorities work through a stadium bomb explosion incident scenario to test available resources (without deploying assets).
Full-scale exercise (FSE)	The command group and local responding authorities work through a stadium bomb explosion incident scenario by deploying real-world assets and testing available resources.

organizational policies and procedures, protocols, response resources, or concepts and ideas. Orientations normally last a maximum of one to two hours.

• **Workshops** increase participant interaction and are effective for solving complex problems, team building, information sharing, and brainstorming. Workshops differ from seminars in that they emphasize producing a product or goal such as a new policy or plan (e.g., emergency action plans [EAPs], mutual aid agreements, and standard operating procedures [SOPs]). Workshops also involve greater participant discussion and often uses breakout sessions to explore parts of an issue with smaller groups.

• **Tabletop exercises** (**TTXs**) consist of informal facilitated discussions of simulated emergencies among key personnel. Basic TTXs involve a constant, unchanging simulation, whereas advanced TTXs present the group with inserts (messages) that progress the initial scenario. TTXs are a useful tool for facility managers who want to assess current plans and identify gaps in security operations. The purpose of a TTX is to test existing plans without incurring costs associated with deploying resources. The TTX can involve many people and many organizations who can contribute to the planned discussion items, typically those entities with a planning, policy, or response role. A TTX usually lasts one to four hours. A sample TTX is provided in appendix 8.1.

• **Game simulations** are computer simulations of operations that involve two or more teams, usually in a competitive environment, using rules, data, and procedure designed to depict an actual or assumed real-life situation. Simulations conduct what-if analyses of existing plans and potential strategies without deploying resources to explore the processes and consequences of decision making. For example, participants are able to respond to a bomb explosion in a stadium by deciding how to allocate personnel and resources and how to evacuate spectators safely.

Operations-Based Exercises

Operations-based exercises are more complex than discussion-based exercises. Operations-based exercises represent the next level of the exercise cycle. They are used to validate the plans, policies, agreements, and procedures solidified in discussion-based exercises. Operations-based exercises validate plans and policies, clarify roles, and identify resource gaps in security operations. Operations-based exercises normally involve the deployment of resources and personnel. Operations-based exercises include drills, functional exercises (FEs), and full-scale exercises (FSEs) (U.S. Department of Homeland Security, 2007a):

- **Drills** are coordinated, supervised activities used to test a specific operation or function within the organization. Participants may gain training on new equipment, practice, and maintain skills. An example of a drill run by a sport or event organization may be to test the stadium's alert and notification system. Management tests the alert system and staff members respond accordingly, depending on the situation. For example, if a tornado is approaching, spectators must seek shelter, so staff members need to relocate spectators to a covered section of the facility. Staff members would then assume their designated positions and act as if the alert were real. This type of drill is conducted without requesting additional resources (as would happen in a full-scale exercise). The time required to conduct a drill operation is usually one half to two hours.

- **Functional exercises** (FEs) examine and validate the coordination, command, and control between various agencies responding to an incident. This exercise involves a simulated deployment of resources and personnel in a highly stressful environment requiring rapid problem solving. Functional exercises can be used to evaluate management of emergency operations centers (EOC) and facility command posts. An FE normally requires three to eight hours to complete.

- **Full-scale exercises** (FSEs) are multiagency, multijurisdictional exercises involving a functional "boots on the ground" response. Real-world deployment of assets occurs in support of the exercise scenario. Participants are able to assess plans and evaluate coordinated responses under crisis conditions. An FSE may be designed to last two to four hours or as long as a day or more. An example of a full-scale exercise scenario can be viewed at www.dhs.gov/files/training/gc_1179430526487.shtm.

Table 8.2 on page 138 describes typical characteristics of discussion-based and operations-based exercises in general and of each of the exercise types described earlier.

Steps in Exercise Project Management

Successfully conducting an exercise involves considerable coordination among participating agencies and officials. The DHS Exercise and Evaluation Program methodology divides individual exercises into five overarching phases: (1) foundation, (2) design and development, (3) conduct, (4) evaluation, and (5) improvement planning (U.S. Department of Homeland Security, 2007a).

Step 1: Establishing a Foundation

Establishing a foundation for a successful exercise involves developing an exercise planning timeline, establishing an exercise planning team, and scheduling planning conferences. Exercise planning helps establish timeframes for attaining significant milestones, such as planning conferences, training, exercise conduct, after-action reporting, and improvement planning. Timelines vary based on exercise scope and

Table 8.2 Characteristics of Exercise Types

Type of exercise	Utility or purpose	Type of player action	Duration	Real-time play?	Scope
Discussion based	To familiarize players with current plans, policies, agreements, and procedures; to develop new plans, policies, agreements, and procedures	Notional; player actions are imaginary or hypothetical	Rarely exceeds 8 hours	No	Varies
Seminar	To provide an overview of new or current plans, resources, strategies, concepts, or ideas	Not applicable	2–5 hours	No	Multi- or single agency
Workshop	To achieve a specific goal or build a product (e.g., exercise objectives, SOPs, policies, or plans)	Not applicable	3–8 hours	No	Multiagency or multiple functions
Tabletop exercise	To assist senior officials in the ability to understand and assess plans, policies, procedures, and concepts	Notional	4–8 hours	No	Multiagency or multiple functions
Game	To explore decision-making processes and examine the consequences of those decisions	Notional	2–5 hours	No (some simulations provide real-time or near real-time play)	Multiagency or multiple functions
Operations based	Test and validate plans, policies, agreements, and procedures; clarify roles and responsibilities; identify resource gaps	Actual; player action mimics reaction, response, mobilization, and commitment of personnel and resources	May be hours, days, or weeks depending on purpose, type, and scope	Yes	Varies
Drill	Test a single operation or function	Actual	2–4 hours	Yes	Single agency or function
Functional exercise	Test and evaluate capabilities, functions, plans, and staffs of incident command, unified command, intel centers, or other command or operations centers	Command staff actions are actual; movement of other personnel, equipment, or adversaries is simulated	4-8 hours or several days or weeks	Yes	Multiple functional areas or multiple functions
Full-scale exercise	Implement and analyze plans, policies, procedures, and cooperative agreements developed in previous exercises	Actual	One full day or longer	Yes	Multiple agencies or multiple functions

Reprinted from U.S. Department of Homeland Security, 2007, *Homeland Security exercise and evaluation program* (HSEEP), Volume 1.

The Five Phases of the Exercise Cycle

1. **Foundation:** The following activities must be accomplished to provide the foundation for an effective exercise: create a base of support (i.e., establish buy-in from the appropriate entities or senior officials), develop a project management timeline and establish milestones, identify an exercise planning team, and schedule planning conferences.

2. **Design and development:** Building on the exercise foundation, the design and development process focuses on identifying objectives, designing the scenario, creating documentation, coordinating logistics, planning exercise conduct, and selecting an evaluation and improvement methodology.

3. **Conduct:** After the design and development steps are complete, the exercise takes place. Exercise conduct steps include setup, briefings, facilitation, control, evaluation, and wrap-up activities.

4. **Evaluation:** The evaluation phase for exercises includes a formal exercise evaluation, an integrated analysis, and an after-action report (AAR) and improvement plan (IP) that identify strengths and areas for improvement in an entity's preparedness, as observed during the exercise. Recommendations related to areas for improvement are identified to help develop corrective actions to be tracked throughout the improvement planning phase.

5. **Improvement planning:** During improvement planning, the corrective actions identified in the evaluation phase are assigned with due dates to responsible parties, tracked to implementation, and then validated during subsequent exercises.

Reprinted from U.S. Department of Homeland Security, 2007, *Homeland Security exercise and evaluation program* (HSEEP), Volume 1.

complexity. For example, planners generally employ longer timelines for tabletop exercises (TTXs) than for workshops and seminars. Timelines may also vary based on the entity's experience in conducting exercises and available resources (U.S. Department of Homeland Security, 2007a).

The exercise planning team is responsible for the execution of all aspects of an exercise, including exercise planning, conduct, and evaluation. The planning team determines objectives; decides what scenario meets the organization's needs; and develops documents used in exercise conduct, control, and evaluation. The exercise planning team should include representatives from each major participating entity and kept to a manageable size (U.S. Department of Homeland Security, 2007a). The exercise planning team should include representatives from key agencies, organizations, and jurisdictions. The sport or event organization should request members from key stakeholder groups and the command group (CG) to be part of the planning team. Members may include facility operations, local law enforcement, the local county emergency management director, local fire and HAZMAT, sheriff, public health, public relations, and emergency medical services. The membership of an exercise planning team can be modified to fit the type or scope of an exercise. For example, a full-scale exercise may require more logistical coordination—and therefore more operational personnel on the planning team—than a discussion-based exercise. Planning team members also help develop and distribute preexercise materials and conduct exercise briefings and training sessions. Because of this level of involvement, planning team members are ideal candidates for facilitator, controller, and evaluator positions during the exercise (U.S. Department of Homeland Security, 2007a). The sidebar on page 140 shows DHS recommended planning team members for discussion-based and operations-based exercises.

Exercise planning team members should be determined based on the scope and type of exercise as well as the scenario or subject. The following lists should be modified to meet the needs of the jurisdiction or organization.

Discussion-Based Exercises

Emergency Management

- Emergency management
- Homeland security

Public Safety

- Fire
- Hazardous materials (HAZMAT)
- Law enforcement
- Emergency medical services (EMS)
- Special operations
- Bomb squad
- Federal Bureau of Investigation (FBI)

Public Health

- Public health department
- Communicable disease
- Epidemiologists
- Infectious disease
- Pathology
- Poison control

Medical

- Hospital administrators
- Coroner or medical examiner
- Hospital infection control
- Hospital lab managers
- Hospital emergency room
- Medical society
- Private practitioners
- Veterinary

Other

- Public works
- Public information officer (PIO)
- Volunteer organizations (e.g., American Red Cross)
- Communications or dispatch
- Government officials
- Environmental quality

Operations-Based Exercises

Note: The agencies marked with asterisks are most critical to have present during all planning conferences.

Emergency Management

- Emergency manager*
- Homeland security*
- Public health*
- Public works
- Transportation or transit authority
- Public affairs
- Exercise venue or site management (e.g., stadium security)

Fire

- Fire department*
- Communications or dispatch*
- Special operations (e.g., hazardous materials [HAZMAT], Metropolitan Medical Response System [MMRS])*
- Mutual aid fire*

Law Enforcement

- Police*
- Special operations (e.g., bomb squad, special weapons and tactics [SWAT])*
- Sheriff's department*
- Local branch of Federal Bureau of Investigation (FBI)*
- Mutual aid law enforcement*

Medical

- Hospital representatives (primary trauma center or hospital association)*
- Emergency medical services (EMS) (public and private)*
- Mutual aid
- Medical examiner or coroner

Reprinted from U.S. Department of Homeland Security, 2007, *Homeland Security exercise and evaluation program* (HSEEP), Volume 1.

The planning team schedules planning conferences to define exercise objectives, develop the scenario, and coordinate logistics (Federal Emergency Management Agency, 2009a). In designing an exercise for a sport or event organization, the planning team must first assess their needs to analyze where exactly they need to focus their exercise design efforts. A sample needs assessment can be found in appendix 8.2. After the planning team identifies why the exercise is being staged and what it intends to achieve, then they can consider the type, scale, and content. Reasons for an exercise may derive from factors such as a need identified by a risk assessment, an incident, evaluation of a previous exercise, a need to assess whether personnel are sufficiently trained, changes to the physical structure or layout of the facility, or a legislative requirement (Football Licensing Authority, 2007). For example, the exercise will test the validity and viability of the stadium's emergency response plan in the event of an active shooter incident. The needs assessment may have presented this emergency as a potential threat because of past incidents at the facility, current trends, an elevated DHS warning, identification of terrorist activity in the local community through a facility or event risk analysis, or facility vulnerabilities.

Organizations should use a building-block approach when establishing an exercise program (see figure 8.2). The exercise planning team should start with a less complex exercise such as a seminar orientation and gradually progress to a more complex, fully involved exercise that deploys assets such as an FSE. For example, if a facility wanted to test its ability to deal with a mass casualty incident, planners may start with an orientation seminar with key stakeholders to inform and review response plans and gain support from local authorities. Planners could then host a workshop in mass casualty incident response for key personnel. The next step may

Figure 8.2   A building-block approach starts with less complex discussion-based exercises and progresses to more complex operations-based exercises.

be to conduct a tabletop exercise to work through an incident and discuss resource capabilities. Finally, planners could implement a full-scale exercise involving all agencies and deployment of assets.

Step 2: Designing and Developing the Exercise

When planning exercises, emphasis is placed on functions, not the emergency itself. Regardless of the type of emergency tested, the response functions must be evaluated to ensure an efficient and effective response (see examples later). "Functions are actions or operations required in emergency response or recovery" (Federal Emergency Management Agency, 2008a, p. 8). The Federal Emergency Management Agency (FEMA) defines 13 functions in its emergency management exercise reporting system: emergency alert notification, public warning, communications, coordination and control, emergency public information, damage assessment, health and medical, individual and family assistance, public safety, public works, transportation, resource management, and continuity of government (Federal Emergency Management Agency, 2008a). The sport or event organization may exercise a different set of functions or subfunctions. For example, the emergency response focus may relate to efforts such as the following:

- Risk communication protocol—notifying internal staff and dealing with the media through a public relations representative after an incident
- Mutual aid agreements—ensuring that resources and logistics from supporting agencies, both private and public, are secured and efficiently distributed to the incident scene in a timely fashion
- Coordination with other organizations to provide mass care
- Mass evacuation and traffic control coordination.
- Conversion of the sport or event facility to a shelter facility in a time of crisis, such as a hurricane relief effort

Detailed objectives are identified in the design and development stage and cover the actions and decisions to be taken by participants (i.e., heighten awareness of the crisis communication plan and standard operating procedures; identify resources available to facility operations). Capability and resource implications should also be considered at this stage. Planners must know whether they have the necessary resources—skills, finances, personnel, time, facilities, and support. Deficiencies in any of these areas will likely dictate what type of exercise they can implement. Questions to ask include (Federal Emergency Management Agency, 2008b) the following:

- What exercise experience is available in the organization? What is the experience of the manager and the staff?
- How much time can the manager (and the planning team) afford to allocate to the exercise process?
- What skills does the planning team provide?
- What facilities are needed to conduct an emergency operation? Are they available for the exercise?
- What communication systems does the organization use in a real emergency? Will they be available for the exercise?
- Will management and administrative support be available for the exercise?

The type of exercise, its location, and its duration will determine how much it costs. Cost considerations include staff salaries, equipment and materials, contract services, and miscellaneous items (paper, pencils, coffee, and so on) (Federal Emer-

Statement of Purpose

The purpose of the football stadium emergency management exercise is to improve the following emergency operations:

1. Evacuation notification and procedure
2. EMS response and coordination of mass care
3. Pedestrian and traffic control outside the stadium
4. Multiagency coordination

The following agencies are involved:

1. Facility management
2. Emergency management
3. Emergency medical services
4. Fire department
5. Health department
6. Law enforcement
7. Hazmat team
8. Biological and chemical experts
9. Local city hospitals
10. Media relations

These entities will be tested on November 1 in a tabletop exercise that simulates the release of a biological agent in the stadium. The exercise will be approximately two hours in length.

---

gency Management Agency, 2008b). The planning team determines the timelines for completion of the exercise plan, acquisition of necessary resources, and development of the support material. The exercise scope and statement of purpose should be clearly defined. A statement of purpose identifies the issue to be addressed in detail. This problem may have been identified based on experience, problems, or simple observations. A sample statement of purpose is provided in the sidebar. Appendix 8.3 provides a more detailed template for developing an exercise plan.

Scenario

A detailed exercise scenario must be developed based on the statement of purpose. A scenario provides the storyline that drives an exercise. It can be written as a narrative or depicted by an event timeline. For a discussion-based exercise (i.e., TTX), a scenario provides the backdrop that drives participant discussion. For an operations-based exercise (i.e., FSE), a scenario provides background information on the incident catalysts of the exercise. A number of factors should be taken into consideration when developing a scenario, including level of realism, type of threat or hazard, site selection, and optimal date and time for exercise conduct. The scenario selected for an exercise should be a realistic representation of potential threats faced by the sport or special event and realistically test the resources and capabilities that a sport or event organization or facility is attempting to improve through its exercise program. Furthermore, scenarios should be constructed to avoid any sensitivity that may arise, such as the use of real names of terrorist groups or sensitive venues (i.e., private company) (U.S. Department of Homeland Security, 2007b).

The first step in designing a scenario is determining the type of threat or hazard (e.g., active shooter) to be used in an exercise. Each type of emergency highlights different aspects of the disaster management cycle—prevention, protection, response, and recovery. The exercise planning team should choose a threat or hazard that best validates the capabilities, tasks, and objectives on which the exercise will focus. For example, if facility management wants to test its evacuation capabilities, they might design a tornado scenario. The identification of the threat or hazard scenario is based on the sport or event organization's facility threat and vulnerability analysis. For example, the threat of a chemical or biological terrorist attack may be considered a greater risk in a highly populated, high-profile community than it is in a predominately rural area. Likewise, the threat of hurricanes is far greater in the southeastern United States than it is in other areas (U.S. Department of Homeland Security, 2007b).

The next step in designing a scenario is to determine the venue (i.e., facility or site) to host the exercise play. Discussion-based exercises require a room set up to accommodate a specific number of participants and areas for breakout sessions if needed. Conference rooms and banquet halls are ideal. When selecting an appropriate site for an operations-based exercise, planners should consider the need for the following (U.S. Department of Homeland Security, 2007b, p. 14):

- A large area for tactical operations during the exercise
- A designated area (either at or near the site) large enough to accommodate the prestaging or assembly area for apparatus and equipment
- Minimal disruption from normal, everyday services such as traffic, public activities, and construction
- A designated area or room for victim actors to receive instructions before the exercise and, in some instances, to be moulaged (i.e., to have mold or makeup applied to simulate real injuries during an exercise)
- A designated area for media, observers, and very important personnel (VIPs) to view the exercise without interfering with exercise play
- Adequate parking for control staff, media, observers, victim actors, and support staff

The date and time of scenarios affect exercise play. Many communities have different population demographics on weekdays, weekends, holidays, and during sport and special events. These population changes may affect players' expected actions. For example, when a major sporting or special event is held at a stadium, a community's population may temporarily increase and traffic patterns may change, thus affecting evacuation routes or response times (U.S. Department of Homeland Security, 2007b).

Exercise Players and Documentation

In both discussion-based and operations-based exercises, facilitators and controllers guide exercise play. During a discussion-based exercise, the facilitator is responsible for ensuring that participant discussions remain focused on the exercise objectives and that all issues and objectives are explored as thoroughly as possible within the available time. Exercise play is governed by the facilitator, who coordinates the exercise and ensures that participants stay on task and within the designated timeframe. The facilitator sets the pace by injecting messages at predetermined times and resists introducing new material that is not part of the original exercise design. In an operations-based exercise, controllers plan and manage exercise play, set up and operate the exercise incident site, give key data to players, and may prompt or initiate certain player actions. All controllers are accountable to one senior controller.

Evaluators are selected from participating entities to evaluate and comment on designated functional areas of the exercise. Evaluators are chosen based on their expertise in the functional areas that they evaluate. Evaluators have a passive role in the exercise and should only record the actions and decisions of players; they should not interfere with exercise flow. Evaluators use exercise evaluation guides (EEGs) to record observations and notes. Evaluators are key people during this stage. They are responsible for keeping detailed and accurate records of all decisions and actions taken by participants. During functional and full-scale exercises, the use of CCTV and the recording of radio, telephone, and face-to-face discussions assist the evaluators and recorders in reviewing and debriefing the exercise.

The players are the participants who represent agencies that would normally respond to an incident. These players discuss their roles and responsibilities in the exercise scenario and are familiar with the facility's standard operating procedures and emergency operations plans being tested. Players have an active role in responding to an incident by either discussing (in a discussion-based exercise) or performing (in an operations-based exercise) their regular roles and responsibilities. For a sport or special event scenario this would include the command group and external agencies such as facility operations, local law enforcement, the local county emergency management director, local fire and HAZMAT, the sheriff, public health, public relations, and emergency medical services. Actors are volunteers who simulate specific roles, such as disaster casualty victims, to add realism to an operations-based exercise. These individuals can be recruited from the public. Simulators, generally controllers, perform the roles of individuals, agencies, or organizations that are not actually participating in the exercise to drive realistic exercise play (U.S. Department of Homeland Security, 2007a).

Exercise planners should develop documentation in accordance with the exercise chosen. A situational manual (SitMan) is a participant handbook for discussion-based exercises, particularly tabletop exercises. It provides information of exercise scope, schedule, and objectives. It presents the scenario narrative that will drive the facilitator's discussions during the exercise (see chapter case study on page 150). The exercise plan (ExPlan) is typically used for operations-based exercises. It provides a synopsis of the exercise, its scope, safety procedures, and logistical considerations. It is distributed to players and observers before the exercise and does not include a detailed scenario. The exercise plan ensures that the players will have to react during the exercise without planning or notification of projected events, as they would during a real incident.

The controller and evaluator (CE) handbook supplements the ExPlan and contains detailed information about the exercise scenario and roles and responsibilities of the controllers and evaluators. The master scenario event list (MSEL) is a chronological timeline of expected actions and scripted events to be inserted by controllers into the operations-based exercise play. It ensures that events happen so that objectives are met. A player handout is a one- to two-page quick reference document for exercise players distributed on the morning of an exercise. An exercise evaluation guide (EEG) helps evaluators collect and interpret relevant exercise observations. The EEG provides information on tasks to be accomplished, space to record observations, and questions to address after the exercise. The EEG guides the evaluator's observations to focus on capabilities and tasks related to the exercise objectives. Exercise policies are implemented to prevent or, at a minimum, mitigate the impact of an action that may cause bodily harm to participants, destruction of property, or embarrassment to the entity conducting the exercise (U.S. Department of Homeland Security, 2007b). Table 8.3 on page 146 describes documents commonly used in discussion-based and operations-based exercises.

Step 3: Conducting the Exercise

Major steps in exercise conduct for both discussion-based and operations-based exercises include (1) setup, (2) briefings and management of exercise personnel, and (3) wrap-up activities.

Conducting Discussion-Based Exercises

The exercise planning team assigned to set up should visit the chosen site at least one day before the exercise begins to arrange the room and test audio and video (AV) equipment. On the day of the exercise, the planning team arrives several hours

Table 8.3   Exercise Documents

Document title	Exercise usage	Distribution audience	Key document features
Exercise evaluation guides (EEGs)	All evaluated exercises	Limited: evaluators	Helps evaluators assess performance of capabilities, tasks, and objectives during an exercise
Situation manual (SitMan)	Discussion based	Not limited: all exercise participants	Textual background for multimedia, facilitated exercise Includes administrative information as well as scenario details
Multimedia presentation	Discussion based	Not limited: all exercise participants	Supports SitMan, concisely summarizing written information Enhances exercise realism with audio or visual depiction of the scenario Focuses and drives exercise
Controller and evaluator (CE) handbook	Operations based	Limited: controllers, evaluators	Supplements ExPlan with exercise administration information and scenario details
Exercise plan (ExPlan)	Operations based	Not limited: players, observers	Includes general exercise information but does not contain scenario details Enables players to understand their roles and responsibilities in the exercise
Master scenario events list (MSEL)	Operations based	Limited: controllers, evaluators, simulators	A chronological listing of the events and injects that drive exercise play Produced in both short (i.e., quick reference) and long (i.e., all-encompassing) formats

Reprinted from U.S. Department of Homeland Security, 2007, *Homeland Security exercise and evaluation program* (HSEEP), Volume 1, pg. 16.

before the start of the exercise to handle any remaining logistical or administrative items pertaining to setup and prepare for registration.

Before the exercise begins, the planning team must deliver the necessary exercise materials and equipment, which include the following (U.S. Department of Homeland Security, 2007b):

- Exercise manuals (SitMans) for participants
- Multimedia presentation
- AV equipment (including televisions, projectors, projection screens, microphones, and speakers)
- Table tents
- Name tents for participants
- Badges identifying the role of each exercise participant (e.g., player, observer, VIP, facilitator, evaluator)
- Sign-in sheets and registration information
- Participant feedback forms

Presentations and briefings are important tools for delivering necessary exercise-related information to participants. All participants (players) must be briefed on the exercise and given an opportunity to ask questions. The briefing should cover topics such as the reason for the exercise, its aims and objectives, rules, and a timetable of events. It will also identify the main participants and their responsibilities; details of how messages will be received; and available support materials, plans, maps, and so forth. A discussion-based exercise generally includes a multimedia presentation to introduce the scenario and accompany the SitMan. People selected to present should be able to speak well in front of large audiences and demonstrate their expertise of the subject matter. The presentation starts with brief remarks by members of the exercise planning team, sponsoring entity, or senior officials from the governing jurisdiction. After opening remarks, a brief introductory and explanatory phase led by a moderator should introduce attendees to facilitators and evaluators, provide background on the exercise process, and inform them of their individual roles and responsibilities. The moderator presents the multimedia briefing, which describes the scenario and any relevant background information. The moderator also leads the discussion, poses questions to the audience, and ensures that the schedule remains on track (U.S. Department of Homeland Security, 2007b).

Facilitated group discussions occur at individual tables organized by discipline or agency. A facilitator is responsible for keeping the discussion focused on the exercise objectives and ensuring that all issues are explored. Participants discuss their responses based on their knowledge of current plans, procedures, and capabilities. Designating a recorder to take notes allows the facilitator to focus on key discussion issues. Facilitated discussions take place before moderated discussions. In moderated discussions, a representative (spokesperson) from each table presents all participants with results from a group's facilitated discussion. The spokesperson is selected before the facilitated discussion so that she or he can prepare to speak on behalf of the group. During moderated discussions, spokespersons summarize the facilitated discussion, present key findings and issues, and discuss unresolved issues or questions. At the end of the moderated discussion period, the floor becomes open for questions (U.S. Department of Homeland Security, 2007b).

Facilitators compile notes relevant to their groups' facilitated and moderated discussions. This information is used to generate after-action reports (AAR) and improvement plans (IP). In addition, participants and observers receive a participant feedback form before the end of the exercise that requests information regarding the exercise's strengths and areas for improvement. Information collected from feedback forms contributes to the issues, observations, recommendations, and corrective actions in the AAR and IP. A "hot wash" is sometimes conducted immediately following the exercise, during which time facilitators conduct an informal conversation with players to capture their perspectives on the key strengths and areas for improvement identified during the exercise. In addition, immediately following the exercise, a short debriefing is conducted with the exercise planning team to determine their level of satisfaction, discuss issues or concerns, and propose improvements (U.S. Department of Homeland Security, 2007b).

Operations-Based Exercise Conduct

The exercise planning team begins setup as many days before the event as necessary, depending on the scope of the simulated disaster. Setup entails arranging briefing rooms and testing AV equipment and communications, placing props and effects to add realism to the incident, marking the appropriate areas and their perimeters, and checking for potential safety issues. Safety is the most important consideration in planning an operations-based exercise. The following actions must take place to ensure a safe environment (U.S. Department of Homeland Security, 2007b, p. 24):

- Identify safety controllers (not to be confused with a safety officer designated by the incident commander as part of the response to the exercise scenario)

- Dedicate advanced life support or basic life support ambulance units for real-world emergencies only
- Identify real-world emergency procedures with a code word or phrase
- Identify safety requirements and policies
- Consider other safety issues outside the scope of exercise control (e.g., weather, heat stress, hypothermia, fire or pyrotechnics, weapons)

On the day of the exercise, planning team members arrive several hours before the start of the exercise to handle any logistical or administrative items pertaining to setup, prepare for registration, and conduct a communications check. Before an exercise, a radio frequency or designated exercise channel is identified for player use. The selected frequency should not interfere with normal operations that are outside the scope of the exercise (U.S. Department of Homeland Security, 2007b) (see appendix 8.4, Exercise Checklist).

An operations-based exercise may include briefings for controllers and evaluators, actors, players, and observers. Briefings and presentations are good times to distribute exercise documentation, provide necessary instructions and administrative information, and answer any questions. An exercise that involves members of the public or movement of EMS resources (i.e., a full-scale exercise) may attract media attention; therefore, the media should be informed of the exercise objectives in advance.

Debriefings at the end of the exercise provide an opportunity to review the general exercise process. The extent of debriefing depends on the scale of the exercise. Large-scale exercises involving multiple constituencies, resources, and deployment of assets require a more sophisticated in-depth analysis both collectively and by each participating individual or agency. Regardless of the type of exercise, an immediate debriefing should occur as soon as the exercise is completed before memories fade and details are confused. This process should focus on the events, coordination, and responses to exercise developments (see table 8.4). A blank version of this log is provided in appendix 8.5.

Table 8.4   Sample Debriefing Log

Problem summary	Recommended action	Responsible agency
Inadequate EMS responders to number of casualties and insufficient triage capabilities	Assign more EMS personnel to stadium operations or to be on-call during event day	Local hospital point of contact
Site restoration capabilities and business recovery plans are lacking	Develop mutual aid agreements with local responding agencies and contractors to ensure adequate equipment, supplies, and resources are available post-incident	Sport organization

Adapted from Federal Emergency Management Agency, 2008, Exercise evaluation.

Step 4: Evaluating the Exercise

Initial debriefing is not normally a lengthy process, but it should be supplemented by a further detailed debriefing and critique at the evaluation stage. The critique and evaluation stage is critical to learning from exercise lessons and revising necessary plans. It should focus on the aim and objectives of the exercise and include input from participants, evaluators, recorders, and subject matter experts (a sample exercise critique is provided in appendix 8.6). The goal is not to criticize but to identify solutions for areas that need improvement. A written critique should be prepared by the planning team specifically addressing whether the exercise went according to plan, whether participants were able to coordinate their responses effectively, and whether the communication systems and plans being tested endured the incident scenario. The outcome of this process should include

1. a final report based on the evaluations;
2. details of plans, policies, and procedures requiring improvement and recommendations to be implemented; and
3. details of further training or exercises required.

Information gathered and summarized at this stage will be reported in a formalized after-action report.

Evaluation is the cornerstone of exercises; it documents strengths and areas in which sport or event programs could improve their preparedness in dealing with all hazards. The outputs of the evaluation phase lead to improvement planning activities. The evaluation process for all exercises includes a formal exercise evaluation, analysis of feedback, and drafting of an after-action report (AAR) and improvement plan (IP). The evaluation process must have a clear outcome such as an action plan. All key stakeholders need to commit to implementing the required improvements. An after-action report captures observations and recommendations based on exercise objectives. An improvement plan identifies specific corrective actions (e.g., additional training), assigns them to responsible parties (e.g., facility management), and establishes target dates for completion (e.g., within three months). The exercise planning team drafts the AAR and submits it to participants before an after-action conference with all agencies (U.S. Department of Homeland Security, 2007a). A sample AAR outline is shown in the sidebar (Federal Emergency Management Agency, 2008c, p. 25).

AAR Report Outline

- **Executive summary**: summary of report
- **Introduction**: main purpose of the report, preview of main topics, evaluation methodology
- **Statement of the problem**: purpose of the exercise
- **Exercise summary**:
  - Aims and objectives
  - Preexercise planning activities
  - Participants—individuals and agencies
  - Description of exercise incident scenario
- **Accomplishments and shortfalls**:
  - Evaluation of group review
  - Summary of postexercise debriefing and critique
- **Recommendations**:
  - Training needs
  - Gaps in capabilities
  - Changes needed in emergency plans
  - Corrective actions

Adapted from Federal Emergency Management Agency, 2008, Exercise evaluation.

Step 5: Planning for Improvement

During the improvement planning phase, corrective actions from the AAR and IP—such as additional training, planning, or equipment acquisition—are assigned to responsible parties with expected due dates. Corrective actions are tracked to completion, ensuring that exercises result in tangible benefits to preparedness. Participating entities may use the following questions as a guide for developing corrective actions (U.S. Department of Homeland Security, 2007c, p. 20):

- What changes need to be made to plans and procedures to improve performance?
- What changes need to be made to organizational structures to improve performance?
- What changes need to be made to leadership and management processes to improve performance?
- What training is needed to improve performance?
- What changes to (or additional) equipment are needed to improve performance?
- What lessons can be learned that will direct how to approach a similar problem in the future?

The improvement plan converts lessons learned from the exercise into measurable steps that result in improved response capabilities. It specifically details the actions that need to be taken to address each recommendation presented in the AAR and IP, who or what agency will be responsible for taking action, and the timeline for completion. After recommendations, corrective actions, responsibilities, and due dates are identified in the IP, the exercise planning team ensures that each corrective action is tracked to completion. The Department of Homeland Security offers two online courses that address exercise planning: IS-120, An Introduction to Exercises, and IS-130, Exercise Evaluation and Improvement Planning.

CASE STUDY

2004 Summer Olympic Games

The Summer Olympic Games ceremoniously concluded on August 29, 2004, in the heart of Athens, Greece. The culmination of the event was celebrated as testimony to peace and world unity. In retrospect, what factors were employed to ensure a safe and secure event? This question requires a close examination of the measures taken to address sport venue safety and security. It also reveals the necessity to begin security preparations early, well before the event, to allow adequate time to address potential training requirements, exercise emergency response capabilities, and implement appropriate corrective actions. Multiagency and multinational cooperation, coordination, and communication are critically important pieces of the security equation.

The environment for terrorism changed dramatically throughout the world after Greece was awarded the 2004 Summer Olympic Games in 1997. In fact, the tragic events of September 11, 2001, escalated the threat of terrorist attacks against U.S. citizens and interests. The risk of deadly aggression during special events increased as the capability of mass media improved, allowing live broadcasts on a worldwide scale. Further, an elevated tendency for terrorist groups to resort to acts of violence and the continued proliferation and accessibility of weapons of mass destruction (WMDs) contributed to the threat.

In preparation for the 2004 Summer Olympic Games, with the intent to test existing emergency response plans and associated annexes, a series of exercises were implemented.

EXERCISE PHASE

Exercises constituted a critical mechanism for testing capabilities during preparations for the 2004 Summer Olympic Games and were conducted in a variety of formats, which assisted with focusing on specific areas of preparedness and response.

Olympic Guardian I and II were discussion-based tabletop exercises (TTXs) with scenario injects that included crisis response planning, antiterrorism, counterterrorism, and consequence management considerations. Both TTXs were conducted to allow interagency decision makers the ability to meet in one location and openly discuss the variables and options available in response to numerous scenarios. Many times, the TTXs were the first time that multiagency executives met to discuss a coordinated response to a crisis. The exercises allowed decision makers the opportunity to test individual agency standard operating procedures and memoranda of understanding (MOUs) between each other before the actual event.

Hercules Shield was a multinational-sponsored full-scale exercise (FSE). The Hercules Shield objective was to prepare for potential worst-case critical tasks during the 2004 Summer Olympic Games. Hercules Shield tested command and control and was expanded to evaluate all aspects of command, control, communication, coordination, and information and intelligence flow and dissemination (C4I). The FSE setting was inside the event's designated location for the multiagency command post. The FBI referred to this location as the joint operations center (JOC), and it included representatives from each affected agency participating in the special event. The JOC included multiagency decision makers assigned to a command group and prepared to make coordinated critical decisions.

Hercules Shield validated all aspects of crisis response and consequence and crisis management. The FSE required a significant commitment by participating agencies to test relevant capabilities. Scenarios closely portrayed an actual crisis, and all elements of crisis response were activated and tested. First responders were dispatched to the incident, and medical facilities exercised mass casualty contingencies. Expertise in handling a hazardous material incident, an explosive device, and a WMD were tested and evaluated. Appropriate personnel staffed command posts, and lessons learned from previous TTXs ultimately assisted decision makers while they evaluated the circumstances associated with the FSE scenarios.

All exercises concluded six months before the beginning of the 2004 Summer Olympic Games. After the completion of all training and exercises, the original vulnerability and threat assessments were updated and reflected improved computer technology capabilities by the host country.

Following the exercises, each involved entity provided input for an after-action report (AAR)—a critical review of the exercise planning and execution strategies. The AAR acknowledged tactics that worked and identified procedures that needed to be corrected, changed, or revised before the beginning of the Games.

LESSONS LEARNED

The TTXs Olympic Guardian I and II and the FSE Hercules Shield demonstrated that numerous security gaps needed to be addressed before the beginning of the 2004 Summer Olympic Games. These gaps included

- a need for a consistent, tested, reliable, compatible communications system;
- improved dissemination of actionable intelligence;

(continued)

Case Study   *(continued)*

- a need to conduct risk assessments;
- a need to develop an overall crisis response plan;
- a need to conduct training in furtherance of developing relationships that would be critical during the event; and
- the importance of exercises to test readiness and preparedness at all levels.

The exercise identified problems that otherwise might not have been uncovered and allowed organizers to address the problems before the 2004 Games. In addition, future Olympic organizers were able to identify potential security issues for their events.

QUESTIONS TO CONSIDER

1. Explain the value of implementing a sequence of exercises into the planning and preparations for a special event.
2. What are the various exercise formats? What is the purpose of each format?
3. Should the media be involved in the exercise process? Why or why not?

REFERENCES

McGee, James A., 2006, International special events, *FBI Law Enforcement Bulletin*.

Key Chapter Points

- An exercise is an activity that places participants in a simulated disaster situation and requires them to function in the capacity that would be expected of them in a real event.
- Exercises help facility managers clarify roles and responsibilities, improve interagency coordination and communication, reveal resource gaps, develop individual performance, and identify opportunities for improvement.
- Exercises are not one-time events; they must be conducted continuously to address the changing elements of the industry.
- Types of discussion-based exercises include seminars, workshops, tabletop exercises, and game simulations.
- Types of operations-based exercises include drills, functional exercises, and full-scale exercises.
- Key personnel involved in the exercise process include planners, players, facilitators, controllers, evaluators, actors, simulators, and observers.
- The exercise planning team should start with less complex exercises such as a seminar orientation and gradually progress to more complex, fully involved exercises such as a full-scale exercise.
- The exercise planning team should include representatives from key agencies, organizations, and jurisdictions. The sport or event organization should request members from key stakeholder groups and the command group (CG) to be part of the planning team.
- Exercises consist of five stages: (1) foundation, (2) exercise design and development, (3) exercise conduct, (4) exercise evaluation, and (5) improvement planning.
- An after-action report (AAR) captures observations and recommendations based on exercise objectives and highlights areas that need improvement.

- An improvement plan (IP) identifies specific corrective actions, assigns them to responsible parties, and establishes target dates for completion.

Application Questions

1. Discuss the various types of exercises available to the sport or event exercise planning group.
2. What is the purpose of conducting exercises?
3. How does the exercise planning group determine what kind of exercise is needed and what functions or plans need to be exercised?

Activity

Review exercises conducted by the U.S. Department of Homeland Security and Federal Emergency Management Agency (descriptions are available at www.dhs. gov) and discuss (1) the purpose, (2) activities and agencies involved in the process, and (3) lessons learned.

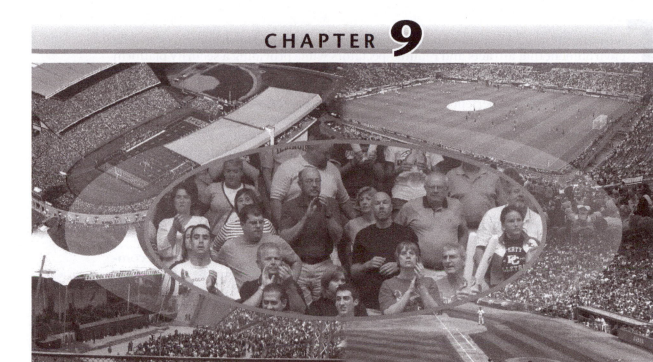

CHAPTER 9

The Future of Safety and Security Management for Sports and Special Events

CHAPTER GOALS

- Present training and educational opportunities in sport and event security.
- Discuss safety and security measures that affect the spectator experience.
- Highlight sport and event security technology solutions.

The overarching goal for sport and event organizations is to create an audience-friendly environment that attracts and retains spectators while providing a security platform to manage risk. A highly trained leadership team and staff must be in place to integrate best practices and technologies that will enhance the balance between security and the spectator experience. Administrators, owners, and operators must ensure that spectators enjoy access to their facilities. This chapter discusses the future of the sport and event safety and security industry. This topic includes a discussion of education and training opportunities in this relatively new field of study, an exploration of the balance between security and the spectator experience, and a review of innovative security technologies.

Training and Education

The future begins with excellence in sport and event security leadership. The complexity of security issues for large venues means that managers must have leadership skills and expertise in sport and event security. They will face numerous challenges, such as integrating risk management into the culture of the organization and its environment, establishing credibility and trust, and building relationships within both the organization and the local community. Another important aspect of the future leader is excellence in the performance of best practices. The future credential expectation in the sport and event security industry will be expertise in the security domain as well as strong leadership skills and the ability to contribute to organizational goals.

Leadership Training

A recent *Security Director News* survey identified real-world experience as the primary background necessary for security practitioners, although many respondents cited that both experience and a college and postgraduate education were important. Most professionals working in the field possess a military or law enforcement background but lack the educational and managerial component. The new professional must become well versed in business processes and able to present a business case for return on investment for security and management solutions (Stelter, 2009).

According to *Homeland Security* magazine, it is estimated that by 2012 nearly 25 percent of all new federal jobs will be related to homeland security. Currently, despite a down economy and high unemployment, nearly 2,000 openings in homeland security are listed on a primary government jobs website. These figures are for federal jobs alone. Clearly, more people will be looking for the best way to secure these positions, and they will need training, degrees, and certifications to do so. Sport and event management educational programs in the future must consider implementing safety and security courses as part of their curriculum or include safety and security knowledge content as a module or unit in sport facility or event management classes.

The University of Southern Mississippi was the first institution in the United States to offer sport-specific safety and security courses. Many degrees are offered in homeland security, emergency management, or some combination thereof, but none focuses specifically on sport and special events. Understanding the competencies needed for future sport and event security managers, the University of Southern Mississippi introduced a concentration area in sport event security management as part of the master's of science program in sport management. The program is designed to provide current and future sport directors and special event managers with the basic leadership skills and subject matter expertise to lead in the sport security industry. In addition to the master's in sport management with a concentration in sport event security management, the National Center for Spectator Sports Safety and Security (NCS[4]) at the University of Southern Mississippi has implemented an online sport security management certificate. It is designed to provide current and future sport and special event professionals with the specialized capabilities and knowledge needed to meet the management challenges of sport and special event security management.

Staff Training

Previous research indicates that key personnel responsible for responding to emergency incidents at major sporting events lack training and education (Cunningham, 2007; Baker et al., 2007; Beckman, 2006; Hall, 2006). According to Cunningham (2007), 62 percent of assistant athletic directors for facilities at Division I football schools reported having no formal training, education, or certification in event security management. Baker et al. (2007) reported similar findings while conducting a study of risk management practices at Division IA schools. Nearly half (47 percent) of all respondents have not received training to guard against terrorist attacks at their facilities, even though managers for NCAA Division IA football stadiums strongly agreed that terrorism is a foreseeable threat to U.S. sport facilities.

A 2006 Delphi study by Hall identified standards for effective security management of sport venues. Training of key personnel emerged as a critical requirement, and training should be provided in the following areas: threat assessment, inspection procedures, credential recognition, and security awareness. Furthermore, Hall et al. (2010) assessed the needs, concerns, and future challenges in security management at National Collegiate Athletic Association (NCAA) Division I football events. Critical needs identified include

1. assistance in conducting vulnerability assessments,
2. training for emergency response planning,
3. crowd control workshops,
4. an annual conference on sport event security best practices, and
5. risk and threat assessment training.

National Center for Spectator Sports Safety and Security (NCS[4])

The National Center for Spectator Sports Safety and Security (NCS[4]) has been a leader and pioneer in the provision of training opportunities related to sport security. In 2006 the University of Southern Mississippi established the first interdisciplinary center specifically focused on research, education, and outreach efforts in sport event security. The University of Southern Mississippi's National Center for Spectator Sports Safety and Security was developed through a grant initiative funded by the Mississippi Office of Homeland Security and the Mississippi Emergency Management Agency. The NCS[4] has worked closely with government agencies, specifically the U.S. Department of Homeland Security (DHS), to develop and deliver training programs relative to sport and special events. In 2007 the NCS[4] was awarded a DHS grant to design, develop, and deliver a national sport risk management course to National Collegiate Athletic Association (NCAA) institutional command groups across the country. The training program builds capabilities for multiagency collaboration at colleges relative to threats, incident management, risk assessment, planning, training, exercising plans, and recovery and business continuity. The college command groups are composed of specialists from five distinct areas: campus police, athletic department, emergency management, fire and HAZMAT, and emergency medical and health services. The overall goal for this training program is the standardization of sport event security risk management practices at intercollegiate athletic events.

The NCS[4] also established a training institute to develop and deliver national and international courses in sport risk management, sport evacuation training and exercises, and sport incident management. Specific courses in venue staff training and behavioral analysis are offered. To augment training, a national sport safety and security conference and exhibition is held annually to enhance professional growth.

Several other agencies are working to sustain future training opportunities in terms of information sharing, threat awareness, risk assessment processes and tools, exercises and training, best practices, facilitating public and private sector interaction, and national incident management activities.

U.S. Department of Homeland Security (DHS) Resources

The role of the Department of Homeland Security (DHS) is to leverage partnerships and relationships within the sport industry and state and local government entities to achieve success. This engagement supports a balanced approach that fairly addresses both public and private sport venues and, more important, ensures that risks are appropriately and reasonably mitigated. Ultimately, security and emergency response planning is the primary responsibly of the venue staff and state and local officials. The role of DHS is to augment and facilitate this planning process.

Vulnerability Assessments and Site Security Planning

DHS has developed a series of programs and initiatives that involve on-site sport venue engagement. One of the most successful programs is the site assistance visits for stadiums, arenas, and racetracks. Site visits are "inside the fence" vulnerability assessments jointly conducted by the department in coordination and cooperation with federal, state, and local authorities and the sport venue operators. These assessments identify critical components, specific vulnerabilities, and security enhancements. The goal is to mitigate identified vulnerabilities.

Another program coordinated by the Infrastructure Protection Program in conjunction with FEMA is the Buffer Zone Protection Program (BZPP). This program is designed to provide local law enforcement and emergency responders and other public sector entities with the resources necessary to enhance security and responsiveness "outside the fence." Local entities are able to apply for grant funding for protection and prevention equipment for first responders to mitigate the identified vulnerabilities, thereby directly contributing to the hardening of the stadiums, arenas, and tracks.

DHS provides computer-based assessments for stadiums, arenas, and racetracks. These assessments make use of a 360-degree, spherical camera system that captures the facility, routes, and specific areas and provides situational awareness during vulnerability assessments. DHS also conducts enhanced critical infrastructure protection visits to stadiums, arenas, and racetracks. The goal is to discuss options for consideration and potential protective measures to address any identified vulnerabilities.

Planning Documents and Tools for Stadium, Arena, and Racetrack Operators

DHS has created a suite of planning and informational resources that assist stadium, arena, and racetrack owners and operators in enhancing security around the facilities. An important document is *Protective Measures Guide for U.S. Sports Leagues*, specifically designed for use by participating representatives of the sport leagues.

The guide provides an overview of protective measures that can be implemented to assist sport teams and owners or operators of sporting event facilities in planning and managing security at their facilities.

The department has developed Common Vulnerability (CV), Potential Indicators of Threat (PI), and Protective Measures (PM) Reports based on data gathered from site assistance visits and the Buffer Zone Protection Program for use by local law enforcement and asset owners and operators to support their efforts in securing their stadiums, arenas, and racetracks.

The Risk Self-Assessment Tool (RSAT) makes assessing risks and vulnerabilities at stadiums, arenas, and racetracks fasters and easier. Developed by the department's Office of Infrastructure Protection, RSAT can assist stadium, arena, and racetrack managers in identifying, evaluating, and mitigating threats and vulnerabilities, including vulnerabilities to foreign and domestic terrorist attacks and natural hazards. Provided free to facility managers, it enables managers to balance resiliency with focused, risk-informed prevention, protection, and preparedness activities so that they can manage and reduce their most serious risks.

Information Sharing

The department's Homeland Infrastructure Threat and Risk Analysis Center (HITRAC) conducts all-source intelligence research and analysis to assess the potential threat to critical infrastructure and key resources like stadiums, arenas, and racetracks, as well as develop lessons-learned products derived from attacks on commercial venues abroad. HITRAC's goal is to provide owners and operators of stadiums, arenas, and racetracks with strategically relevant and actionable bulletins on threats that they face, primarily from terrorists. DHS disseminates these bulletins by the Homeland Security Information Network (HSIN), the department's primary platform used to facilitate the information sharing necessary for coordination, planning, mitigation, and response by the government and the private and public sector regarding threats identified by DHS.

Training Opportunities

Besides providing assessments, self-assessment tools, and threat and intelligence information, DHS provides a series of training opportunities. DHS conducts training courses for stadium, arena, and racetrack personnel that include the Soft Target Awareness (STA) Course, Surveillance Detection (SD) Course, and Protective Measures Course.

DHS has developed *Evacuation Planning Guide* to ensure the safety of the public, increase the level of preparedness, allow personnel to respond to an incident quickly and appropriately, and assist stadium, arena, and racetrack owners and operators with preparing a plan to determine when and how to evacuate, shelter in place, or relocate stadium spectators and participants.

Active shooter materials have been designed to be used as training guidance to address how employees, managers, training staff, and human resources can mitigate the risk of and appropriately react to an active shooter.

In addition, DHS and FEMA provide free training resources through the EMI. A full list of courses and resources can be viewed at http://training.fema.gov/.

Other Resources

Other professional security organizations have developed training programs and resources to aid security management professionals. The International Association of Assembly Managers (IAAM) is dedicated to the proficient operation of public assembly facilities, such as stadiums and arenas, convention centers, performing arts venues, and auditoriums. The IAAM host the Academy for Venue Safety and Security (AVSS). This training includes security planning and life safety management for the public assembly venue industry. The core educational tracks are risk management, emergency planning, security operations, and training. These tracks familiarize trainees with the many types of emergencies that can occur at public assembly facilities, and they offer techniques for planning, implementing, and ensuring the safety of patrons, staff, and facilities.

Information on the IAAM training and educational programs can be found at www.iaam.org. Another professional body devoted to security management of facilities is the American Society for Industrial Security (ASIS) International. ASIS is a global security management organization for security management professionals. ASIS International has issued standards and guidelines related to business continuity management, facility physical security management, risk assessment, organizational resilience, information asset protection, and workplace violence prevention and response (asisonline.org, 2008). Information on ASIS International and security resources can be found online at www.asisonline.org (Schwarz, Hall, & Shibli, 2010).

Safety and security are important issues for international sport governing bodies, as evident by the International Olympic Committee's bid documentation under the safety and security theme. Countries operate in different ways and have different requirements for the training of personnel. Furthermore, some organizations have in-house training and education programs, whereas others outsource, as described in chapter 7 of this textbook. Britain has been a pioneer in the implementation of safety and security practices through government regulation. Hooliganism in English football (soccer) forced the British government to introduce legislative changes to help control the problem. The safety legislation requires each football club in the top four divisions in England to hold a stadium safety certificate. The government produced and published a set of safety requirements in *Guide to Safety at Sports Grounds* (2008) for every club to adhere to and comply with, including the training of safety officers and stewards. Each football club is designated a safety officer to assist facility management with safety strategies on match day. Safety officers are responsible for the recruitment and training of all stewards. The sidebar gives an overview of the training requirements and duties of stewards. Safety officers formed the Football Safety Officer's Association to share best practices. Information about this organization can be found at www.fsoa.org.uk (Schwarz, Hall, & Shibli, 2010).

Balancing Security and the Spectator Experience

Effective customer relationship management is the key to continued support and attendance, which many times results in huge economic benefits. Given the threat of terrorism to sport and special event venues worldwide, the challenge of balancing the fan experience with optimal security management practices has been greatly magnified. The dilemma that faces most sport and event organizations is how those responsible for safety and security can create a somewhat transparent yet highly efficient and effective security management system that does not become excessively obtrusive.

A variety of sport and special events frequently draw large, highly emotional crowds. Every event has a unique set of circumstances, differing in fan demographics, number of spectators, and unanticipated outcomes. Highly emotional crowds, such as those at rock concerts, can be challenging for security management. With high emotion comes the possibility of aggression and spectator violence. Madensen and Eck (2008) identified several event characteristics associated with spectator violence:

crowd demographics, event significance, performance quality, alcohol availability, crowding, performer behavior, and event duration.

According to Madensen and Eck (2008), males are more likely to engage in violent behavior; therefore, events that attract males are more likely to involve violence. Organizers can combat this tendency by promoting the event as a family experience. In addition, sport events that attract many visiting supporters and have highly dedicated fans can engender acts of violence. Event significance also plays a role in spectator aggression. Events of known significance, such as a championship match, can provoke celebratory rioting. Poor performance by a team may provoke crowds to engage in verbal abuse and throw objects at each other or onto the playing area. Some of these incidents may occur (or escalate) because of alcohol consumption. In addition, performance behavior has been noted to affect spectator behavior. Spectator violence normally follows player violence during soccer and football games (Madensen & Eck, 2008).

Crowding plays a factor in aggressive behavior and the likelihood for violence because crowding limits spectators' mobility, increases the likelihood of unwanted physical contact among spectators, and increases wait times for entry, exit, and purchases. Pre- and postevent activities such as tailgating can also create opportunities for spectator violence. Spectators congregate before and after games and normally consume alcohol (Madensen & Eck, 2008). Different sports and events pose different problems, so security personnel should rely on assessments of risks and lessons learned from previous incidents to know what to expect. Security personnel should be prepared to handle crowd management problems such as field or stage invasion, rioting, and assault on players or performers.

The sport or event marketing and operations department must be committed to planning and working effectively with security operations. Achieving an optimal balance between entertainment (enjoyment) and security must always be considered. The operations side of a sport or other event includes such aspects as site preparation, parking, signage, ticketing, concessions, announcing, and press coverage. These elements are somewhat easily recognized and evaluated based on satisfaction or dissatisfaction of those involved. The focus is on customer relations management, and the desired result is to optimize entertainment and enjoyment.

The challenge becomes how an organization can maximize the event experience for the customer while also assuring that optimal safety and security policies and procedures are in place. One side or the other not may not understand or respect the responsibilities of the other. Organizations often seem to have two teams competing against each other—entertainment versus security—rather than one team made up of several components that cooperate. For example, the need arises at university football games to use the Jumbotron to communicate key safety and security messages, including evacuation information if needed. In tough budget times, marketing departments are charged with maximizing fund-raising efforts through ads. Pregame time is prime time exposure. The goal should be to increase fan awareness of security policies and procedures without forgoing critical fund-raising opportunities. The marketing department is ultimately responsible for selling tickets and providing an enjoyable fan experience. This aspect is enhanced through sponsorship deals. The marketing team is also responsible for venue signage, video screenings, Jumbotron announcements and commercials, halftime shows, competitions and prizes, and giveaways.

Facility management wants to ensure a safe and secure environment as well as a fun and enjoyable one. Therefore, they may implement policies that may not be fan friendly in some way. For example, they may conduct pat-downs and bag checks and limit alcohol sales. Pregame and halftime shows may also generate a conflict if the marketing department wishes to use small aircraft to fly over the stadium for promotional purposes (e.g., parachuting, good luck signs) and the security team

U.K. Guide to Safety at Sports Grounds: Guidelines for Stewards

The Need for Stewards

Effective safety management requires the employment, hire, or contracting of stewards in order to assist with the circulation of spectators, prevent overcrowding, reduce the likelihood and incidence of disorder, and provide the means to investigate, report, and take early action in an emergency. In carrying out these duties, stewards should always be aware of and ensure the care, comfort, and well-being of all categories of spectators.

Definition of a Steward

A steward (also referred to at certain sports grounds as a marshal) is a person who has obtained a level-2 stewarding qualification within the relevant qualifications framework, or is undergoing training and assessment for such a qualification and who is employed or contracted by management to act in accordance with the general recommendations of the *Guide*, and, where appropriate, the specific requirements of the safety certificate.

Duties of Stewards

While these may vary, depending on the size and configuration of the ground and the nature of the event, the basic duties of stewards (whether in house, hired, or contracted) should be to enforce the management's safety policy, the requirements of the safety certificate, where applicable, and all ground regulations. There are 10 basic duties for stewards, summarized as follows:

a. To understand their general responsibilities towards the health and safety and welfare of all spectators, other stewards, ground staff, and themselves

b. To carry out safety checks

c. To control or direct spectators who are entering or leaving the ground, to help achieve an even flow of people to and from the viewing areas

d. To assist in the safe operation of the ground, not to view the activity taking place

e. To staff entrances, exits, and other strategic points, such as segregation, perimeter, and exit doors or gates that are not continuously secured in the open position while the ground is in use

f. To recognize crowd conditions so as to ensure the safe dispersal of spectators and the prevention of overcrowding, particularly on terraces or viewing slopes

g. To assist the emergency services as required

h. To provide basic emergency first aid

i. To respond to emergencies (such as the early stages of a fire); to raise the alarm and take the necessary immediate action

j. To undertake specific duties in an emergency or as directed by the safety officer or the appropriate emergency service officer

Training

It is the responsibility of management to ensure that all safety personnel, whether employed in house or under contract, are trained and competent to undertake both their normal duties and their roles under its emergency and contingency plans. The training should also cover the specific needs of vulnerable and juvenile spectators.

Training must be conducted by occupationally competent persons using suitable training resources and material that will provide the relevant underpinning knowledge to satisfy the requirements of the National Occupational Standards for those relevant vocational qualifications.

During the training program, stewards should be assessed by occupationally competent assessors to demonstrate their competency against the National Occupational Standards and performance criteria of the relevant vocational qualification. It is recognized that, at any given time, some stewards will probably not have had the opportunity to complete their training and assessment. However, no steward should be deployed at the sports ground until they have undertaken all aspects of relevant familiarization and induction training. Stewards should not work unaccompanied until they have satisfied the following criteria:

a. They have received training to provide the underpinning knowledge for the following units in the National Occupational Standards for Spectator Safety:

   i. C29—prepare for spectator events,

   ii. C35—deal with accidents and emergencies, and

   iii. C210—control the entry, exit and movement of people at spectator events.

b. They have attended four events as a steward.

All stewards should complete their training, assessment, and qualification within 12 months thereafter.

Supervisors should receive additional training that develops their skills and competencies especially when responding to unplanned incidents. It is recommended that supervisors hold a level-3 spectator safety qualification on the relevant qualification framework.

All training and assessment records must be complete and fully maintained to ensure the training and assessments can be verified by the relevant awarding body and, where a safety certificate is in force, the local authority.

Reprinted from U.K. Department of Culture, Media and Sport, TSO Stationary Office, 2008, *Guide to safety at sports grounds* (5th ed.).

(and sometimes the FAA) wants to institute a no-fly zone in times of heightened alert of a potential terrorist attack scenario (e.g., a small aircraft dispersing chemical or biological agents across the playing area). The facility management team should ensure that all responsible parties are present during the planning of an event so that all needs and perspectives are addressed to form a common policy on such matters.

One of the advancements made in sport and event security is the embracement of spectators as first responders. Through new technology, spectators can now instantly and discreetly alert venue security personnel to any problem, whether it is a health emergency or an unruly fan sitting nearby, by sending a brief text message. Within seconds, venue personnel will receive the message and then can monitor and respond to the issue. The Department of Homeland Security has established the "If You See Something, Say Something" campaign to raise public awareness and strengthen security in the sport industry. The goal is to remind spectators to report indicators of terrorism, crime, and other threats to the proper authorities at sport venues.

Integrating Technology With Best Practices

The evolution of technology will bring dramatic changes in the way that venue managers approach protective security measures. Advances in technology and the entry of innovative firms into the marketplace will provide sport and event security professionals with enhanced tools, physical resources, and best practices to protect against threats and mitigate incidents. Venue safety and security is a prime issue for stadiums, arenas, tracks, and open venues worldwide. The NCS[4] at the University of Southern Mississippi established a National Sports Security Laboratory (NSSL) in 2010 to meet the operational and technological needs of venue operators and security personnel at sport venues. The primary mission of the NSSL is to advance sport security by providing opportunities for security observation and practice, technology tests and experimentation, and evaluations of feasible security solutions applicable to sport operations. The lab environment helps sport security operations and security personnel become more aware and knowledgeable of sport security issues. The NSSL conducts impartial, vendor agnostic, and operationally relevant assessments and validations of safety and security solutions (systems) based on the requirements of the community of interest (stakeholders).

The program is supported by a network of subject matter experts who perform assessment and validation activities. The program also provides evaluation reports that enable venue operators and security personnel to select and procure suitable solutions, and to deploy and maintain solutions effectively. In some cases process evaluations are performed to provide newly devised procedures. An outreach project of the NSSL is Industry Day, a biannual event that offers vendors an opportunity to showcase safety and security solutions for pregame crowd surge issues to sport industry management and security personnel, as well as a chance for security and stadium operators to explain operational and technological needs for safety and security issues at sport venues.

The first step in the process is to identify operational priorities for security. The National Center for Spectator Sports Safety and Security conducted a focus group consisting of the National Advisory Board. The board is composed of security representatives from the National Football League, National Basketball Association, Major League Baseball, Major League Soccer, United States Tennis Association, National Association for Stock Car Auto Racing, Indy Racing League, National Hockey League, National Association of Collegiate Directors of Athletics, National Collegiate Athletic Association, Stadium Managers Association, and the Department of Homeland Security (DHS). Based on feedback received from the board, NCS[4] identified the following operational priorities for security:

- **Screening**: contraband detection of persons and vehicles, with additional consideration of chemical, biological, and radiological (CBR) detection
- **Access control**: verification of credentials and granting of access rights pertaining to vendors, staff, and temporary employees
- **Video surveillance and analytics**: capabilities to support detection, recognition, and deterrence needs

These findings coincide with the general protective security measures promoted by DHS. The general protective security measures promoted by DHS can be categorized into four areas: (1) communication and notification, (2) planning and preparedness, (3) access control, and (4) surveillance and inspection. Security measures specific to sport events being shared as best practices by DHS include

1. conducting security assessments,
2. increasing perimeter security,
3. enhancing detection monitoring capabilities,
4. establishing access control, and
5. reinforcing employee procedures to ensure knowledge of emergency protocol.

After operational priorities for security are identified, the laboratory offers opportunities for security observation and practice, technology tests and experimentation, and investigations of feasible robust security solutions applicable to sport venue operations. The primary mission is to advance global sport security by serving as the epicenter for the enhancement of technology, training, research, and best practices. In this chapter, the emphasis on technology will be tied to the best practices just described.

Command and Control: The Art of Integration

The key technology component for the future sport or event security manager will be a single command center that integrates the most advanced security technologies with innovative networking capabilities to bring security solutions applicable to a venue of any size. Integration of video surveillance and analytics, access control, intrusion, and other functions into one system will provide capabilities to enhance best practices.

These smarter systems are leveraging existing information technology (IT) platforms as a standard business function with measurable accountability. As sensor technologies continue to develop, they will soon become managed by the IT function much the same as traditional information system components are. Many sport and special event security managers are also seeking to reduce capital expenditures by integrating existing systems with new systems. An important factor in the future will be the capability to couple existing systems with megapixel and high-definition (HD) cameras and video analytics. This integration will permit the management and correlation of information from an access system.

The functionality and capabilities of these new automated solutions have risen over the last few years. In recent years, the economy has become intensely focused on return on investment. The key to return on investment is automation that extends workforce efficacy. This trend will include more security automation, which will leverage the strengths of networked intelligent sensors and streamline the effectiveness and timeliness of security information. In essence, automation will increase the effectiveness of security and reduce its cost.

With the advent of networked automated sensors, a sport or event organization will not have to own and maintain all the elements of a security system. Instead, in the future, improved cost effectiveness will be obtained by outsourcing security systems in the way that network operations are outsourced today. By moving equipment and systems off site, a model of security as a service will shift capital expenses to operational expenses. Accordingly, security investments will be amortized over time, and sport and event organizations will benefit from best practices and the latest technologies.

Video Surveillance and Analytics

Administrators, owners, and operators seek to ensure that spectators enjoy access to events, and venue managers are required to achieve well-managed risk programs. One of the most significant technology advancements is video management. High-definition network video management software platforms and megapixel cameras provide security personnel with full situational awareness and actionable image detail. By immediately producing indisputable video evidence, these systems reduce investigation time and improve the accuracy of investigations. Future video management systems will provide exceptional usability and image clarity throughout the venue, ultimately providing cost savings by reducing the personnel needed to monitor protected areas on event days.

Emerging video technologies can improve the effectiveness of the monitoring activity. A standard stadium command and control center has a limited number of monitors, each displaying footage from several video surveillance cameras. A "push" video or audible alerts will dramatically raise the effectiveness of the monitoring system. Recent advances in video analytics will aid security staff in object tracking, detection of abandoned objects, and audio alert with respect to detection of gunshots, sirens, and screams.

The high-definition systems provide powerful zooming capabilities to capture the most precise image details using video management control software with high-definition cameras. Security personnel can instantly identify the details necessary for positive identification, leading to faster response times and better overall protection. The process of detection currently being performed by security personnel will be enhanced by the accuracy of intelligent evidence. New technology will equip security staff with the tools to make effective and efficient response decisions. This technology is especially important when protecting large areas, such as stadiums, arenas, tracks, and outdoor open spaces. A perfect example of why the new technology is important involves the pan–tilt–zoom (PTZ) cameras in use today at sport venues. Even with highly trained operators, during an incident these cameras are likely to be out of position to be able to respond effectively.

An important goal of the security staff is to maintain the balance between a good experience for fans and their safety and security. The new video management systems provide the ideal platform for powerful analytics to be completely integrated into the system, making them an integral part of its operation. Today, leading manufacturers of video management systems support analytics that can be performed in two fundamental modes: live (to detect events as they occur) and postprocessing (to test various scenarios on recorded footage). Analytics will detect suspicious movement. Motion detection is the most basic form of analytics. The use of video analytics will assist with this evaluation.

From a strategic perspective, stadium security personnel can track response time to incidents. They can also look for correlations between the number of incidents, such as fights and alcohol-related incidents, and attendance size. As indicated earlier, return on investment will be an important selling point for security personnel. The new technology combines video and audio and is focused on creating solutions to everyday security problems. The technology can detect, verify, resolve, and investigate security-related incidents and improve business processes. For example, in the case of a fight in the stands or a medical issue, video analytics paired with wireless devices can help security gain instant access to the trouble spot. Megapixel cameras would provide quality image details to identify the spectators causing the incident. The access system will identify the section, row, and seat and forward that information to stadium security near the incident. Intervention will be fast enough to prevent a severe problem, and positive identification from video can ensure proper handling of the incident.

Business processes can be improved by using video analytics; for example, in the pregame crowd surge, recorded or live video images can be scanned using video analytics to determine when an entry gate is at its busiest or when lines start to build. Operations personnel can then better understand crowd traffic and apply proper resources.

As we discussed, incident identification is one of the primary benefits of implementing video analytics software. Cost effectiveness or ROI (return on investment) is also a major benefit. By comparison, manual monitoring can be inconsistent and expensive, and it requires a significant investment in resources without being scalable or cost effective. Professional security staff will always be required in a video surveillance operation, but video analytics can help to relieve the burden of monitoring and improve the overall effectiveness of the system.

Access Control

Sport and event security managers must have the ability to regulate the movement of people into and within the organization's facilities to help protect employees and the organization's information. There is growing interest in implementing smart cards for physical and network access as well as other purposes. This method can provide significant security benefits compared with traditional passwords. Credentialing can also be accomplished through biometric technologies that include fingerprint, facial recognition, iris recognition, retinal scan, voice recognition, and hand geometry.

In the sport and event industry, temporary staff on the day of the event may range from 400 to 4,000 part-time employees. The issue facing security managers is authorization of these part-time employees. Research is being conducted at the National Sports Security Laboratory in biometric authorization. Identification is critical for entrance to media areas, locker rooms, housekeeping, suites, and offices.

The threat of attack has certainly heightened in recent years. Security management has become a focal point, and the need to build teamwork capabilities within sport and event organizations and with external constituencies has been identified. The provision of human resources and advanced technology as well as the implementation of multiagency training to assure the proper balance between event entertainment and security remains a major challenge. Those responsible for safety and security management must communicate effectively and build trust and respect with those on the event operations side, including the marketing and media staff, and explore ways to assure a spirit of mature teamwork.

The future success of sport and special event security requires that the security leadership and trained staff carry out their responsibilities in a consistent manner aligned with best practices. Personnel involved include law enforcement, contract security professionals, ticket takers, ushers, gate security, parking attendants, emergency management, and emergency medical staffs. Because the sport and special event industry is based on profit margins, best practices must be in place to protect the human and physical asset of the event. Based on the business model of the sport and special event industry, the security manager's highest priority will be to keep the fans, players or entertainers, coaches, and employees safe while working in their venues. Clearly, today's spectators value their total experience while attending the event.

In concluding, key considerations for safety and security stakeholders include risk management, staff training, multiagency collaboration, testing of plans through exercises, and the implementation of measures to combat threats and risks. The use of technology can also assist in safety and security efforts. Managers must be proactive and act in a reasonably prudent manner to protect participants, spectators, and staff. The issue is simply a matter of whether management, when an incident occurs, has taken the necessary precautions and is prepared to respond in an efficient and effective manner to saves lives and mitigate the consequences. We hope that this book will serve a current need in the field to educate current and future managers.

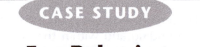

CASE STUDY

Fan Behavior

A Major League Baseball organization established an AA affiliate in a city that has a population of 200,000. The franchise is located in a suburban environment in the southeastern United States. The franchise has been in existence for six seasons, and the team plays in a stadium that has a capacity of 12,000. A postseason evaluation indicated a decline in spectator attendance. The first five seasons had shown an average attendance increase of 3 percent annually. The attendance decline in the just-completed season was the first in the history of the franchise.

(continued)

Case Study   *(continued)*

During a postseason meeting, the operations and security staff met to discuss the decline in attendance during the previous baseball season. Written feedback and oral comments from fans indicated that fan conduct had become a main issue.

Families with children made up at least 50 percent of the attendance during the previous season. An increase in alcohol impairment during the season had resulted in irresponsible behavior, foul language, and obscene gestures. Many families with children cited those behaviors as their reason for not attending. The owner charged the operations and security staff with developing a plan to reduce irresponsible fan behavior and create a friendlier family environment for the next season. The highlight of the new plan was the development of a new code of conduct for the fans, an alcohol policy, the installation of a texting system, and an increase in security staff.

For the next season, the franchise was committed to creating a safe, comfortable, and enjoyable experience for all their fans in the stadium and in the parking lot. Their goal was to create an environment that would allow those attending to enjoy the experience in a responsible fashion. For the next season, fans will be required to refrain from the following behaviors:

- Behavior that is unruly, disruptive, or illegal in nature
- Intoxication that results in irresponsible behavior
- Foul or abusive language or obscene gestures
- Interference with the progress of the game
- Failing to follow instructions of stadium personnel
- Verbal or physical harassment of fans of opposing teams

The new safety and security philosophy emphasized that all patrons will be responsible for their conduct as well as the conduct of their guests. Stadium staff will promptly intervene to support an environment where fans and their guests can enjoy the game free from irresponsible behavior.

Besides the new code of conduct, an alcohol policy will be implemented to reduce the number of alcohol impairment cases. The policy will cut off beer purchase after the seventh inning, and a spectator may purchase a maximum of two beers at point of purchase.

The installation of a texting system will represent an important step in the venue safety and security plan. The text messaging system will be a "time of need" communication tool. Patrons will be able to report safety and security issues as they occur, allowing security staff to intervene before situations escalate. This system will improve safety and security and promote a positive guest experience. Appropriate personnel will be able to receive large quantities of high-quality messages and respond to issues as they happen, thus reducing response times with minimum safety and security personnel.

With this technology, trained observers and supervisors will be able to monitor reported suspicious behavior in areas surrounding and within the venue and extract sufficient detail to support further tracking of suspicious objects, behavior, vehicles, or individuals. The texting system will provide the command and control center with the capability to identify safety, security, and medical issues instantly, as well as systematically collect evidence data.

LESSONS LEARNED

- It took a decline in attendance to initiate changes in stadium safety and security operations.
- The key to maintaining a successful operation is reacting to situations in the environment as quickly as possible.

- The widespread use of mobile phones and texting can, in some situations, help spectators contribute to safety and security goals.
- Alcohol consumption can play a major role in the attitude of fans.
- Policies and procedures play an important part in the management of a game.
- The fan is the most important ingredient in game management.

QUESTIONS TO CONSIDER

1. Why did it take a postseason meeting to identify the issue?
2. What should management have done the previous season?
3. How can the fans be assured that the code of conduct will be carried out?
4. What type of staff recruitment and training should be in place?
5. Should management segment family sections?
6. What should the policy be for violations of the code of conduct?
7. How will two-way communication with fans by text be expanded to marketing?

Key Chapter Points

- Advances in technology and training and educational programs will provide sport and event security professionals with enhanced tools, resources, and procedures to protect against threats and mitigate incidents.
- Operational priorities for security identified by key industry stakeholders include (1) screening of persons and vehicles, (2) access control for verification of credentials and granting access, and (3) video surveillance capabilities to support detection, recognition, and deterrence of criminal and illegal activity.
- One of the most significant technology advancement in the industry is video management.
- Real-time surveillance monitoring will greatly improve operational effectiveness through heightened situational awareness by automatically and immediately drawing attention to the incident.
- The dilemma facing most sport and event organizations is to create a somewhat transparent yet highly efficient and effective security management system that does not become excessively obtrusive to spectators' enjoyment.
- Previous research indicates that key personnel responsible for responding to emergency incidents at major events lack training and education. Sport and event management educational programs should consider implementing safety and security courses as part of their curriculum, or include safety and security knowledge content as a module in sport facility or event management classes.

Application Questions

1. How can technology enhance the safety and security of sporting and special events?
2. What new technologies could be developed to assist security stakeholders?
3. What suggestions would you offer to a stadium manager who is attempting to balance safety and security measures with an entertaining spectator experience?
4. What training and educational opportunities are available to someone in the field of sport or event security?

Activity

Research at least two innovative security solutions in the sport and event industry. Provide a description of the product or service and present a summary of their effect on the sport and event industry.

Appendixes

Appendix 1.1
Janet Napolitano Presentation: NCS⁴ Conference August 2–4, 2010

Everything is spoken by Napolitano unless otherwise noted.

Thanks, Todd (Todd Keil, assistant DHS secretary for infrastructure protection). Thank you so much for that introduction. Let me extend thanks to the conference organizers for having me here today. It's always a pleasure to be back in New Orleans, but it was particularly gratifying to be here today not just for this conference, and the reason I am, and that I ask your indulgence for being a little bit late, is that I have just been at the unified area command here in New Orleans. This is the unified command area for the entire Gulf region for the Deepwater Horizon oil spill response. I thought what I would do before I got into my prepared remarks was to tell you a little about where that sits because it has been a massive effort in terms of building a response beyond what anyone had seen before beyond the surface of the sea, in terms of number of vessels.

We have over 6,000 vessels either skimming or laying boom or burning something on the surface of the sea. Right now on the Gulf Coast they have laid over 2,200 miles of boom and have more now in place to establish the supply chain as you might imagine to allow that amount of boom to come to one area of the world and we have today about 35,900 people working on the spill. At our height it was close to 60,000 people working at any given time. It has been a massive organizing activity and is one in which we have worked tirelessly to make sure that BP does its job and caps the well and that the ocean is cleaned and the extent that the oil hits the shoreline that it is picked up and that the persons that have been impacted have their claims paid. It's all being run out of a building on Poydras Street. So that's where I have been.

Tomorrow they are going to start a process known as the static kill which will be the first near death of the well. That will be followed in several weeks by the completion of a relief well, which will be the true death of the well. In the meantime, they have done so much burning, skimming, and booming that right now the surface is clean. We hope by the end of today, based on estimates by not just government scientists but a group of scientists we have brought together from outside government as well, to give an estimate of how much has actually been deposited in the Gulf. That's called the flow rate and it will be generated by the Flow Rate Estimates Group. We didn't have a lot of time to spend on names. Tomorrow, of course, we hope is the so-called static kill and then hopefully after that we can provide for you and for the public at large the scientific analysis of where the oil has gone and what has happened to the oil that has spilled. Then we want to make sure that BP, as the responsible party, pays what it owes for this environmental disaster.

So, it's appropriate that we are here in New Orleans. The Gulf has gone through a lot in recent years and I think it's important to note that sports have been an important part of the recovery in this area of the country, particularly from events like Katrina. I would be remiss if I didn't mention we are in the home of the Super Bowl champion New Orleans Saints. I understand they may be having a visit to the White House soon. On behalf of the president, we are very committed to the Gulf, to the people, to the way of life here, and so this is not just for us about response to an oil spill. This is about recovery and restoration to a situation that is even better than the status of the Gulf on the day before the spill. That's our promise to the people in Louisiana, that's our promise to the people across the Gulf, and that's our promise to those in this room today.

Now, this my eighth trip to the Gulf in the last 100 days, and I venture to say it will not be my last. But I am very grateful that this trip has given me the opportunity to address you because being secretary of DHS is a very unusual position in our federal government, and I use the term "unusual" broadly. One minute you are coordinating the response of the largest oil spill in history. The next, you are dealing with a breach of our transportation security. The next, you may be called upon to help coordinate security for events like the Super Bowl or the Winter Olympics. Sometimes I can actually go to the sporting event that we are providing security for, at which point I say, "It's good to be the secretary." But at all of them, it's very important that we think ahead and plan ahead because the fact of the matter is that this industry is an important partner with us in defending the country against terrorism and disasters. You possess a special role in society's mind and you possess a special visibility and you possess special assets that from time to time are called upon to perform functions as you were just hearing that perhaps they were not designed to do but were called upon to do.

So, let me if I might, turn to the subject of attacks and of terrorism. The past 18 months, what this administration has seen, what I have seen, is an evolving terrorist environment. We no longer just see big conspiracies that evolve over time that give us the opportunity to intercept and interrupt them. We are seeing more and more individuals who are trained, who receive their tradecraft perhaps in the Fatah, perhaps somewhere else, and have become radicalized by a group or by the Internet, sitting at home. We more and more are seeing U.S. citizens themselves acting out in furtherance of Islamic jihad.

So the issue about terrorism, the prevention of attack, is something that this industry in particular needs to be paying attention to and this industry in particular, I think, has an important role to play. Todd mentioned partnerships when he was discussing how we have been getting at this new and evolving threat picture at DHS and I will tell you this: this is something that needs to be more than just a slogan or a word. These need to be active, ongoing intersections between the federal government; state, local, tribal governments; and the private sector because we cannot ever predict with certainty where a particular threat will emanate or where a particular risk will effectively come to pass. And, as I mentioned, sports, just because of the symbolic nature of the industry and its importance to the way of life, obtains a special value here.

Since I have been secretary, I have met with commissioners and security directors of every major sports league on security issues. We are engaged directly in the work Todd mentioned: the evacuation planning guide, the risk self-assessment tool. We don't do those just to occupy our time. We have lots of things that we could be doing. We do them because they fit the threat environment that, unfortunately, is the environment in which we live. So let's deal with that reality and be proactive about it and be thinking ahead.

In May we launched an outreach and awareness initiative to visit all of the major sports leagues and the Division I facilities in the NCAA. We have already visited and worked with owners and operators at approximately 260 of the 300 sites that are either the major professional sites or the NCAA Division I sites in our country. We conducted a table-top exercise relating to stadium security which had representatives from most of the major leagues and a number of the teams present there. I want to thank everyone who helped us design that exercise and who also participated in it and all the lessons learned.

And of course while overall, being a spectator at a sports event is very, very safe. And we know that. People from all over the world came safely to the World Cup recently in South Africa. They gathered safely in Vancouver for the Winter Olympics. But, you only have to step back a little bit and think about what happened in Uganda after the World Cup: a tragic bombing carried out by a group that harbors radical views against the United States. To be reminded again that sporting events can get the attention of not just fans but also violent extremists, be they terrorists acting out in furtherance of radical Islam or in furtherance of other groups as well. When you think of incidents like Munich in 1972 or Atlanta in 1996, it's easy to see that this is a long-standing risk. Indeed, I suspect you wouldn't be having this conference if you yourselves didn't recognize the kinds of risks and the fact that they are part of our threat environment.

So we need to work together to keep your venues secure. We need to make sure that the fans are safe and we need to make sure that in doing so, we are protecting the economic and social benefits of sports in our society. The partnerships we have built are ones that we want to continue to expand: state and local law enforcement, local emergency responders, public health authorities, and with the private sector.

Now, one other area of partnership that we are expanding is one not just with teams, not just with security officials, but with individuals themselves, with the fans, with the citizenry of our country. That is, making sure that everyone understands that security is a shared responsibility. You can't do it by yourself. We can't do it by ourselves. But the plain fact of the matter is that educated citizenry, alert stadium employees, properly trained, properly supervised, can be force multipliers way beyond what the people in this room can accomplish. When you think about, for example, the Times Square attempted bombing this year, what brought that to law enforcement's attention was a hotdog vendor who noticed there was smoke where smoke shouldn't be and alerted law enforcement and law enforcement immediately jumped on that matter. Indeed, we went from law enforcement being alerted by that street vendor to capturing the Times Square bomber in 53 hours. We went from a faux pas to a capture and identification in 53 hours. Now, I don't know whether you all watch TV. On TV they have a show called *24*. I'll tell you, *24* may be a television show, but 53 was real life, and it was very, very effective law enforcement.

So what does it mean when we say we want to involve the citizenry, we want to involve fans, we want to involve everybody in the shared responsibility of our security. Well, one of the things that means is that we carry out or conduct campaigns that reach out in that fashion. The most successful of recent campaigns in this regard is one that was started by the New York City Municipal Transit. It was called, "See Something, Say Something." The S campaign was started by the Metropolitan Transit Authority with funding provided in part from the Department of Homeland Security. Many other cities, states, and localities have gone to similar campaigns, but one reason why the campaign works is because it is easy to remember. If you see something, say something. If you see something out of the ordinary, say something to law enforcement. If you see an unattended package, say something to law enforcement. If you see people conducting surveillance of critical infrastructure, say something so that can be inquired into. If you see vehicles parked where they shouldn't be parked, say something to law enforcement. If you see smoke coming out of anything, say something immediately to law enforcement. If you see something, say something.

So, if you are in a public space like a stadium and you see something that looks suspicious, like an unattended bag or package or an individual acting in a suspicious manner, say something. Say something in the stadium environment to the stadium attendant, to law enforcement. By the way, if it's the stadium attendants, we need to make sure they are trained and know to whom to report, so stadium employees need to be trained as well. But by that simple mechanism, the adoption of a shared responsibility and a see something, say something mentality, we can be a force multiplier far beyond what law enforcement can provide.

Last month I was at Penn Station in New York City announcing the expansion of See Something, Say Something to Amtrak. So when you ride on Amtrak right now, you will see See Something, Say Something signs and other indicators of the campaign: posters, publication materials, and other outreach tools. If you're in shopping malls, we have reached out to the shopping mall community. If you see something, say something. Last year, before the holiday shopping season began, we conducted training online for shopping mall employees. We have literally thousands of shopping mall employees receiving that training before the holiday shopping season began.

We have, as I already mentioned, met with the major sports leagues and the NCAA. We met with them about involving the fans. Making sure stadium and venue employees know what to do beyond just your security force. It's your vendors, your concessionaires, men and women going up and down the aisles all need to know if you see something, say something.

See Something, Say Something is combined with another thing we're doing and that has a law enforcement report focus. That is a system around the country for suspicious activity reporting, or SAR. We piloted this now in several states. It is a special partnership involving trained law enforcement to share information about suspicious incidents that may indicate true terrorist planning or other criminal activity. Information, that when locally collected, analyzed, and shared, is one of the most powerful tools we have, if we have any, to prevent one of the risks present in our environment from materializing itself into an actual event where there could be loss of life, serious injury, or serious damage to property. So See Something, Say Something is for the citizenry and SAR is for law enforcement. Now what we're working on is growing both and merging the two together as complementary systems that augment each other. That is ongoing at DHS.

I want to pause on one thing, because the press often asks me about this. The SAR initiative does not collect information based on ethnicity. It is focused solely on suspicious actions and behaviors associated with crime. The front line personnel who have access to the system are given extensive training to distinguish between those, between legal and illegal behavior. I think that's important to say. It has rigorous civil liberties protections built in, but we're not starting SAR from scratch. SAR is piloted in a number of places and it is very effective in focusing law enforcement where it needs to be focused, sharing information where it needs to be shared, and making sure that we are being proactive about our threat environment, not just reactive after the threat has occurred. SAR is ongoing. See Something, Say Something is ongoing.

Let me return to sports. I think that teams have a big and special ability to communicate with the fans. You can help fans as well as stadium staff connect with their responsibility when it comes to our security. Not just at the game, but when they get it in their minds, it will move to other environments as well. You can help encourage them that if they See

Something, Say Something anywhere, not just if they are attending a game. You can help instill a broader understanding about how important it is to be prepared for an unexpected event or disaster.

Sports teams are important messengers in our society. They have a unique role to play here. Let me conclude my remarks with an ask because I think, in light of this special role, there is an ask I would like to make of you. And the ask is very straightforward. I would like our sports franchises, our sports leagues, as well as NCAA Division I to formally enter into agreements with us using their own marketing talents and brands to help us expand the reach of the See Something, Say Something campaigns because we're all about the games and we're all about protecting the millions of fans who enjoy the product and the safety and security of the product is what we are all seeking together. So in the aftermath of this and other meetings and in the spirit of teamwork and partnership, we would like to see the See Something, Say Something campaign move from transportation and transportation venues to shopping malls and into sports as well. That way, we help to expand, as I mentioned at the beginning of my remarks, the architecture we are constructing for the security of us all. Thank you all very much.

Questions From the Audience

Question from the emcee: How critical has the SAFETY Act been to increase security and need for awareness at sporting events?

Napolitano: I think it is among a number of things, among a whole universe of things that are critical. But here's the thing about safety and security. And that is we have a tendency in our country to go to a conference or a meeting or even to a table top and then it's done. Okay, now we've done our safety and security thing and we can move on to what we really want to do, which is to put on a great sports product. Well, we want to make sure safety and security are core competencies of any team or league hosting sports. You can tell this one, the picture's behind me, these are huge venues and we want to be trained and we want to be resilient, because if this were to happen the number one thing we need to do is prevent this from happening.

Statement from the audience (no question): The Safe American Foundation has been working with the governor of West Virginia and using the West Virginia-Marshall football game to conduct the first ever stadium-wide texting drill on September 10. We applaud what you're doing in our organization, trying to bring grassroots readiness to all America using sports venues, so we'll be working with Verizon and other companies on September 10. Our program is called Drill Down for Safety and last year we had 400,000 people actually conduct individual drills. This year we're expanding it to include texting and we think that this is an important tool especially at sports venues where there are so many employees and spectators.

Napolitano: Thank you. That's great. And let me just add to that that one of the things that FEMA has done over the past year is greatly expand the use of social media in disasters and disaster response, including texting and other capabilities that we didn't have after Hurricane Katrina and we have now in an effort to give people easier access to information, easier ability to find out what they need to do, where they need to go, how they get help, easier abilities or ways to find family members or others who may be lost in the course of a disaster. So social media can be a very, very, and is a very, very useful tool.

Emcee: Madame Secretary, just so you know, the security directors for all the major sports leagues are sitting here in the first two rows. The support the Center has gotten from the leagues has been incredible, along with your department, DHS. I think your ask has a lot of effects on the first two rows and I think we're going to take that up with the Board of Advisors at the next meeting to assist you in that arena.

Napolitano: Great.

Ron from Eastern Michigan University: Regarding the ask for the NCAA and the venues, is there anything in particular we can do to participate in that? How could we participate specifically?

Napolitano: I think the easiest thing to do is to contact our department and we will leave with the conference organizers some contact information on how to do that. I don't have the phone number and email address in my head directly but we will have information that we will leave for you. Just call them up and say, "We want to do something" and we'll get at it.

Emcee: We'll end with one question and the secretary is incredibly generous with her time. Madame Secretary, if there's one message you would like all the NCS⁴ participants here today to bring back to their campuses and facilities to hear with all the efforts and support the DHS has done, what would that message be?

Napolitano: I don't think it would be a message about what we have done. We have done a lot. I'm perfectly pleased to stand up and give you a laundry list of things that have gone on, but I think the key message to take away from this is that security is a shared responsibility and if we can empower people, then we can empower teams and communities to help us, to help law enforcement, to help those of us who are in security. As I said many times this afternoon, that is a powerful force multiplier. It has to be done in the right way. We think the initiatives we created do it in the right way. It has to be done in a way that recognizes that if you are prepared, you're not as fearful as you might be. And it has to be done in a way that recognizes, I think, the special role that athletics plays in our culture and our society. So I would not take away from this about the long list of DHS activities. I would take away two words: shared responsibility. And how it put me on those words, on those bones, is really going to be how secure we get.

Emcee: Please join me in thanking Madame Secretary.

Transcribed from J. Napolitano, Presentation given at NCS⁴ Conference, August 2-4, 2010.

Harris County, Texas, Citizen Corps Response to Hurricane Katrina

Summary

In the wake of Hurricane Katrina, the Harris County, Texas, Citizen Corps—under the leadership of Harris County Judge Robert Eckels—coordinated a massive volunteer effort to provide evacuees with temporary housing at make-shift shelters throughout the Houston metropolitan area. The volunteers sheltered roughly 15,000 Louisiana residents in Houston's Reliant Astrodome, while thousands more were housed in the nearby Reliant Arena, Reliant Center, and George R. Brown Convention Center.

Harris County Citizen Corps Council

Established on August 26, 2002, the council's membership includes the Harris County Judge, the Mayor of Houston, the Harris County Sheriff and Fire Marshal, the Superintendent of the Houston Independent School District, the Chairman of the American Red Cross, the Area Commander of the Salvation Army, and some 15 other members.

Background

On August 29, 2005 Hurricane Katrina made landfall near Buras, Louisiana. Despite mandatory evacuation orders by Mayor Ray Nagin of New Orleans, an estimated 100,000 residents could not, or would not, leave their homes for safer ground. Many of those trapped by the storm flocked to hurricane shelter points set up by the American Red Cross (ARC) at the New Orleans Superdome and other sites around the city. Approximately 30,000 Louisiana residents took shelter from 145 mph winds and torrential rains at the Superdome complex.

Within days of the storm, 80 percent of the city had flooded, and the shelters set up by the ARC and other organizations had far exceeded their capacity. At the Superdome, the air conditioning failed, the water pressure dropped, and the turf field, plastic seats, and concrete ramps and corridors were overflowing with hungry, dehydrated, and exhausted evacuees. The deteriorating situation forced emergency managers to transport remaining residents out of New Orleans to make-shift shelters in cities throughout the Southwest, including Houston, San Antonio, and Dallas, Texas.

Goals

The obstacles encountered during the New Orleans hurricane response prompted a concerted effort on the part of cities to provide the storm's victims with comfortable, convenient, and safe living accommodations. The Harris County Citizen Corps mobilized thousands of Houston-area volunteers to assist in the shelter efforts. Citizen Corps volunteers assisted in greeting and processing 65,000 evacuees from the New Orleans area.

At the Reliant Astrodome and surrounding buildings, the Citizen Corps volunteers created an evacuee "city"—complete with its own zip code—capable of sustaining over 27,000 people.

Description

In a matter of hours, the Harris County Judge's Office and the Harris County Citizen Corps prepared the Reliant Astrodome to receive evacuees displaced from their homes. Exemplary aspects of the Citizen Corps response included:

- the use of the Harris County Citizen Corps online member directory to call for volunteers;
- the formation of an organized process for enlisting, training, and assigning the thousands of volunteers to specific tasks; and
- the seamless integration of Community Emergency Response Team (CERT) members and other Citizen Corps members familiar with the National Incident Management System (NIMS) into the Reliant Park Incident Command (IC).

Summary of Events

Two days after Katrina's landfall, the Harris County Citizen Corps began mobilizing to accept volunteers. At approximately 6:00 am on August 31, Mark Sloan, the Coordinator for Homeland Security Special Projects at the Harris County Judge's Office, participated in a conference call with officials from the Texas Department of Emergency Management (DEM) and the Harris County emergency responder community. During that call, Harris County officials were instructed to prepare for the arrival of 23,000 to 25,000 Louisiana residents, who, at that time, were being sheltered in the New Orleans Superdome. Texas DEM representatives warned Harris County officials that buses full of victims were set to leave the Superdome, and that the County would have to support the ARC in its efforts to prepare the Astrodome as a shelter.

Four hours later, at 10:30 am, the ARC asked the Harris County Citizen Corps how many volunteers were available to help prepare the Astrodome. Using the Harris County Citizen Corps directory of member e-mail addresses, Sloan sent out a general e-mail announcing that New Orleans evacuees were on their way to Houston, and that Harris County "must build a city ready to receive them." Sloan got 1,000 responses per hour, flooding his inbox and crashing his personal e-mail system and the Harris County Citizen Corps website. When the site came back online a short time later, the directory contained over 2,800 new members and 38 new organizations.

Evacuees began trickling into the Astrodome shelters the night of August 31, but it was not until late in the evening on September 1 that the Citizen Corps was officially activated. At 10:00 pm, the ARC sent a second message to Harris County, this time alerting them that 60 buses—each with 50 passengers—were expected to arrive at the Astrodome and that volunteers were needed to process evacuees and staff the shelter. In response, Sloan turned again to the Harris County Citizen Corps website member directory to issue a call for volunteers. Within the hour, over 1,000 people had arrived at the dome ready to help.

For the next several weeks, the Harris County Citizen Corps assisted the ARC in the complicated volunteer coordination effort. Members of the area CERT, Medical Reserve Corps (MRC), Volunteers in Police Service (VIPS), and Neighborhood Watch groups established volunteer check-in points, where spontaneous volunteers were received, enrolled, and assigned to shelter tasks. In the first 24 hours, the Harris County Citizen Corps processed over 8,000 volunteers to assist the ARC in its activities. Over the course of the county's operations, volunteer coordinators averaged 3,500 spontaneous volunteers processed each day.

By Wednesday, September 7, the number of evacuees still sheltered in Houston area sites had dropped from almost 27,000 to only 8,096. In a matter of days, the ARC had transitioned New Orleans evacuees from temporary shelters in the Astrodome and other Reliant Park sites to more permanent housing arrangements in cities around the country.

Using the Member Directory

The Harris County Citizen Corps member directory proved invaluable to the Hurricane Katrina response effort. Since the launch of the Citizen Corps website, it has been used as both a public information tool and a resource-tracking mechanism. Volunteers visiting the website are asked to login using a member name and password. They are also asked to create a member profile with their contact information and emergency response skill sets (e.g. language skills, medical skills, veterinary skills, etc.). Area organizations and businesses can also create member profiles detailing the type and amount of resources at their disposal in the event of an emergency. This member directory allows the Citizen Corps to accurately track the location and availability of potential volunteers and emergency response supplies in their area.

When the ARC requested volunteers to staff the Reliant Park shelters, the Harris County Citizen Corps used the member directory to quickly mobilize area residents. In addition to the e-mail sent to 10,000 subscribers issuing a general call for aid, Citizen Corps also sent out more detailed messages asking volunteers not to self-deploy and describing the number of volunteers needed, when they should arrive, and the skills they should have. Including specific instructions in volunteer requests allowed the Citizen Corps to control the flow of volunteers into the Reliant Park shelter area.

Organizing Volunteers

Once the Citizen Corps had issued its call for volunteers, the complicated task of organizing and deploying those who responded began. Using CERT members and representatives from other local Citizen Corps organizations, the Harris County Citizen Corps established a volunteer integration procedure to lead the thousands of spontaneous volunteers through the enrollment, training, and deployment process. The volunteer integration procedure involved three primary steps:

- First, upon arrival at the designated volunteer area, organizers asked potential volunteers to provide a valid photo identification, reminded them that they must be 18 years or older to work on-site, and asked them to fill out the appropriate NIMS sign-in sheet. Individuals accepted for service were issued a wristband identifying them as registered volunteers and were directed to the Reliant Center's orientation area.

- Second, groups of accepted volunteers participated in short orientation sessions on the policies and procedures of volunteer duty. Orientation leaders encouraged volunteers to first take care of their own physical and emotional needs, to always work in pairs, and to work only as long as they felt comfortable. They said that, if volunteers found themselves incapable or uncomfortable of performing their assigned tasks, they should return to the assignment area where they could be redeployed.

- Third, at the end of each orientation session, organizers sent volunteers to staging areas, where they awaited deployment orders. When volunteer job opportunities arrived, an organizer announced the nature of the work involved and asked for a specific number of volunteers to perform the task. Finally, coordinators escorted groups of volunteers to their assigned worksite.

Using this system of volunteer integration, the Harris County Citizen Corps was able to identify and meet areas of need in a timely and effective manner.

The Benefit of NIMS and ICS Training

According to emergency responders on the scene, Citizen Corps members previously trained in the National Incident Management System (NIMS) and the Incident Command System (ICS) were of great value to the hurricane response. Due to their pre-incident training, many Citizen Corps volunteers were already familiar with NIMS/ICS terminology (e.g., Joint Information Center, Joint Operations Center, IC, etc.) and understood the responsibilities of emergency responders at the incident site. Because of this knowledge, coordinators could place well-trained Citizen Corps volunteers in positions of responsibility. These responsibilities included conveying information from site to site in the shelter area; controlling access to doors, elevators, and escalators; providing directions to volunteers and emergency responders; and moving volunteers from staging areas to areas of need.

Incident Command also recognized the value of NIMS-trained volunteers in the Hurricane Katrina response. On the morning of Friday, September 2, the Reliant Park Incident Commander requested that 4 NIMS-trained volunteers be made available to staff the Reliant Park IC Post. Volunteers continued to operate under NIMS/ICS guidelines at the IC Post 24 hours per day, 7 days a week throughout the response effort.

Requirements

Keys to Success

Long before Hurricane Katrina ever made landfall, the Harris County Citizen Corps laid the groundwork for success with its pre-incident organization and its partnerships with local volunteer groups and area businesses. These two factors allowed the Harris County Citizen Corps to mobilize and organize its resources quickly and efficiently to serve the thousands of evacuees sheltered in Houston-area sites.

- Pre-Incident Organization: The Harris County Citizen Corps organized itself for large-scale emergencies through the formation of a Citizen Corps Council and the tracking of Council member capabilities. Upon joining the council, Citizen Corps Council members complete a survey which describes the resources and capabilities they can provide. This awareness of capabilities allowed Hurricane Katrina responders to gain easy access to information on where resources were located and how they could be employed.

- Establishing Partnerships: The Harris County Citizen Corps also established partnerships with volunteer organizations and area businesses. Included among these partners were the United Way, Catholic Charities, and Volunteer Houston, the major clearinghouse for volunteer opportunities in the Houston area. When the number of spontaneous volunteers arriving at Reliant Park leveled off during the Hurricane Katrina response, Volunteer Houston was tasked with managing corporate volunteer commitments. These commitments included local businesses (e.g., Shell, Halliburton, etc.) that provided groups of employees willing to volunteer for shelter activities for a specific period of time. These partnerships became "force multipliers," as pre-incident contacts with a few area organizations led to the mobilization of large groups of volunteers.

Links

- Harris County Citizen Corps: www.harriscountycitizencorps.com
- Office of the Harris County Judge: www.judgeemmett.org

Disclaimer

This website and its contents are provided for informational purposes only and do not represent the official position of the US Department of Homeland Security or the National Memorial Institute for the Prevention of Terrorism (MIPT) and are provided without warranty or guarantee of any kind. The reader is directed to the following site for a full recitation of this disclaimer: www.llis.gov.

Reprinted from Federal Emergency Management Agency, 2006, *Harris County, Texas, Citizen Corps response to hurricane Katrina.*

Appendix 3.2
Worksheet to Identify Organizational Structure Needs

The following questions will help event planners develop an organizational structure to meet the management needs of the planned event:

1. Does the event involve a single agency or multiple agencies? _____

   If multiple, describe:_____

   _____

2. Does the event involve a single jurisdiction or multiple jurisdictions? _____

   If multiple, describe:_____

   _____

3. What command staff needs exist? _____

   _____

4. What kind, type, and amount of resources are required by the event?_____

   _____

5. Are aviation operations projected?   ☐ Yes   ☐ No

   If yes, describe: _____

   _____

6. Are there any staging areas or other required facilities?   ☐ Yes   ☐ No

   If yes, describe: _____

   _____

   What kind and type of logistical support needs are required by the event? _____

   _____

7. Are there any known limitations or restrictions of local resources?   ☐ Yes   ☐ No

   If yes, describe: _____

   _____

8. What kind and type of communications resources are available?_____

   _____

From S. Hall, W. Cooper, L. Marciani, and J. McGee, 2012, *Security management for sports and special events* (Champaign, IL: Human Kinetics).

Appendix 4.1
Sample Facility Security Survey

A. Facility Description

Name and address of facility:_____

_____

Type of facility: _____

Number of employees and support staff: _____

Square footage of facility space: _____

Facility design and structure (i.e., wood frame, brick buildings, steel frame): _____

_____

Is the facility subject to natural disasters?   ☐ Yes   ☐ No   If so, describe in detail.

_____

_____

What major road and railroad arteries serve the facility?_____

_____

B. Perimeter Security

Describe the type of perimeter barriers (i.e., fence, wall, bollards). _____

_____

Is the perimeter regularly maintained and inspected?   ☐ Yes   ☐ No

How many entry and exit points are located on the perimeter? _____

Are access points properly secured?   ☐ Yes   ☐ No

How are gates and doors of the facility controlled? _____

_____

Are alarm devices used?   ☐ Yes   ☐ No

Is closed circuit television (CCTV) used to observe gates and doors?   ☐ Yes   ☐ No

Are any areas unprotected?   ☐ Yes   ☐ No

Is lighting adequate at entrances and the surrounding perimeter?   ☐ Yes   ☐ No

C. Building Security

Are administrative offices locked?   ☐ Yes   ☐ No

How and where are critical records stored? _____

_____

Does the organization have a secure computer file server? ☐ Yes ☐ No

Are shipping and receiving areas secured? ☐ Yes ☐ No

What type of supervision and record keeping is exercised at receiving? _____
_____

Describe the locking and key system. _____
_____

Is there a master key system? ☐ Yes ☐ No

Is some type of credentialing system in place? ☐ Yes ☐ No

If yes, describe. _____
_____

How are outside contractors, visitors, and vendors controlled? _____
_____

D. Area Security

Is parking allowed inside perimeter? ☐ Yes ☐ No   If so, is it controlled? ☐ Yes ☐ No

Where do employees, officials, athletes, and visitors park? _____
_____

What type of security controls are in place for parking? _____
_____

Do roads within the perimeter or outside the facility present a traffic problem? ☐ Yes ☐ No

If yes, describe. _____
_____

E. Emergency Procedures

Do employees understand emergency and evacuation protocols? ☐ Yes ☐ No

Are emergency drills conducted? ☐ Yes ☐ No

Is the facility designated a public disaster shelter? ☐ Yes ☐ No

Are mutual aid agreements in place for repair and recovery operations if needed? ☐ Yes ☐ No

If yes, describe. _____
_____
_____

From S. Hall, W. Cooper, L. Marciani, and J. McGee, 2012, *Security management for sports and special events* (Champaign, IL: Human Kinetics). Reference: Broder, J.F. (2006). Risk analysis and the security survey (3rd ed.). Oxford, United Kingdom: Butterworth-Heinemann Business Books.

Checklist for Analyzing Vulnerabilities at a Sport or Special Event Venue

	Yes	No
1. Emergency preparedness		
Do you have a written emergency response plan?		
Do you have a written evacuation plan?		
Have you practiced your emergency response and evacuation plans?		
Do you have a bomb threat protocol?		
Are crowd control policies in place and communicated to staff and spectators?		
Are emergency medical services readily available or present at the facility?		
2. Perimeter control		
Do you have adequate lighting in and around the facility?		
Do you have controlled parking areas for visitors?		
Do you search the facility before an event?		
3. Access control and credentialing		
Have you developed a list of prohibited items for the facility?		
Do you search fans and their belongings?		
Do you have adequate personnel at entry to the facility?		
Are concessions properly secured?		
Is a visitor management system in place?		
4. Physical protection systems		
Do you have an adequate number of cameras and alarms for facility coverage?		
Are dangerous chemicals stored at the facility effectively protected?		
5. Personnel		
Is local law enforcement present at events?		
Do you outsource security?		
Are ushers, ticket takers, checkers, and so forth trained in security awareness?		
Do you perform background checks on all staff?		

From S. Hall, W. Cooper, L. Marciani, and J. McGee, 2012, *Security management for sports and special events* (Champaign, IL: Human Kinetics).

General Components of a Risk Management Plan

1. **Organizational structure:** the role of employees and the person in charge (chain of command)

2. **Goals and objectives:** prioritizing risks and threats identified in the risk assessment process highlighting the probability, frequency, and potential consequences

3. **Contract policies:** licenses, leases, insurance, permits, and rental agreements included as documentation for the treatment of identified risks

4. **Conduct of programs and services:** highlighting facility standards, warnings, medical exams, use of waivers, and participant forms as documentation for the treatment of risks identified

5. **Human resource policies:** occupational safety standards and procedures for hiring, firing, sexual harassment, and violence in the workplace

6. **Supervisory functions:** including a supervisory plan (who, what, when), and crowd management plan (discipline, crowd control of large events, violence in sport, intoxicated participants, spectators, visitors)

7. **Emergency plans and procedures:** specific protocol in response to personal injury of participants, spectators, and visitors (rendering first aid, medical services, accident reports); large-scale natural disasters (inventory and location of equipment and materials; evacuation procedures; displacement plans for facility staff and activities; psychological assistance for staff postincident); civil disturbances; bomb threats; fires; power failures; and crisis management (dealing with victims and their families from a public relation standpoint, establishing cooperative agreements with other programs and community organizations)

8. **Protection against criminal acts and security:** actions to ensure safety of persons and property, adequate security, and provision of law enforcement

9. **Transportation and vehicles:** policies regarding travel regulations, driver safety, and vehicle maintenance

10. **Equipment:** procedures for purchase or rental, authorization to use, and repair

11. **Environmental conditions:** ensuring recreation safety by recognizing hazards and providing warnings

12. **Developed areas and facilities:** implementing an inspection system to assess lighting, signage, and sanitation

Reference: Kaiser, R., & Robinson, K. (2005). Risk management. In *Management of park and recreation services*. Washington DC: National Recreation and Park Association.

Checklist of Considerations Before, During, and After an Event

	Y	N	N/A
Preevent considerations			
Develop risk management plan.			
Implement training program for event staff.			
Identify nearby dangerous and explosive sites.			
Determine quantities of antidotes within the region.			
Coordinate plans with local and state police.			
Conduct employee background checks (including students and part-time employees).			
Verify that response agencies possess drugs and medications for rapid response to a biological attack.			
Use surveillance system.			
Lock down the venue before the event.			
Prohibit concessions deliveries 90 minutes before the event.			
Use bomb-sniffing dogs.			
Issue personal identification cards for all media.			
Use clear refuse bags and receptacles.			
Supervise cleaning crews.			
Game or event time considerations			
Secure no-fly zones over the venue when needed.			
Patrol air space above the venue, parking lots, and adjacent access roads when needed.			
Secure the services of an onsite mobile emergency room.			
Use portable biological detection equipment.			
Use undercover surveillance teams.			
Hire a crowd observer for every 250 spectators.			
Use radio-equipped security personnel in parking lots and entry points.			
Have key personnel wear inexpensive HAZMAT smart strips to detect the presence of nerve agents, cyanide, and other chemicals.			

(continued)

Appendix 5.2 *(continued)*

	Y	N	N/A
Game or event time considerations *(continued)*			
Conduct broadcasts detailing security practices and restricted areas within the facility.			
Implement electronic scanning system for tickets.			
Frisk or wand spectators.			
Ban carry-ins and backpacks.			
Prohibit reentry.			
Postevent and general considerations			
Implement a postevent debriefing for all personnel.			
Consider varying security practices to avoid creating a pattern for adversaries.			

From S. Hall, W. Cooper, L. Marciani, and J. McGee, 2012, *Security management for sports and special events* (Champaign, IL: Human Kinetics). Based on M.J. Pantera et al., 2003, "Best practices for game day security at athletic and sport venues," *Sport Journal, 6*(4).

Appendix 5.3

Checklist for Routine Nonevent Security Measures

Security measure	Yes	No	Unsure
Facility management should designate a security director who will lead the daily security matters.			
Conduct risk assessment to determine threats, vulnerabilities, and consequences.			
Develop a facility emergency action plan (EAP) that addresses event preparation, incident response, evacuation, and communications.			
Create a command post within the facility to manage security of events and use an incident command system.			
Maintain awareness of current threat conditions and intelligence information available from local, state, and federal agencies.			
Establish procedures to enhance protective measures when threat levels increase.			
Develop mutual aid agreement or memorandums of understanding with local jurisdictions in case additional resources are needed after an incident.			
Hold routine meetings with sport league, facility management and owners or operators, and public safety agencies before an event to determine protective security measure requirements, roles, and responsibilities.			
Ensure adequate communication capabilities among responding agencies before an event.			
Conduct regular exercises with facility staff to test safety and security plans and assess resource capabilities.			
Inspect all safety and security communication systems, such as the PA system, before an event.			
Establish a secure perimeter around the facility, that is, a buffer zone that has controlled access points for vehicles and people.			
Create a vehicle parking system with allocated parking areas for players or performers, employees, and visitors.			
Issue photo credentials for all staff, vendors, and contractors indicating various levels of access.			
Protect critical system controls such as lighting and CCTV.			
Develop procedures for shutting down the facility in case of event cancellation.			
Prepare a business continuity and recovery plan.			
Review insurance coverage.			

From S. Hall, W. Cooper, L. Marciani, and J. McGee, 2012, *Security management for sports and special events* (Champaign, IL: Human Kinetics). Adapted from U.S. Department of Homeland Security, 2008, *Protective measures guide for U.S. sports leagues.*

Planning Considerations for Special Events

High-Risk Events

Some events pose more risk than others and may require special planning well in advance of the event. Promoters and sponsors are generally aware of the types of risk involved. Planners should work with the promoter or sponsor to ensure that the jurisdiction is prepared to respond appropriately to the hazards presented by the event.

Powerboat Races and Similar Aquatic Events

Aquatic events, particularly those involving motorized watercraft, require careful planning. Areas that planners must consider carefully include:

- Medical support for participants.
- Setup of spectator areas.

Power Boat Races—Medical Support

A designated medical response boat should be available in the water at all times when boats are operating. The boat should include trained medical personnel and be equipped with a spinal board and resuscitation equipment. The medical boat should also be linked by two-way radio to the rescue boats and onshore medical personnel.

A rescue boat should be available, with experienced divers who are trained to remove personnel trapped underwater.

Landing locations appropriate for the transfer of patients from boats to ambulances should be identified in advance.

Power Boat Races—Spectator Areas

Where spectators will be permitted to line piers and breakwaters along areas of deep waters, planners should create a physical barrier or mark a line to warn spectators away from the edges fronting deep water.

It is also a good idea to have a dedicated boat to patrol the shore adjacent to the spectator area. The boat should be equipped with a loudspeaker to warn spectators who venture too close to the edge. The boat should be equipped for water rescue and resuscitation of injured persons.

Power Boat Races—Rescue Boats

All boats intended for rescue or designated to provide medical attention should be clearly marked and equipped with hazard lighting to warn other vessels off.

Any boat intended for medical assistance or water rescue should contain sufficient clear space to resuscitate a patient. These boats should also include a range of medical supplies and equipment, including:

- an Automatic External Defibrillator (AED),
- a spinal board for full-body immobilization and cervical collars,

- ventilation equipment, and
- large pressure dressings.

Automobile and Similar Races

Sponsors of organized auto races conducted by professional racing organizations at permanent facilities normally meet safety guidelines and have sophisticated contingency planning information. For events conducted by local clubs, however, no formal guidelines may exist.

Motocross races, bicycle races, and auto rallies are a source of great concern because of:

- limited control over spectators and
- the often remote locations where they are held.

Automobile and Similar Races—Medical Support for Participants

In the event of a crash, an ambulance with trained staff should be available immediately. Medical support staff must understand racing rules and be able to recognize the various flags and warning lights used by race officials.

The standby ambulance should be positioned for controlled, rapid access to the track. A communications system and procedures should be in place to activate an immediate response to a track emergency.

Firefighting and rescue equipment should also be available at the track.

Automobile and Similar Races—Spectator Areas

Barriers should be in place to isolate spectators from out-of-control vehicles. Experience shows, however, that these barriers can be moved or broken upon impact, causing injuries to spectators. Safety can be enhanced by keeping spectators away from the barriers.

Individuals responsible for barrier design should consider the possibility that one vehicle may mount another or somersault end over end. Barriers should be designed to retard penetration into spectator areas in these situations.

Planners and promoters should remember that parts of automobiles involved in collisions can become projectiles. To protect spectators, a strong wire-mesh debris screen should be attached to the barrier fencing and to the tops of retaining walls.

Major problems have occurred when spectators access the track after the winner has crossed the finish line, but while other competitors are still racing. All officials should be briefed on:

- ways to control spectators who intend to access the track and
- what to do if those control measures fail.

Automobile and Similar Races—Pit Areas

In-race refueling in pit areas creates a potential for fire. To counter this threat, fire extinguishers or other equipment suitable for extinguishing fire must be available at refueling sites.

Vehicles entering the pit lane at high speeds and with limited driver visibility increase the risk to both drivers and pit crews. Organizers should consider enforcing speed limits (and penalties for drivers who ignore them) in the pit areas. If possible, organizers should also implement a warning system when vehicles are entering the pits.

Air Shows and Displays

Air shows are usually staged in accordance with aviation rules and regulations. Event organizers, emergency managers, and health personnel should take several steps to reduce the risk of a serious incident. Special precautions are included for:

- aerobatic areas,
- parachute jump areas, and
- fire-suppression requirements.

Air Shows and Displays—Aerobatic Areas

Aerobatic maneuvers should not take place over built-up areas. They should be conducted over fields, water, airstrips, or other uninhabited areas.

Aircraft should not fly over spectator areas. Where aircraft execute a maneuver laterally, the direction of execution should be away from, or parallel to, the spectators.

Air Shows and Displays—Parachute Jump Areas

Parachutists can be blown off course and suffer injury or death as a result. Spectators can also be injured in the scramble to avoid a descending jumper. Events that feature parachute jumps should include designated landing zones that are safely away from spectators and create no obvious hazards to the jumpers.

Air Shows and Displays—Fire-Suppression Requirements

There are several general safety precautions that should be taken at all air shows.

Onsite fire services should be capable of delivering fire-suppressant foam into a crashed or burning aircraft. If the air show does not take place at an airport where this equipment is available, alternate arrangements should be made to ensure that foam equipment is available.

Organizers should also clearly understand the requirements of the coroner and air crash investigators and be prepared to assist them in the event of a crash.

Fireworks and Pyrotechnics Displays

Shows involving fireworks or pyrotechnics also present specific risks. When event organizers plan public fireworks or pyrotechnics displays, they should notify and work with local authorities including:

- law enforcement,
- fire, and
- emergency medical services.

Most pyrotechnical providers follow Occupational Safety and Health Administration (OSHA) safety standards for the placement of spectator seating and fireworks launch sites.

Fireworks and Pyrotechnics Displays—Launch Site Placement

Most major incidents involving fireworks can be avoided through careful design of the launch site. Organizers should pay close attention to the anticipated or prevailing wind direction and strength. Both may affect the flight path of fireworks and the area where debris will fall. When establishing site placement and design, an emergency egress route should be identified in case of an emergency.

There is also substantial debris from fireworks displays. The launch site should be situated to ensure that no damage occurs from debris and, if possible, to make cleanup and a search for unexploded fireworks easier.

- Whenever possible, locate the launch site on water (for example, on a barge or pier). Locating the launch site on water enables personnel to abandon the site easily if an accident occurs and the pyrotechnic supply ignites.
- Erect a barrier between the crowd and the launch site to protect the crowd if fireworks tip over after ignition, resulting in a lateral, rather than a vertical, projection.
- Do not allow fireworks to be projected over the heads of spectators because debris is often hot and can injure spectators if it falls into their eyes or onto their heads.
- Anticipate potential respiratory difficulties, resulting from smoke from the display.
- If launching over water, do not allow fireworks to be projected over flammable trees, bush areas, buildings, or boats.
- Require unused fireworks to be stored in covered metal containers to prevent accidental ignition, either by staff or by descending hot particles from previously ignited fireworks.
- Require fire equipment, including fire extinguishers and trained firefighters, to be immediately available at the launch site.
- Require all personnel who deploy or ignite fireworks to wear protective clothing, including face shields, helmets, and heavy gloves.
- After the event, personnel should inspect the launch site carefully to ensure that no incipient or rekindled fires are possible. All used fireworks should be soaked in water and removed from the site, along with any securing spikes, wires, or other potentially hazardous objects.

Laser Displays

Laser light shows are now often included as entertainment at many special events. Before the light show occurs, onsite health care professionals should:

- understand the kinds of accidents that can occur, and
- identify the potential hazards associated with lasers.

Event organizers should always become familiar with the kind and type of laser that will be used and the risks associated with them.

Spontaneous Events

Occasionally, an event occurs without planning. Local emergency management and public safety agencies need to be aware that:

- spontaneous events create the same need for emergency response contingencies as planned events;

- safety plans or agreed-upon roles and responsibilities for participants will be established; and
- spontaneous events present unique difficulties to public safety personnel because they offer no warning—and no time to plan.

Types of Spontaneous Events

There are four basic types of spontaneous events:

- Events that are planned without official input or permits as a result of an oversight.
- Events that are planned without official input or permits on purpose.
- Events that result from other events (for example, a victory celebration for a local sports team).
- Events that are demonstrations, protests, or picketing (for example, civil disobedience or spontaneous violence).

Because spontaneous events are dynamic, a well-timed and appropriate response is critical to achieving safe outcomes.

Spontaneous Events—Staffing

The use of existing mutual aid and assistance agreements, response plans, training, and resource lists will help communities that are confronted with a spontaneous event. Essential to the outcome, however, is implementing ICS for an orderly and coordinated deployment of resources and personnel.

Additionally:

- Identifying a staging area where additional personnel and resources will be gathered is critical.
- All personnel must be briefed before assignment.
- Span of control must be maintained.

Spontaneous Events—Evaluating Other Events

Another essential element when responding to spontaneous events is the continuing evaluation of other events that could be catalysts for spontaneous events. Many spontaneous events occur with some level of expectation by public safety officials.

The significant difference between an organized special event and a spontaneous event is that no planning time exists before a spontaneous event. It is critical, then, to develop contingency plans for events that are high-risk or high probability.

Events Involving Pre-Teen and Early Teen Audiences

Concerts and other events that attract younger audiences can create a number of difficulties. These spectators can become lost or separated from friends, miss transportation, or lack the money to pay for alternate transportation.

Parents often take their children to these events, then have difficulty finding them after the event. If parents are using their cars to pick up children, traffic jams may prevent close access to the venue.

- Create a "Parents' Oasis" adjacent to the venue where parents can wait during the concert. Coffee, soft drinks, snacks, and newspapers can be available to help parents pass the time while waiting for the event to conclude. The additional cost and effort devoted to providing a Parents' Oasis are more than offset by the reduction in efforts needed to deal with young audiences at the conclusion of the event.
- Provide information booths with access to the public address system to enable clearly identified event staff to assist lost children and their parents.
- Develop contingency plans for the "worst case"—the occurrence of a major incident exacerbated by the problems of parents attempting to gain access to the area to reunite with their children—or trying to find out where their injured children have been taken.

Reprinted from Federal Emergency Management Agency, 2010, *Special events contingency planning for public safety agencies.*

Considerations for a Game- or Event-Day Operations Plan

General Survey and Operations Plan Considerations

The following characteristics of a facility, and of the particular event, should be evaluated and addressed before game or event day.

Transportation Routes

- Delivery routes
- Visiting team routes
- Motorcades
- Emergency routes
- Evacuation routes
- Hospital routes

Site Walk-Through Security

- Game or event schedule
- Delivery schedule
- Personnel and press movements
- Team movements
- Crowd control
- Ingress and egress routes
- Hazards
- Emergencies
- Evacuations
- Risks
- Credentials
- Response

Staff Briefing and Review

These staff counterparts should include, but are not limited to, the following:

- Sport owners or operators and facility managers
- Athletic or event personnel
- Police
- Fire

- Medical
- Emergency management
- Electrical and mechanical technicians
- Facility personnel
- Security supervisors
- Communications personnel
- Physical plant
- Parking management
- Food services
- Entertainment directors
- Private security company representative
- Vendors
- Booster clubs

Access Control

- Criteria for admittance to the event
- Whether the event is ticketed or not
- Open or closed to press or public
- Team or entertainer arrivals and departures
- Arrival times and locations of staff, vendors, teams, game officials
- Arrival times and locations of stage, entertainers, press, public, VIPs, photographers
- Verification of credentialed persons with photo identification
- Provision for guests and credential reenter site

Environment

- Event layout
- Time of event setup
- Seating
- Barricades
- Overflow or open crowd area
- Stage size and buffer zone parameters
- Sound and lighting company
- Vendors

Policy and Procedures

- Name checks
- Credentialing

- Bomb sweep times
- Delivery
- Building security
- Emergency
- Evacuation
- Fire
- Medical
- Threats
- Visitor and escort procedures
- Disturbances
- Criminal incidents
- Presentations

Media Concerns
- Press passes and identification
- Press pool
- Parking for satellite trucks
- Press areas
- Press entrance
- Press movements and containment
- Press movements within buffer area
- Staff escorts for press
- Press risers and platforms
- Press filing center

Site Dynamics
When considering site dynamics the following people should be considered:
- Facility and university personnel
- Event services and vendors
- Catering
- Entertainers and dignitaries
- VIPs
- Teams
- Police and fire
- Emergency services
- Parking
- Public

- Press
- People from nonrelated events

Contacts

Contact numbers should be readily available before, during, and after an event for the following:

- Assistant athletic directors and facility managers
- Director of operations
- Athletic or event personnel
- Police
- Fire
- Medical
- Security supervisors
- Emergency management
- Event sales office
- Electrical and mechanical technicians
- Facility personnel
- Communications personnel
- Physical plant
- Parking management
- Food services
- Entertainment directors
- Lead private security company representative
- Vendors
- Booster clubs

Site Considerations

- Consider effect on other businesses
- Parking issues
- Inform public of no parking areas
- Inform public of restricted areas
- Inform public of street closings
- Consider delivery schedule
- Provide handicap access
- Consider public restrooms
- Consider safety and medical concerns for public
- Request containment assets (ropes, barriers)
- Solve any mechanical issues or technical considerations

Technical Considerations

Facility managers must be familiar with the technical and mechanical aspects of their facility when preparing for an event. Several considerations should be discussed with lead representatives of physical plant, engineering, fire marshal, and law enforcement:

Physical Security Considerations

- Access control
- Locks and master keys
- Alarms
- Video equipment
- Flood lights
- Emergency lighting
- Perimeter lighting

Fire Safety Considerations

- Sprinkler system
- Detection equipment for heat or smoke
- Fire alarm, silent and audible
- Notification procedure
- Fire extinguisher (locations)
- Fire alarm read-out panel (locations)
- Fire personnel or fire marshal
- Water shutoff valve

Mechanical Considerations

- Mechanical room (locked and secured)
- Electricity backup power, generator, delay time
- Air-handling shutoff
- Elevator operation in power outage
- Automatic doors and gates (understand operation)
- Water source
- Natural gas line locations
- Gas feed into kitchen
- Propane on site
- Stage soundness and stage parameters

Environmental Considerations

- EOD sweep
- Car and truck bomb threat

- Hazardous materials on site
- Industrial hazards on site
- Chemicals on site
- Special effects (safety considerations)
- X-ray equipment
- Dumpsters (emptied and removed)

Emergency Preparedness

Facility managers are responsible for the safety and security of staff and spectators at all times. Managers should understand and anticipate any problems that might occur. Emergency preparedness must be coordinated with police, fire, medical, and emergency management agencies before any event. The type of plan and the amount of support will vary between events and sites. The following emergency plan items should be considered when preparing for an event.

Communication Considerations
- Command post
- Frequencies
- Equipment
- Personnel

Incident Management Plan
- Inner, middle, and outer perimeter response
- Evacuation routes and plan
- Evacuation route marked and identified
- Evacuation route cleared

Fire Response and Evacuation Plan
- Fire evacuation plan
- Fire department response time
- Fire response notification system
- Location and identification fire exits
- Location of fire extinguishers and hoses
- Fire personnel on site

Medical Emergency Response Plan
- Evacuation plan (drive and fly)
- Medical personnel onsite
- Paramedic and EMT locations
- Access for ambulances
- Emergency landing zone
- Hospital location

Environmental and Mechanical Considerations

- Master keys
- Crowd control plan
- Explosive device
- Power outage and evacuation plan
- Emergency lighting
- Elevator repair standby
- Elevator extraction capability
- Emergency and evacuation routes cleared
- Hazardous material
- Natural disaster plan

Based on a resource developed by Robert McDavid, training program coordinator, National Center for Spectator Sports Safety and Security (NCS[4]).

How Prepared Is Your Business for an Emergency?

Readiness Assessment

	Yes	No	Unsure
1. Does your business know what kinds of emergencies might affect it—both internally and externally?			
2. Does your business have a written, comprehensive emergency plan in place to help ensure your safety and take care of employees until help can arrive?			
3. Has your business created and practiced procedures to quickly evacuate and find shelter in case of an emergency?			
4. Has your business created a plan to communicate with employees in an emergency? (Examples include a telephone call tree, password-protected page on the company website, e-mail alert or call-in voice recording, and a contact list that includes employee emergency contact information.)			
5. Has your business talked with utility service providers about potential alternatives and identified back-up options?			
6. Has your business determined operations that need to be up and running first after an emergency and how to resume key operations?			
7. Has your business created a list of inventory and equipment, including computer hardware, software, and peripherals (such as backed up or protected records and critical data) for business continuity and insurance purposes?			
8. Has your business met with your insurance provider to review current coverage in case of an emergency?			
9. Does your business promote family and individual preparedness among co-workers (such as emergency preparedness information during staff meetings, newsletters, company intranet, periodic employee e-mails, and via other internal communication tools)?			
10. Have emergency shutdown procedures been developed for equipment such as boilers, automatic feeds, or other operations that simply cannot be left running in an emergency evacuation?			
11. Has your business worked with your community on emergency planning efforts and helped to plan for community recovery?			

Readiness Results

Count your number of "Yes" responses to calculate a score. Your score is a general reflection of how much you know about emergency planning efforts at your business or how prepared your business may be for an emergency.

If you have 8-11 "Yes" responses, you are well on your way to having a comprehensive and effective plan in place.

If you have 4-7 "Yes" responses, while some aspects of your plan may be in place, you have some work to do to fill gaps.

If you have 1-3 "Yes" responses, get started immediately on developing an emergency plan for your business.

From S. Hall, W. Cooper, L. Marciani, and J. McGee, 2012, *Security management for sports and special events* (Champaign, IL: Human Kinetics). Reprinted, by permission, from National Safety Council, 2007. Available: http://www.nsc.org/safety_work/empreparedness/Documents/Emergency%20Preparedness%20Documents/Readiness%20Assessment.pdf.

Emergency Response Plan Template for a College Sporting Event

Objective

- Provide clear course of action in the event of an emergency.
- Outline specific evacuation procedures if needed.
- Prepare employees and event staff for all-hazard incidents and communicate their roles in attempting to prevent or minimize injuries and loss of life or property.

General Guidelines

- Employees and event staff should be familiar with the plan and follow provided directions; however, certain situations may arise that require one to deviate from the documented plan.
- There should be an efficient flow of information from all locations to the command post and staff members should notify supervisors of developments in an emergency situation.
- A public information officer will keep the media informed during an emergency situation. Staff members should not discuss the emergency with the media and should refer media representatives to the designated public information officer.

Emergency Situations Prompting Plan Activation

- Bomb threat
- Explosion
- Fire
- Power failure
- Inclement weather
- Crowd control issue
- Terrorist activity
- Criminal activity within facility
- Disaster incident outside facility perimeter
- Building (structural) collapse

Chain of Command

- Ranking university police officer (ranking fire department officer will assume command of fire-related hazards)
- Athletic director
- Senior associate athletic director

- Assistant athletic director for facilities
- Assistant athletic director for operations
- Assistant athletic director for internal affairs
- Assistant athletic director for ticket operations

Note: All personnel on the chain of command must report to the command post during an emergency situation.

Plan Personnel

The following personnel should report to the command post:

- Incident commander (IC)—ranking university police or fire official
- Principal evacuation officer (PEO)—athletic director
- Alternate evacuation officer (AEO)—assistant athletic director for facilities
- Public information officer (PIO)—assistant athletic director for sports information
- Police supervisor—serves as IC
- Security supervisor—director of security personnel
- Medical supervisor—senior medical staff member of first aid operations director
- Physical plant supervisor
- Assistant athletic director for facilities
- Assistant athletic director for operations

Staging Areas

Command Post [*insert location*] _____: This is the main information and meeting station for an emergency. The following personnel will man the command post (CP):

- Incident commander
- Athletic director
- Assistant athletic director of operations
- Public information officer
- Police dispatcher
- Medical services dispatcher

Responsibilities of personnel at CP should be documented.

The following equipment should be available at the command post:

- Hard wire telephones
- Cell phones
- Two-way radios
- Copy of ERP
- Maps and diagrams of facility
- Bullhorns
- Emergency contact numbers

Security Control Station [*insert location*] _____: The security supervisor is in command of the SCS. This is where they will meet with their staff with instructions regarding an emergency. The security supervisor works closely with IC.

Responsibilities of personnel at SCS should be documented.

Media Station [*insert location*] _____: Media should be directed here in order to obtain information pertaining to the emergency. The PIO or sports information director will be present to handle media activities.

Responsibilities of personnel at media station should be documented.

First Aid Control Station [*insert location*] _____: If the facility is unsafe and a full evacuation is needed, EMS will activate their emergency triage plan.

Responsibilities of personnel at first aid control station should be documented.

Employee Reporting Stations [*insert location*] _____: In the event of a full evacuation, employees should meet at an assigned area to obtain further instructions from their supervisor.

Responsibilities of personnel at employee reporting station should be documented.

From S. Hall, W. Cooper, L. Marciani, and J. McGee, 2012, *Security management for sports and special events* (Champaign, IL: Human Kinetics).

Appendix 6.2
Evacuation Plan Template for Stadiums

Insert the name of the stadium and other appropriate information in the blanks below.

I. Introduction

Events at [*Insert name of stadium*] _____ are considered premier events hosted in [*Insert name of state*] _____. As such, [*Insert name of stadium*] _____ needs to be prepared for any eventuality where it may become necessary to evacuate, shelter in place, or relocate spectators, participants, and staff from within the stadium, or to redirect traffic around the stadium. Assessing risk, reducing vulnerabilities, and increasing the level of preparedness will help to minimize potential threats and consequences. It is essential, therefore, that key security personnel at [*Insert name of stadium*] _____ are well trained in risk factors, planning an appropriate response, informing the public, and implementing the Evacuation Plan. This Evacuation Plan is a supplement to the [*Insert name of stadium*] _____ Emergency Plan (EP). The template for this plan was developed by a working group comprised of Federal agencies, university research organizations, sports leagues, and consultants and professional associations involved in the safety and security of stadiums.

II. Purpose

This Evacuation Plan provides instructions and guidance to effectively address the safety of all individuals in attendance at [*Insert name of stadium*] _____ with regard to evacuation, sheltering in place, or relocation. The Emergency Plan describes procedures for responding to an emergency or critical incident at the [*Insert name of stadium*] _____. The Evacuation Plan provides guidance for developing and implementing procedures to evacuate, shelter in place, or relocate in response to an emergency or critical incident.

This Evacuation Plan was prepared by [*Insert name*] _____, [*Insert name of stadium*] _____ Security or Safety Director and *(Insert name)* _____, *(Insert name of county/city)* _____ Emergency Management Director on *(Insert date)* _____. This document was prepared in coordination and cooperation with the following, and they have signed-off with their concurrence:

Chief of Police _____ , & Staff _____ Police Department

Fire Chief _____ , & Staff _____ Fire & Rescue

Sheriff _____ , & Staff _____ Co. Sheriff's Office

Emergency Management Director _____

Emergency Medical Services Director _____

State Highway Patrol Captain _____ , & Staff _____

State Bureau of Investigation _____ , & Staff _____

FBI Special Agent in Charge _____ , & Staff _____

Bureau of Alcohol Tobacco and Firearms _____

Area Substance Abuse Council _____

Federal Aviation Administration, Flight Standard Office _____

Other—if additional or different people, continue to list. _____

_____

_____

III. Relevant Plans

This section provides an overview of the plans, policies, and guidance documents that are applicable to the [*Insert name of stadium*] _____ . Plans may be maintained by the county or city where the stadium resides.

A. [*Insert name of stadium*] _____ **owner's Security and Safety Guideline Reference Manual**

Insert a brief description of the owner's Security and Safety Guideline Reference Manual.

B. [*Insert name of stadium*] _____ **Emergency Action Plan**

Insert a brief description of the Emergency Plan.

C. [*Insert name of stadium*] _____ **Security and Safety Plan**

Insert a brief description of the Security and Safety Plan.

D. Other (as appropriate)

- *Reference other Stadium Plans.*
- *Reference County Plans (including Mass Casualty Plan).*
- *Reference City Plans.*

IV. Command Structure or Response Organization

The command structure or response organization for evacuation, sheltering in place, and relocation activities should mirror the normal command structure, as found in section [*Insert section number*] _____ of the Emergency Plan.

A diagram depicting the command structure or response organization is also included in the Emergency Plan.

A. Jurisdiction and Liability

- *Identify laws, ordinances, and authorities that affect evacuation activities*
- *Identify any issues of liability associated with evacuation activities*

Reference: Evacuation Planning Guide for Stadiums, 3.1.1 Administration

B. Evacuation Team—Roles and Responsibilities

- *Define for each entity, designate and identify key personnel*

Reference: Evacuation Planning Guide for Stadiums, 2.1 Evacuation Team

C. Direction and Control—Roles and Responsibilities

- *Define for each entity, designate and identify key personnel*

Reference: Evacuation Planning Guide for Stadiums, 2.2 Direction and Control

D. Local, State, and Federal Assistance—Roles and Responsibilities

- *Define for each entity, designate and identify key personnel*

Reference: Evacuation Planning Guide for Stadiums, 2.3 Local, State, and Federal Assistance

E. Surrounding Industry and Private Sector Assistance—Roles and Responsibilities

- *Define for each entity, designate and identify key personnel*

Reference: Evacuation Planning Guide for Stadiums, 2.4 Surrounding Industry and Private Sector Assistance

F. Local Transportation Structure—Roles and Responsibilities

- *Define for each entity, designate and identify key personnel*

Reference: Evacuation Planning Guide for Stadiums, 2.5 Local Transportation Structure

V. Preevent Planning Considerations

Preevent planning considerations need to be considered prior to a scheduled event at the [*Insert name of stadium*] _____. This section of the Evacuation Plan provides further information on the types of potential hazards or scenarios that could occur at the stadium and the number and makeup of the spectators and participants of the stadium.

A. Potential Hazards and Scenarios

Table 1 below includes the potential hazards that the [*Insert name of stadium*] _____
_____ can expect. The table also illustrates the likelihood of the hazard and whether evacuation, sheltering in place, or relocation would be the appropriate response for each hazard.

Table 1: [*Insert name of stadium*] _____ **Hazards and Scenarios**

	Likelihood of Hazard High, Medium, or Low	Evacuation, Shelter in Place, or Relocation Decision
Weather		
Rain		
Lightning		
Tornado		
Heat		
Severe thunderstorm—heavy		
Rain or flooding		
High winds		
Hurricane		
Heavy snow		
Emergency situations		
Accidental release (chemical, biological, radiological)		
IED or bomb threat		
Shooter situation		
Mass casualty event		
Civil disturbance		
Food borne illnesses (e.g., accidental food poisoning [mayonnaise left in sun])		
Fire—Multiple motor homes, track, wildfire, structural, fuel		
HAZMAT		
Structural collapse		
Terrorism—WMD, explosion, chemical or biological event, dirty bomb		

From S. Hall, W. Cooper, L. Marciani, and J. McGee, 2012, *Security management for sports and special events* (Champaign, IL: Human Kinetics). Reprinted from U.S. Department of Homeland Security, 2008, *Evacuation planning guide for stadiums*.

Appendix 6.3

Planning Process and Procedures

Evacuation Planning Guide Meeting Procedures (Using the Evacuation Planning Guide for Stadiums)

The purpose of the evacuation planning meeting is to develop an integrated joint response plan to handle any type of evacuation, sheltering in place, or relocation situation that could occur at a stadium. The Evacuation Planning Guide (template) was developed as the guideline for developing stadium evacuation plans.

The focus of the evacuation planning meeting is to develop an evacuation plan as part of any existing emergency action plans presently in place. For those stadiums that have an evacuation plan already in place, the planning process and template will assist in enhancing those existing plans. It is not envisioned that the evacuation plan will be stand-alone, but it will become part of the stadium's existing emergency action plan. For example, the organizational structure to respond to an evacuation is one of the areas that will be covered by the evacuation plan, but it is envisioned that this response organization would likely be similar to the organization that deals with most other emergency situations within the stadium.

The planning meeting should be facilitated by someone familiar with the stadium and hazards to the stadium. It is suggested that someone be designated to take notes during the meeting, and then provide the pertinent information on plan details, decisions made, and any outstanding planning issues to the entire planning team for their use in developing the stadium's evacuation plan.

Who should attend the planning meeting?

All pertinent stadium, local, state, federal and industry planning partners should be invited to the meeting. These should include those individuals that are able to speak and make decisions on behalf of their agencies, with respect to evacuation planning, and those with knowledge of the current stadium plans. During the course of the planning meeting, a discussion will be held regarding the right mix of members for the planning team, and a determination of who will be responsible for maintaining the plan and planning process.

Some of the local, state, federal, and industry personnel and agencies who may be invited to participate include:

- Stadium
- Law Enforcement
- Fire and Rescue
- Emergency Management
- Health and Safety
- Medical (health care facilities and EMS)
- Transportation (all modes, if relevant)

- Industry neighbors
- Others, as necessary and dictated by your particular track location

How should personnel and agencies prepare for the planning meeting?

- All personnel participating in the planning meetings should review any emergency response plans and procedures, especially those pertaining to evacuation, sheltering in place, and relocation. These plans should include both the stadium emergency action plans as well as the local emergency response plans, since these plans should link together.
- Review and be thoroughly familiar with the Evacuation Planning Guide for Stadiums, since this is the document that will be used in guiding those present through the facilitated meeting.
- Review the special adjacent facilities located near the stadium or within the community.
- Bring along any maps, facility diagrams, pictures, etc. of the stadium, as well as the local area. These will be helpful in planning out such items as resource staging areas, holding areas for evacuees, transportation routes for pedestrians and vehicles, etc.
- Be familiar with the stadium (e.g., the numbers of seats per section, number of people that can view the event from the concourses suites, restaurants, etc.).
- Identify possible areas for shelter in place.
- Send copies of existing emergency plans and procedures to primary participants at least one week prior to the planning meeting so they may become familiar with response operations prior to arriving at the stadium.
- Be familiar with the local area's response capability, including hospital's surge capacity.
- Create a few realistic scenarios to discuss during your planning meeting (see draft Planning Meeting Agenda below). The scenario discussion can be used as part of the analysis to validate the decisions made during the planning process.

What are the logistical requirements for the planning meeting?

Logistics requirements for the planning meeting include a meeting location and minimum audio and visual requirements. The primary need is for a meeting space (tables and chairs) that will hold the requisite number of attendees. The meeting place should also be large enough to be able to lay out maps, diagrams, emergency plans, and anything else you might need. The meeting space should include a white board or flip chart, projector and screen, teleconference capability, and extension cords or power strip for computer hookup. Even though it will not be needed in the meeting room, access to a copier and printer may be necessary.

Planning Meeting Agenda (Draft)

- Welcome and introductions
- Purpose and objectives of the planning meeting
- Review existing emergency plans and procedures
  - Discuss gaps and inconsistencies

- How will the Evacuation Plan fit into the existing plans?
- Conduct site tour of stadium and property familiarity
- Review stadium and local area hazards and vulnerabilities
- Work through Planning Guide
  - Organizational structure
  - Concept of operations
  - Program and plan maintenance
  - Annexes
- Review potential scenario incidents—discuss relocation, evacuation, and shelter in place options
- Discuss next steps

Reprinted from U.S. Department of Homeland Security, 2008, *Evacuation planning guide for stadiums*.

Emergency Management Considerations

Mitigation

- ☐ Conduct risk assessment.
- ☐ Establish mutual aid agreements with local or regional partners.

Preparedness

- ☐ Develop an emergency response plan, including an evacuation plan.
- ☐ Develop public address audio or video scripts for specific emergency announcements.
- ☐ Conduct annual evacuation simulations involving multiple agencies.
- ☐ Conduct tabletop exercises to test emergency procedures.
- ☐ Conduct briefing and debriefing meetings with agencies involved in security for the event.
- ☐ Check communication systems before the event.
- ☐ Conduct continuous staff training to ensure that emergency response practices are updated.

Response

- ☐ Establish a command and control center.
- ☐ Maintain copies of critical plans at the command center.
- ☐ Identify and maintain clear ingress and egress emergency routes at the stadium facility.
- ☐ Conduct an incident assessment report when necessary.

Recovery

- ☐ Designate primary and secondary triage and transport sites.
- ☐ Maintain interoperable communications.
- ☐ Establish plans with local hospitals to ensure adequate response to a patient surge.

From S. Hall, W. Cooper, L. Marciani, and J. McGee, 2012, *Security management for sports and special events* (Champaign, IL: Human Kinetics). Reference: Hall, S., Marciani, L., & Cooper, W.E. (2008). Emergency management and planning at major sports events, *Journal of Emergency Management*, 6(1), 43–47.

Appendix 6.5
Bomb Threat Checklist

Most bomb threats are received by phone. Bomb threats are serious until proven otherwise. Act quickly—but remain calm, and obtain information with the checklist.

If a bomb threat is received by phone:

1. Remain calm. Keep the caller on the line for as long as possible. **Do not hang up**, even if the caller does.
2. Listen carefully. Be polite and show interest.
3. Try to keep the caller talking to learn more information.
4. If possible, write a note to a colleague to call the authorities or, as soon as the caller hangs up, immediately notify them yourself.
5. If your phone has a display, copy the number or letters on the window display.
6. Complete the Bomb Threat Checklist immediately. Write down as much detail as you can remember. Try to get exact words.
7. Immediately upon termination of the call, do not hang up, but from a different phone, contact FPS immediately with information and await instructions.

If a bomb threat is received by handwritten note:

- Call _____
- Handle note as minimally as possible.

If a bomb threat is received by e-mail:

- Call _____
- Do not delete the message.

Signs of a suspicious package:

- No return address
- Excessive postage
- Stains
- Strange odor
- Strange sounds
- Unexpected delivery

Do not:

- Use two-way radios or cellular phone; radio signals have the potential to detonate a bomb.
- Evacuate the building until police arrive and evaluate the threat.
- Activate the fire alarm.
- Touch or move a suspicious package.

Bomb Threat Checklist

Date: _____ Time: _____

Time Caller Hung Up: _____

Phone Number Where Call Received: _____

Ask Caller:

Where is the bomb located? (Building, floor, room, etc.) _____

_____

When will it go off? _____

What does it look like? _____

_____

What kind of bomb is it? _____

_____

What will make it explode? _____

_____

Did you place the bomb?   ☐ Yes   ☐ No

Why? _____

_____

What is your name? _____

Exact Words of Threat:

_____

_____

_____

Information About Caller:

Where is the caller located? (Background and level of noise) _____

_____

Estimated age: _____

Is voice familiar? If so, who does it sound like? _____

_____

Other points: _____

_____

_____

_____

Caller's Voice:

Accent	Deep	Lisp	Rapid
Angry	Deep breathing	Loud	Raspy
Calm	Disguised	Male	Slow
Clearing throat	Distinct	Nasal	Slurred
Coughing	Excited	Normal	Soft
Cracking voice	Female	Ragged	Stutter
Crying	Laughter		

Background Sounds:

Animal noises	Booth	Motor	Office machinery
House noises	PA system	Clear	Local
Kitchen noises	Conversation	Static	Long distance
Street noises	Music		

Threat Language:

Incoherent	Taped	Profane
Message read	Irrational	Well-spoken

From S. Hall, W. Cooper, L. Marciani, and J. McGee, 2012, *Security management for sports and special events* (Champaign, IL: Human Kinetics). Reprinted from U.S. Department of Homeland Security, 2007, *Homeland security exercise and evaluation program* (HSEEP), Volume 1.

Responses to Spectator Violence in Stadiums

1. Venue

Response	How it works	Works best if . . .	Considerations
Creating access barriers	Prevents fans from interfering with performances and protects both performers and spectators	fans cannot easily overcome barriers	The barriers should not reduce visibility or cause safety hazards. They can become death traps if a stampede or similar event occurs, so barriers should be constructed to give way safely under extreme pressure.
Providing adequate facilities and proper placement	Reduces long lines and crowding	facilities are equally accessible to all spectators	Reducing beverage lines could increase alcohol consumption.
Strategically placing stages, sound equipment, and screens	Helps to break up larger crowds and maintain seating assignments	spectators can easily view the stages and screens from their assigned seats	Additional sound systems may increase volume levels and noise-related frustrations.
Providing adequate nearby parking	Reduces opportunities to engage in violent behaviors	multiple entry and exit points exist	Large parking areas provide opportunities for car theft and vandalism. They also create traffic jams and the possibility of conflicts because of frustration at not being able to enter or exit quickly.
Posting signs	Conveys information to spectators to maintain safety and facilitate movement and activities throughout the stadium	the signs are clearly visible above the crowd but are out of the reach of vandals	Signs may need to be printed in several languages, depending on spectator demographics.
Changing venues for high-risk events	Creates a neutral environment and reduces tensions between fans and away teams	fans who cannot get to the alternative venue can watch the event on television	Event promoters may lose money if residents near the alternative venue are less interested in attending the event; changing the venue does not help to prevent postevent celebrations outside the stadium.
Establishing processing and holding areas for spectators who are arrested or refuse to leave the premises	Provides a place to isolate violent spectators from the rest of the crowd	other crowd members cannot see or access the areas	Arrangements must be made to transfer the spectators to the local jail or courthouse without disrupting the event.

(continued)

Response	How it works	Works best if . . .	Considerations
Redesigning stadium features that facilitate violence	Shields possible targets of spectator aggression	spectator aggression is concentrated in particular places in the stadium	Major renovations can be costly, and owners may not want to invest their resources or shut down their venues to allow these changes to be made.
Providing sectioned and personal seating	Helps to break crowds down into smaller and more manageable groups, reducing the crowding commonly associated with festival seating	tickets are sold for each seat and ushers can guide spectators to the appropriate seats to avoid disputes	Personal seating can reduce the venue's overall capacity and result in revenue loss.

2. Event

Response	How it works	Works best if . . .	Considerations
Restricting alcohol sales	Reduces intoxication-related violence	staff are trained to recognize signs of intoxication	Alcohol sales generate revenue, so venue management may have to raise prices to compensate for a decrease in sales; restricting alcohol sales increases spectators' incentive to arrive intoxicated or to smuggle alcohol into the event.
Removing disruptive spectators	Limits the harm that results from their action and prevents further instigation of other spectators	police target only those engaged in disruptive behavior	Removing spectators may require use of force and can instigate other spectators.
Refusing entrance to known troublemakers and intoxicated spectators	Reduces the pool of people willing to engage in violent behavior at the event	staff can recognize those who have been banned and the signs of intoxication	Some fans may not show overt signs of intoxication, despite having consumed large quantities of alcohol.
Screening items brought into the stadium	Prevents spectators from bringing in items that they can use as weapons during altercations	staff can quickly search spectators without delaying entry to the stadium	Female staff may be needed to search female spectators; metal detectors are expensive.
Reducing situational instigators of violence	Eliminates situational factors, both physical and social, that can encourage spectator violence	police are familiar with a particular stadium's fan culture and can identify the emergence of new instigators	Controlling the temperature in open-air stadiums and noise levels in enclosed arenas is difficult.
Controlling the dispersal process	Prevents the crowding that results as spectators leave the stadium	after-event activities attract some, but not all, spectators	After-event activities require additional staffing or personnel hours.

Response	How it works	Works best if . . .	Considerations
Requiring permits and adherence to entertainment ordinances	Notifies authorities in advance of upcoming events, sets restrictions and standards for the events, and holds hosts accountable for meeting basic requirements	city ordinances governing stadium events are already in place	The city council may have to pass new legislation.
Advertising penalties for violent behavior	Deters spectator-related violence	laws and sanctions for such behaviors are in place and spectators view the sanctions as credible	Penalties must be severe enough to offset the perceived benefits of engaging in violent behavior.
Encouraging marketing to age- and gender-diverse crowds	Reduces the pool of young adult males	the event can be marketed as family friendly	This tactic may decrease the popularity of some events. If family groups are in a completely different part of the stadium from where the young men are, then the advantages are lost. Comingling within the venue may be necessary.

3. Staff

Response	How it works	Works best if . . .	Considerations
Establishing an effective command post	Aids prevention efforts by facilitating information flow	representatives from all agencies are stationed at the post	One agency will need to lead the communication efforts.
Training staff to respond appropriately	Prepares staff to deal with the complexities of differing crowd dynamics	experienced personnel are on hand to help those with less crowd experience	Some departments may require more extensive training.
Using different security levels	Reduces the need for police personnel	stadium staff members remain consistent from event to event	Police must be available to provide backup if other personnel cannot effectively handle spectator concerns or conflicts.
Increasing the visibility of security	Provides a visual deterrent to those considering violent behavior	uniformed personnel are placed at strategic points throughout the stadium	Too many uniformed officers may create a hostile atmosphere.
Incorporating technology	Improves surveillance and can eliminate the need for deadly force	security can monitor cameras from a centralized location	Use of nonlethal weapons requires specialized training and can pose safety risks.

Reprinted from T.D. Madensen and J.E. Eck, 2008, *Spectator violence in stadiums* (Washington, DC: U.S. Department of Justice, Office of Community Oriented Policing Services, Center for Problem-Oriented Policing).

Appendix 6.7
Business Recovery Plan Template

Business Continuity and Disaster Preparedness Plan

Plan to Stay in Business

Business name: _____

Address: _____

City, state, zip code: _____

Telephone number: _____

If this location is not accessible we will operate from location below:

Business name: _____

Address: _____

City, state, zip code: _____

Telephone number: _____

The following person is our primary crisis manager and will serve as the company spokesperson in an emergency:

Primary emergency contact: _____

Telephone number: _____

Alternative number: _____

E-mail: _____

If the person is unable to manage the crisis, the person below will succeed in management:

Secondary emergency contact: _____

Telephone number: _____

Alternative number: _____

E-mail: _____

Emergency Contact Information

Dial 9-1-1 in an emergency

Non-emergency police and fire number: _____

Insurance provider: _____

Plan to Stay in Business

The following natural and manmade disasters could impact our business:

_____

_____

_____

_____

Emergency Planning Team

The following people will participate in emergency planning and crisis management:

_____

_____

_____

_____

We Plan to Coordinate With Others

The following people from neighboring businesses and our building management will participate on our emergency planning team:

_____

_____

_____

_____

Our Critical Operations

The following is a prioritized list of critical operations, staff, and procedures we need to recover from a disaster:

Operation	Staff in charge	Action plan
_____	_____	_____
_____	_____	_____
_____	_____	_____
_____	_____	_____

Suppliers and Contractors

Company name: _____

Street address: _____

City: _____

State: _____

Zip code: _____

Phone: _____

Fax: _____

E-mail: _____

Contact name: _____

Account number: _____

Materials / service provided: _____

If this company experiences a disaster, we will obtain supplies/materials from the following:

Company name: _____

Street address: _____

City: _____

State: _____

Zip code: _____

Phone: _____

Fax: _____

E-mail: _____

Contact name: _____

Account number: _____

Materials / service provided: _____

If this company experiences a disaster, we will obtain supplies/materials from the following:

Company name: _____

Street address: _____

City: _____

State: _____

Zip code: _____

Phone: _____

Fax: _____

E-mail: _____

Contact name: _____

Account number: _____

Materials / service provided: _____

Evacuation Plan for _____

(Insert address)

The following natural and manmade disasters could impact our business:

We have developed these plans in collaboration with neighboring businesses and building owners to avoid confusion or gridlock.

We have located, copied, and posted building and site maps.

Exits are clearly marked.

We will practice evacuation procedures _____ times a year.

If we must leave the workplace quickly: _____

_____

_____

1. Warning system:_____

   We will test the warning system and record results _____ times a year.

2. Assembly site:_____

3. Assembly site manager and alternate: _____

   Responsibilities include: _____

   _____

   _____

   _____

4. Shut-down manager and alternate: _____

   Responsibilities include: _____

   _____

   _____

   _____

5. _____ is responsible for issuing all clear.

Shelter in Place Plan for _____

(Insert address)

The following natural and manmade disasters could impact our business:

We have talked to coworkers about which emergency supplies, if any, the company will provide in the shelter location and which supplies individuals might consider keeping in a portable kit personalized for individual needs.

We have located, copied, and posted building and site maps.

We will practice shelter procedures _____ times a year.

If we must shelter quickly: _____

_____

_____

1. Warning system:_____

   We will test the warning system and record results _____ times a year.

2. Storm shelter location:_____

3. "Seal the Room" shelter location: _____

4. Shelter location manager and alternate: _____

   Responsibilities include: _____

   _____

   _____

   _____

5. Shut-down manager and alternate: _____

   Responsibilities include: _____

   _____

   _____

   _____

6. _____ is responsible for issuing all clear.

Communications

We will communicate our emergency plans with coworkers in the following way:_____

_____

_____

In the event of a disaster we will communicate with employees in the following way:_____

_____

_____

Cyber Security

To protect our computer hardware, we will: _____

_____

To protect our computer software, we will: _____

_____

If our computers are destroyed, we will use back-up computers at the following location: _____

_____

Records Back-Up

_____ is responsible for backing up our critical records including payroll and accounting systems.

Back-up records including a copy of this plan, site maps, insurance policies, bank account records, and computer back-ups are stored at the following onsite location: _____

Another set of back-up records is stored at the following off-site location: _____

_____

If our accounting and payroll records are destroyed, we will provide for continuity in the following ways: _____

_____

Employee Emergency Contact Information

The following is a list of our coworkers and their individual emergency contact information:

_____

_____

_____

_____

_____

Annual Review

We will review and update this business continuity and disaster plan in _____.

Additional notes: _____

_____

_____

_____

_____

_____

_____

From S. Hall, W. Cooper, L. Marciani, and J. McGee, 2012, *Security management for sports and special events* (Champaign, IL: Human Kinetics). Reprinted from Ready Business, Business emergency plan. Available at www.ready.gov/business/_downloads/sampleplan.pdf.

Appendix 7.1
Event Staff Capabilities, Tasks, and Key Security Considerations

Parking Attendant

Capabilities

- Prevent unauthorized access to parking areas
- Provide directions to patrons
- Operate park-and-ride shuttles
- Assist guests with disabilities
- Observe and protect against unsafe and unlawful activities

Tasks

- Greet guests
- Provide directions and answer questions
- Verify parking credentials
- Drive shuttles
- Observe and report items of concern:
  - Abandoned vehicles
  - Falsified credentials
  - Illegal parking
  - Altercations and arguments
  - Weapons

Key Considerations

- Preevent sweeps
- Vehicle screening
- Good lighting and visibility
- Effective communication system
- Policy enforcement
- Credential control measures
- VIP arrival points

Common Problems

- Abandoned vehicles
- Counterfeit parking credentials

- Illegal parking
- Unattended fires or grills
- Altercations and arguments

Gate Security

Capabilities

- Prevent unauthorized entrance to venue
- Check for prohibited items
- Answer questions
- Assist security force or law enforcement as needed

Tasks

- Greet and direct guests
- Perform security inspections
- Verify tickets
- Respond to incidents and threats
- Assist law enforcement
- Observe and report

Key Considerations

- Prohibited items (food and beverages, alcohol, backpacks, signs, beach balls and balloons, video cameras, noisemakers, coolers and ice chests, explosives, and fireworks)
- Items of concern:
  - Wires, switches, circuit boards
  - Pipes, tubes, tape, tools
  - Nails, washers, screws
  - Liquids and powders
  - Aggressive response to search request
  - Unattended or abandoned bags
- Gate operations set the tone for most guests.

Common Problems

- Guests attempting entry with prohibited items
- Unusual items such as wires, switches, circuit boards, pipes, tubes, tape, tools, nails, washers, screws, liquids, or powders
- Aggressive response to search request
- Unattended or abandoned bags

Ticket Taker

Capabilities

- Prevent unauthorized entrance to venue
- Assist guests with ticket-related issues
- Maintain accurate gate count

Tasks

- Verify tickets or credentials
- Scan or stub tickets
- Resolve ticket issues
- Maintain gate count
- Observe and report items of concern:
  - Counterfeit tickets or credentials
  - Recycling tickets
  - Scalping and scamming
  - Odd behavior

Key Considerations

- Know the plan for lost tickets, duplicate tickets, will call, and special ticket requirements
- Be prepared with backup scanners
- Deal with ticket problems efficiently
- Ensure that guest lines are moving

Common Problems

- Guests offering cash for access
- Counterfeit tickets
- Counterfeit credentials
- Recycling tickets
- Scalping and scamming

Usher

Capabilities

- Maintain a safe, orderly environment
- Assist guests with problems
- Enforce venue policy
- Safely evacuate designated section if necessary

Tasks

- Greet guests and answer questions
- Verify tickets and credentials
- Keep aisles clear and safe
- Resolve minor issues
- Evacuate section if necessary
- Observe and report items of concern:
    - Heads turned away from playing area
    - Abusive language
    - Taunting, altercations
    - Thrown objects
    - Blocked aisles or stairways
    - Signs of excessive alcohol consumption
    - Offensive signs, banners, or clothing

Key Considerations

- Venue knowledge
- Positioning and presence before, during, and after the event
- Visibility and interaction with the crowd:
    - Minor incident (e.g., foul language)
        - Polite introduction to guest
        - Explain why the behavior is inappropriate
        - Ask guest to stop the behavior and comply with venue policy
        - Record the individual's location
    - Significant incident (e.g., threats)
        - Contact supervisor to issue official warning
        - Identify and interview witnesses
        - Warning may be recorded at command post
    - Major incident (e.g., fighting, medical emergency)
        - Contact law enforcement or emergency medical services
        - Assist responding agency if necessary (e.g., restrain or remove person, identify or interview witnesses)
        - Complete incident report

Common Problems

- Abusive language (slurs, threats, and so on)
- Taunting, arguing, and altercations
- Thrown objects or objects entering the stands

- Blocked aisles and stairways
- Signs of alcohol impairment
- Guests who are sleeping or vomiting
- Offensive signs, banners, or clothing
- Isolated pockets of opposing fans

Concessions and Maintenance

Capabilities

- Maintain clean, safe venue
- Sell food, beverages, and merchandise
- Respond to spills or incidents
- Assist guests with problems
- Secure critical assets during an emergency

Tasks

- Maintain assigned area
- Account for valuable and hazardous materials
- Maintain critical systems
- Observe and report items of concern:
  - Loss of materials, uniforms, keys
  - Vandalism, property damage
  - Unauthorized access by people or vehicles
  - Guests who appear aggressive or impaired
  - Accumulation of trash or hazardous materials

Key Considerations

- Venue knowledge
- Accountability (money, property, actions)
- Key and access control
- Uniforms and staff credentials
- Inspection program
- Preventative maintenance
- Trash removal
- Effective communications

Common Problems

- Locked or obstructed exits
- Abandoned bags and packages

- Loss of materials, uniforms, or keys
- Elicitation of facility information and inquiry
- Vandalism and property damage
- Unauthorized access by people or vehicles
- People who appear agitated or impaired

Field, Playing Area, or Stage Staff

Capabilities

- Prevent unauthorized access to playing area
- Resolve problems for team or performers and staff
- Safely evacuate playing or event area if necessary
- Protect audience (e.g., from body surfing)

Tasks

- Perform escort duties when needed
- Keep playing area clear and safe
- Enforce league rules
- Perform crowd control
- Evacuate playing area
- Observe and report items of concern:
  - Drug or alcohol impairment
  - Counterfeit credentials
  - Demonstrators
  - Mass gatherings or gang activity

Key Considerations

- Event procedures
- Positioning and presence at playing or performance area
- Coordinate response procedures for all hazards, such as weather (lightning, tornado) or encroachment (crowd surfing)
- Coordinate communication and response

Common Problems

- Drug and alcohol impairment
- Crowd problems
- Counterfeit credentials
- Exhibitionists and demonstrators

Security Force

Capabilities

- Prevent unauthorized venue access to patrons and vehicles
- Protect critical assets
- Observe and protect against unsafe and unlawful activities

Tasks

- Present visible security presence
- Conduct preevent sweeps
- Conduct foot patrols
- Respond to and report incidents

Key Considerations

- Ensure that venue policies and procedures are enforced
- Coordinate communication and response activities with command center

Common Problems

- Unauthorized access by people or vehicles
- Abandoned bags and packages
- Crowd control issues

Appendix 7.2
Common Complaints From Volunteers and Staff

Volunteer Complaints

- I'm always told what to do but never asked to participate in planning the work.
- Salaried staff gets or takes the credit for my good ideas.
- No one says, "Thank you."
- I always seem to get the "grunt work."
- I never get feedback on my work.
- Salaried staff is always given the benefit of the doubt in any dispute.
- Can't I have a title other than "Volunteer"?
- I always have to search for a place to do my work. There is nowhere to store my work from week to week.

Staff Complaints

- Volunteers will take salaried jobs.
- Volunteers will do a poor job and I'll get the blame and have responsibility for cleaning it up.
- Volunteers will do a great job and I'll look less effective.
- Volunteers are amateurs.
- Volunteers gossip; they don't understand confidentiality.
- Volunteers are not dependable.
- Volunteers will lower professional standards.
- Volunteers get all the recognition.

Reprinted from Federal Emergency Management Agency, 2006, *Developing and managing volunteers: Independent study.*

Checklist for Determining Volunteer–Staff Climate

Instructions: Review each of the statements listed below and mark those that you think accurately reflect the climate in your organization. When you finish, review the list. If only a few boxes are checked, you have some work to do to develop a healthy volunteer program.

- ☐ My agency is stable, healthy, and free of conflict and survival tension.

- ☐ Top management has issued a clear, specific, forceful policy statement, assigning high priority to involving volunteers in the agency.

- ☐ Roles of staff and volunteers are clearly defined and distinguished, both generally and in terms of specific tasks.

- ☐ Most volunteer job descriptions are based on staff work assistance needs; information about these needs is provided by staff members themselves.

- ☐ We have a wide variety of volunteer jobs and roles from which staff may select those they are most comfortable with.

- ☐ Our goals for increased participation of volunteers are realistic.

- ☐ A significant, well-planned part of volunteer training emphasizes sensitivity and sympathy to staff problems.

- ☐ Volunteers are rewarded and recognized only in conjunction with their staff supervisor.

- ☐ Staff receptivity to volunteers is carefully diagnosed; volunteers work primarily with receptive staff.

- ☐ We have a system of concrete, specific rewards for staff and volunteers who work productively with one another.

- ☐ Receptivity to and experience with volunteers are two of the criteria actively used in recruiting and selecting new staff.

- ☐ We have a well-planned program for orienting and training staff to work with volunteers.

From S. Hall, W. Cooper, L. Marciani, and J. McGee, 2012, *Security management for sports and special events* (Champaign, IL: Human Kinetics). Reprinted from Federal Emergency Management Agency, 2006, *Developing and managing volunteers: Independent study.*

Appendix 8.1
Sample Tabletop Exercise

Scenario: Improvised Explosive Device(s) Bombing at a College Sport Venue

Background

The Department of Homeland Security (DHS) has identified collegiate stadiums and arenas as potential targets for terrorist activity. Other potential threats include non-terrorist criminal acts, crowd control, and natural disasters. Catastrophic events impacting stadiums and arenas could potentially result in mass casualties and severe economic loss. Based on the potential vulnerability, collegiate athletic departments in coordination with local emergency responders are tasked with addressing simulated crisis scenarios to further enhance multiagency interoperability when responding to a stadium or arena crisis situation.

Purpose

The purpose of this exercise is to provide participants with an opportunity to evaluate current response concepts, plans, and capabilities for response to an explosive terrorist event at a venue.

Exercise Objectives

Exercise design objectives are focused on improving understanding of a response concept, identifying opportunities, or potential problems. This exercise will focus on the following design objectives selected by the Exercise Planning Team.

- **Intelligence and Information Gathering and Dissemination:** Discuss plans, policies, and procedures for ensuring the proper gathering, analyzing, sharing, and dissemination of incident-related information as it pertains to critical infrastructure and citizen protection during all the stages of a possible terrorist attack.

- **Incident Command System (ICS) and Unified Command:** Responders will demonstrate the ability to implement the ICS, transition to Unified Command, and effectively direct, coordinate, and manage a response to a terrorist attack at a university sports venue. Responders will activate their respective Emergency Response Plans (ERP) and all relevant Annexes (Evacuation Plan, Stadium and Arena Emergency Response Plan (ERP).

- **Citizen Protection and Mass Care:** Discuss plans, policies, and procedures for ensuring fans are evacuated and provided with sheltering, food, medical care, and other related services as needed during and after a major terrorist attack at a university sports venue.

- **Public Information:** Assess the adequacy of local plans for the flow of public information and the interface with, and use of, media resources. Discuss options to provide timely information to the population and assist in minimizing confusion.

- **Communications:** Understand communication channels and procedures to conduct incident management activities at the university with support of federal, state, and local resources. Identify the emergency proclamation process at the local and state levels. Determine strengths and weaknesses in the communication of response activities. Identify critical issues and potential solutions. Identify and activate a primary and alternate communication system.

Exercise Structure

To run the exercise effectively you must ensure it is properly structured. Participants will be divided into Command Groups (CGs) to discuss aspects of the situation as presented. Tables will represent CGs. Distribute name tags and a marker to each table (Command Group). Have each Command Group designate one person to represent each of the following agencies listed below:

- University Athletic Department
- Campus Police Department or Local Law Enforcement
- Local Fire Department or Hazardous Materials Response
- Local Emergency Management
- Local Emergency Medical Service and Public Health

Instruct individuals to write their agency's name on a name tag so that other instructors and facilitators will be able to recognize what role each person is playing during the exercise. Use a flip-chart for individuals as they stand to brief the class about their decisions during the scenario.

Before beginning the exercise, the facilitator should explain that the exercise will require the use of assumptions and artificialities. Time will be controlled by the facilitators and will accelerate as the scenario progresses. There is no hidden agenda and there are no trick questions. The intent of the exercise is to model the implementation and utility of a table top exercise and, as such, to get the participants to make decisions in the face of incomplete or inaccurate information. Mistakes are welcomed as learning opportunities.

Timeline

00:00 – 00:15	Introduction and general situation briefing
00:15 – 00:35	Inject 1 and discussion
00:35 – 00:45	Inject 2 and discussion
00:45 – 00:55	Inject 3 and discussion
00:55 – 01:15	Inject 4 and discussion
01:15 – 01:25	Inject 5 and discussion
01:25 – 01:35	Inject 6 and discussion
01:35 – 01:50	Inject 7 and discussion
01:50 – 02:00	End of exercise, debrief

General Situation

Regent University is a mid-size school located in the southeastern United States. It has an undergraduate enrollment of approximately 20,000 students and is located in a small rural town with a population of about 50,000 residents. The campus of Regent University is fairly compact. The football stadium is located on campus and is surrounded by a number of other campus buildings that include several residence halls, classroom buildings, and at least three science laboratories that contain significant amounts of chemicals and other hazardous materials. A four-lane, divided highway runs along the east side of the campus adjacent to the stadium. Event parking is dispersed throughout the campus with a significant concentration located south of the football stadium for game day parking.

Regent University has a fairly successful football program. The school hosts six to seven games each season and each game has an average attendance of approximately 45,000 spectators. The biggest game of the year is usually the last game of the season when Regent University plays its biggest in-state rival, Fairview University. The Regent vs. Fairview game is usually sold out; attendance exceeds 50,000 and approximately 5,000 additional spectators, who were unable to get tickets, remain in the parking areas to tailgate.

Approximately thirty days ago, the campus police chief and President of Regent University received a bulletin from the local FBI/DHS fusion center. The bulletin described an incident at a college football game in California where two improvised explosive devices (IEDs) were found hidden in backpacks. One backpack was found hidden near some bushes in the stadium parking lot, approximately 100 meters from the building. The other backpack was found behind a trash can near an entrance gate. Both devices were found during the preevent lock down and security sweep and were rendered safe. The devices were very similar and were each found in a navy blue, student-style backpack. The FBI believes the devices were constructed and placed by the same group or individual. The FBI has encouraged all domestic universities to review their safety and security measures for all of their large public assembly venues.

Further investigation by the FBI has determined that the devices may be linked to a group known as the True Revolution Brigade (TRB). The TRB is a relatively unknown organization that has been under FBI surveillance following a series of attacks on university research facilities in the Pacific Northwest. Members of the group communicate through various websites and blogs. The FBI has issued a second bulletin regarding recent activity on the Internet in which suspected TRB members mentioned "blowing up a stadium full of people."

Inject 1

It is Friday morning. The final home game of the season, Regent v. Fairview, is scheduled for a 3:30 PM kickoff in a little more than fifteen days. The campus police department receives a telephone call from the local FBI office. The FBI informs the campus police chief that further investigation of the TRB has resulted in the arrest of a TRB member with ties to Regent University. The individual in custody was enrolled at Regent University three years ago but withdrew after one semester. The individual is described as a 23-year-old, white male with a medium build and very short brown hair. The arrest revealed this individual also had an outstanding federal warrant for a weapons violation and a series of traffic violations in California. A search of his California residence uncovered a lot of information regarding college football.

Command Group Task 1

Within your table discuss this latest information and decide on a course of action. Be ready to answer the questions below during a brief back. You have 10 minutes.

- Who is in charge?
- What are you going to do (what is your objective)?

- What would really happen with regards to?
  - Time
    - What can you do now?
    - What is the best way to use your time?
  - Communications
    - Who needs this information?
    - Is there any information you need?
  - Resource tactics and SOP
    - Are there other resources you need?
    - How would you respond to an IED incident like this?
    - What plans, policies, and procedures do you need?
  - Crowd behavior
    - What will happen when this news gets out?

Inject 2

The big game between Regent and Fairview is 5 days away. Further investigation by the FBI has uncovered evidence, including a series of Internet chat room messages, confirming the identity of the TRB suspect in custody as Jeremy Potts, a one-time Regent student who transferred to State College near San Jose, California. The investigation has also uncovered specific information linking the TRB to the failed attack in California. National media has been covering the TRB case but, thankfully, the local angle of this case (and any specific ties to Regent University) has not been picked up by local media.

At 11:30 AM the special agent in charge of the local FBI office contacts the campus police chief and communicates some sensitive information. Acting on a tip, the FBI raided a TRB safe house in California. The raid uncovered additional evidence linking the TRB to potential attacks against college football games. Specifically, several college football schedules were recovered. A white board inside the residence listed what, according to the FBI, appeared to be a target list that included Regent University's game against Fairview and six other prominent games. The FBI also contacted the President of the University and requested a meeting.

At 2:30 PM the president of Regent University conducted a conference call with the athletic director and the campus police chief. The president angrily underscored the economic importance and tradition of the Regent v. Fairview football game. The president clearly communicated his decision, "I will not allow this institution to give in to the terrorists! This is why I pay you folks. This event will continue as scheduled, and if you don't feel you can do so, then please submit your resignation by the end of the day."

At 3:15 PM the Regent University Athletic Department's sports information office received a call from the local NBC news affiliate, Channel 12. The caller identifies themselves as a news reporter and wants to interview the athletic director about chances the big game will be cancelled.

Command Group Task 2

Within your table discuss this latest information and decide on a course of action. Be ready to answer the questions below during a brief back. You have five minutes.

- Who is in charge?
- What are you going to do (what is your objective)?
- What would really happen with regards to?
  - Time
    - What can you do now?
    - What is the best way to use your time?
  - Communications
    - Who needs this information?
    - How will you communicate?
    - Is there any information you need?
  - Resource tactics and SOP
    - Are there other resources you need?
    - What plans, policies, and procedures do you need?
  - Crowd behavior
    - What will happen when this news gets out?
    - How might this information impact your game day operation?

Inject 3

It is 9:00 AM on game day. Kickoff between Regent University and Fairview University will take place in approximately six and one half hours. In response to recent events, the stadium was locked down twelve hours ago. All personnel were evacuated from the facility, all entrances were locked or placed under guard, and bomb detection teams swept the building and its immediate perimeter for any suspicious devices. There are some RV trailers in the outer parking areas, but all of the parking areas near the stadium are clear. Any vehicles remaining in these areas were towed at lock down. All parking areas will open to the public in one hour. Local police have established traffic control points to handle the expected crowd. Stadium employees are arriving at the stadium via shuttle bus and are entering through the employee entrance. All employees are being briefed on the situation and asked to be extra vigilant.

The stadium command center is staffed and monitoring radio traffic. Student volunteers are working in the stadium ticket office when one of them receives a threatening phone call. The student calls 911 on her cell phone and tells the dispatcher that someone called her at the stadium and said there was a bomb inside the stadium.

Command Group Task 3

Within your table discuss this latest information and decide on a course of action. Be ready to answer the questions below during a brief back. You have five minutes.

- Who is in charge?
- What are you going to do (what is your objective)?
- What would really happen with regards to?
  - Time
    - What can you do now?

- What is the best way to use your time?
- Communications
  - Who needs this information?
  - Is there any information you need?
- Resource tactics and SOP
  - Are there other resources you need?
  - What plans, policies, and procedures do you need?
- Crowd behavior
  - What will happen when this news gets out?
  - Do you need to evacuate—who and where to?

Instructor Note: From this point on any resource requests should be assessed a reasonable time frame. For example, a bomb dog might take an hour or more to arrive.

Inject 4

It is 1:00 PM, and stadium gates will open to the public in 30 minutes. Both football teams and all of the league officials have arrived and are inside. Media truck and camera crews are conducting live shots from inside the media compound on the south side of the stadium. The parking lots are reaching capacity as traffic continues to stream in from the highway.

In response to recent events, Regent University has decided to prohibit all backpacks and large bags from entering into the stadium. Extra law enforcement has been positioned around the venue and additional private security officers have been posted at all entrances. Several thousand fans wander throughout the parking lots and around the stadium's perimeter. Roaming patrols of uniformed law enforcement, plain-clothes officers, and uniformed private security move in and around the stadium.

At 1:12 PM a private security officer reports an abandoned backpack in a large planter near the NW corner of the stadium. The planter is approximately 25 yards from a stadium entrance gate. The backpack is described as a "standard book bag."

Command Group Task 4

Within your table discuss this latest information and decide on a course of action. Be ready to answer the questions below during a brief back. You have 10 minutes.

- Who is in charge?
- What are you going to do (what is your objective)?
- What would really happen with regards to….?
  - Time
    - What can you do now?
    - What is the best way to use your time?
  - Communications
    - Who needs this information?
    - Is there any information you need?

- Resource tactics and SOP
  - Are there other resources you need?
  - What will the deployed resources do, specifically?
- Crowd behavior
  - How will the crowd react? What happens if the media shows up?
  - Do you need to evacuate—who and where to?

Instructor note: Reveal the contents of the backpack in the middle of next inject (#5). The backpack was a green gym bag that contained chemistry text books, a cell phone, a roll of duct tape, and a campus map. There is no device and there was no personal identification found in the bag.

Inject 5

It is 1:40 PM. All stadium gates, except for the gate at the NW corner, are open. A few spectators have entered the stadium, but most of the building remains empty. The parking lot and all pedestrian areas around the stadium are very busy. The Regent University marching band is performing a short concert just south of the stadium. Traffic on the highway to the east of the stadium is at a virtual standstill.

Plain clothes officers deployed outside of the stadium's SE entrance are observing a suspicious person wearing a dark blue backpack. The suspect, a white female who is walking alone, is moving towards the stadium.

Command Group Task 5

Within your table discuss this latest information and decide on a course of action. Be ready to answer the questions below during a brief back. You have five minutes.

- Who is in charge?
- What are you going to do (what is your objective)?
- What would really happen with regards to?
  - Time
    - What can you do now?
    - What is the best way to use your time?
  - Communications
    - Who needs this information?
    - How will you communicate?
    - Is there any information you need?
  - Resource tactics and SOP
    - Are there other resources you need?
    - What will the deployed resources accomplish specifically?
  - Crowd behavior
    - How will the crowd react? What happens if the media shows up?
    - Do you need to evacuate—who and where to?

Instructor Note: Reveal the contents of the backpack in the middle of next inject (6). The backpack in this inject contains a number of text books, clothing, granola bars, and two bottles of water.

Inject 6

It is 3:00 PM. The game kicks off in 30 minutes. The Command Post receives a report of smoke on the main concourse. Using a radio, a roaming security officer reports a strong smell of smoke coming from a dumpster near one of the concession stands on the east side of the stadium. The dumpster is located behind a fenced enclosure that is locked. The security officer does not see any flames, but he thinks smoke is coming from the dumpster. The security officer cannot get into the enclosure. He is asking for assistance.

Minutes later the Command Post receives a cell phone call from an usher working inside the stadium's north end zone. The usher relays the following information: "Hello, is this the Command Post? I need EMTs to respond to the men's restroom near section 115. There is a fan that appears to be having a heart attack. He is lying on the floor in the bathroom and is unresponsive. My name is Walter Ryan, and I am an usher near section 115 in the north end zone. The gentleman is a white male, approximately 50 years old with a heavy build and gray hair."

Command Group Task 6

Within your table discuss this latest information and decide on a course of action. Be ready to answer the questions below during a brief back. You have five minutes.

- Who is in charge?
- What are you going to do (what is your objective)?
- What responsibilities are assigned to each member of the table?
  - University Athletics and Scribe
  - Campus Police or Local Law Enforcement
  - County Emergency Management
  - Fire and Rescue, EMS, HAZMAT
  - Public Information
- What would really happen with regards to?
  - Time
    - What can you do now?
    - What is the best way to use your time?
  - Communications
    - Who needs this information?
    - How will you communicate?
    - Is there any information you need?
  - Resource tactics and SOP
    - Are there other resources you need?
    - What will the deployed resources do, specifically?
  - Crowd behavior

- How will the crowd react? What happens if the media shows up?
- Do you need to evacuate—who and where to?

Inject 7

It is 3:25 PM. The game kicks off in five minutes. Long lines of spectators extend from each gate, and in some cases, into the parking areas as spectators, tailgating until the last minute, now begin to enter the stadium. The longest line is located in the SW corner of the stadium. The stadium is nearly full as a capacity crowd files in for the game. Traffic on the highway has begun to ease up but there is still a lot of congestion.

A man wearing a backpack is standing in line to enter the stadium at the SW entrance gate. A uniformed private security officer approaches the individual and asks him to step out of line. A local unit of the Air National Guard is on station to provide a pre-game fly over of the stadium. As the planes fly low over the stadium the crowd inside, and outside at the gates, lets out a loud cheer. In the confusion of the moment the man with the backpack darts away from the security officer and heads towards the NW corner of the stadium. The security supervisor from the SW gate describes the individual as a "white male in his 20's with very short black hair, and wearing a dark blue backpack." A few minutes later, as the game kicks off, a loud explosion is heard outside of the west side of the stadium. Within seconds, panic erupts as frightened people flee from the area.

The source of the explosion is unknown but it occurs on the west side of the stadium near a chemistry building. There are several people who are wounded and they report seeing other more seriously injured casualties lying near where the explosion took place. The stadium command center and the local 911 dispatch lines become choked with calls. There are numerous conflicting reports. A police officer on the west side of the stadium continues to call for medical support. The police officer reports three fatalities and five people with serious, life threatening injuries.

Inside the stadium the public is restless. Almost everyone is standing up looking at the smoke rising from the stadium's west side. Several individuals are moving quickly up and out of the seating area. Sirens can be heard approaching the stadium.

Command Group Task 7

Within your table discuss this latest information and decide on a course of action. Be ready to answer the questions below during a brief back. You have 15 minutes.

- Who is in charge?
- What are you going to do (what is your objective)?
- What responsibilities are assigned to each member of the table?
  - University Athletics and Scribe
  - Campus Police or Local Law Enforcement
  - County Emergency Management
  - Fire and Rescue, EMS, HAZMAT
  - Public Information
- What would really happen with regards to?
  - Time

- What can you do now?
- What is the best way to use your time?
  - Communications
    - Who needs this information?
    - How will you communicate?
    - Is there any information you need?
  - Resource tactics and SOP
    - Are there other resources you need?
    - What will the deployed resources do, specifically?
  - Crowd behavior
    - How will the crowd react? What happens if the media shows up?
    - Do you need to evacuate—who and where to?

Instructor Note: This is the final inject so begin to finalize notes for the post-exercise debrief.

Capstone Debrief

The Capstone debrief is an important part of the overall exercise. The instructor and facilitators should have made several detailed notes that can be used to moderate the debriefing. The intent of the debriefing is to use the value of hindsight and get the students talking about three essential questions:

1. What did you do right?
2. What did you do wrong?
3. What would you do differently?

The debriefing should also serve to review material presented in many of the modules. The instructor should make use of the module review charts to get the students thinking about several of the topics presented, to include:

1. NIMS or ICS and multiagency coordination
2. Decision making
3. Threat analysis
4. Planning and preparation
5. Risk assessment
6. Protective measures and venue policy
7. Staff training and exercise

Reprinted from U.S. Department of Homeland Security, 2010, Sport Event Risk Management Module 10: Capstone. Developed by James A McGee.

Appendix 8.2
Needs Assessment

1. Risks

List the various risks to your sport or event venue and surrounding community. What risks are you most likely to face? Use the following list as a starting point:

- Hostage or shooting
- Bomb threat (IED/VBIED)
- Hurricane
- Tornado
- Biological, chemical, or radiological release
- Power failure
- Terrorism
- Crowd disaster
- Event cancellation
- Others _____

2. Secondary Risks

What secondary effects from those identified risks are likely to affect your organization? Use the following list as a starting point:

- Communication system breakdown
- Sustained power outage
- Transportation issues
- Mass evacuation
- Others _____

3. Risk Priority

What are the highest priority risks? Consider such factors as

- frequency and likelihood of occurrence and
- potential consequences (severity of impact).

#1 priority risk: _____

#2 priority risk: _____

#3 priority risk: _____

4. Plans and Procedures

What plans and procedures will guide your organization's response to an emergency incident?

- Emergency response plan (ERP)
- Evacuation plan
- Game-day operational plan
- Continuity of operations plan (COOP)
- Standard operating procedures (SOP)

5. Functions

What emergency response functions are in need of rehearsal? For example, what functions have not been exercised recently or where have difficulties occurred in the past? Use the following list as a starting point:

- Alert notification
- Communication systems
- Coordination and control
- Transportation
- Resource management
- Continuity of operations
- Health and medical
- Others _____

6. Participants

Who needs to participate in an exercise (i.e., personnel, agencies, operational units, or state and federal entities)? The following questions should guide the process for participant inclusion:

- Have any parties updated their plans or procedures?
- Have any parties changed policies or personnel?
- What agencies does your organization need to coordinate with in the event of an emergency?
- What do regulatory requirements state?
- What personnel can you devote to developing the exercise process?

7. Program Areas

Mark the status of your emergency plans, procedures, and protocols to identify those most in need of exercising.

	New	Updated	Exercised	Used in an Emergency	Not applicable
Emergency plan					
Game-day operations plan					
Evacuation plan					
Cyber plan					
CBRNE plan					
Terrorism plan					
Active shooter protocol					
Alert notification					
Crisis communication					
Continuity of operations					
Resource list					
Mutual aid agreements					
EOC or command center					
Damage assessment					

8. Past Exercises

Has your organization participated in exercises before? What did you learn and what did the after-action reports indicate about future training and exercise needs? Consider the following questions:

- Who participated in the exercise and who did not?
- Were exercise objectives achieved?
- What were the lessons learned?
- What problems were identified and what measures were taken to resolve them?
- What improvement recommendations were made and have they been tested?

From S. Hall, W. Cooper, L. Marciani, and J. McGee, 2012, *Security management for sports and special events* (Champaign, IL: Human Kinetics). Adapted from Federal Emergency Management Agency, 2008, Introduction to exercise design.

Exercise Plan Template and Examples

General Section

This Exercise Plan identifies policies, procedures, administrative requirements, and exercise roles and responsibilities that will support exercise-planning initiatives.

Exercise Type

State what type of exercise is going to be conducted:

1. Orientation
2. Drill
3. Tabletop
4. Functional
5. Full-Scale

Exercise Purpose

This Exercise Plan provides exercise developers with guidance concerning procedures and responsibilities for exercise design and support. It explains the exercise concept, establishes the basis for the exercise, and establishes and defines the communications, logistics, and administrative structure needed to support the exercise—before, during, and after.

Describe the purpose of the plan itself and the mission and goals of the exercise. Provide specific information to exercise developers on the exercise objectives, points of review, administrative procedures, and methods of control for simulation and evaluation. Most importantly, lay out the exercise methodology, including Control and Evaluation Team structure, team member responsibilities, and procedures.

Scenario Narrative

Briefly describe the hazard and related events and conditions setting the stage for the exercise. Provide background information for the emergency to enhance the realism of the situation.

Scope

Describe the type of exercise, scope of exercise, dates of exercise, primary exercise locations, hours of operations, participating organizations, and the briefing or narrative summary that will start the exercise as follows.

Exercise play will officially begin on [*insert time, day of week, date*] _____ and end at approximately [*insert time, day of week, date*] _____ as determined by the exercise director. The exercise will be played [*insert number of hours*] _____ per day at all primary exercise locations; however, some locations [*insert if some are out of sequence*

or have limited extents of play] _____. On [*insert date*] _____
the exercise will be initiated by a [*describe whether briefing, incident, or video and provide a general description of the information. Example: The briefing will begin with a description of the situation as it currently exists. The briefing will describe background actions that have been taken by emergency response organizations as well as a review of the weather situation. This background briefing will be based on the information in Scenario Narrative]* _____
_____. There will be a post-exercise meeting at each player location on [*insert date*] _____. (May use calendar to illustrate scheduled activities.)

List of Exercise References

[*The following are types of references to be listed.*]

- Student manual
- Model community manual
- Location's EOC staffing pattern
- Location's EOC positions descriptions
- Exercise control plan
- Exercise evaluation plan
- Exercise scenarios
- Job aids

Assumptions, Artificialities, and Simulations

[*The following assumptions are fairly generic; you may modify or add specifics for your own exercise.*]
   The assumptions, artificialities, and simulations applicable during the exercise are provided in the following paragraphs.

Exercise Assumptions

The following assumptions must be made in order to ensure that the exercise is as realistic as possible. It is intended that exercise events progress in a logical and realistic manner and that all exercise objectives be achieved during exercise play.

- Exercise participants are well versed in their own department and agency response plans and procedures.
- The term *participants* includes planners, controllers, simulators, evaluators, and players.
- Players and controllers will use real-world data and information support sources.
- Players will respond in accordance with existing plans, policies, and procedures. In the absence of appropriate written instructions, players will be expected to apply individual initiative to satisfy response and recovery requirements.

- Implementation of disaster response plans, policies, and procedures during the exercise will depict actions that would be expected to occur under actual response conditions and, therefore, will provide a sound basis for evaluation.
- Actions to direct unit, personnel, or resource deployments will result in simulated movement during the exercise unless live deployment in real time is stipulated to achieve an exercise objective.
- Real-world response actions will take priority over exercise actions.

Exercise Artificialities

It is recognized that the following artificialities and constraints will detract from realism; however, exercise planners should accept these artificialities as a means of facilitating accomplishment of exercise objectives.

[*This section will be based upon your extent of play agreements and include any pre-exercise player activity or pre-positioning of equipment. The following are examples.*]

- The exercise will be played in near-real time; however, to meet exercise objectives, some events may be accomplished by participants before the exercise, and other events may be accelerated in time to ensure their consideration during play.
- Many alert, notification, initial activation, and emergency response procedures, as well as some early response actions, will not be a part of the exercise.
- Responses obtained by players from simulations may not be of the quality or detail available from the real organization or individual.
- During the exercise, actions may occur to direct unit, personnel, or resource deployments, and subsequent movement of resources may be played; however, these actions may be simulated with no live movement occurring in the exercise.
- Some personnel and equipment may be pre-positioned at exercise locations rather than moved in real-time during the exercise, and they will enter play at predetermined times from their pre-positioned locations. When this exercise artificiality occurs, it will be referred to in exercise documentation as exercise pre-positioning to differentiate it from the live deployments that will be evaluated.

Exercise Simulations

Simulation during exercises is required to compensate for nonparticipating individuals or organizations. Although simulations necessarily detract from realism, they provide the means to facilitate exercise play.

Describe, in general, any areas that will be simulated. Examples include weather information, simulation of nonparticipating organizations, media, victims, and evacuees.

Exercise Objectives

Each developed exercise requires objectives that provide the foundation and guidance for exercise development. Objectives are designed to reflect the validity of community plans, procedures, and systems, and provide the basis for exercise control, simulation, and evaluation. The following are examples of exercise objectives:

- Demonstrate the capability to initiate public warning procedures at the EOC, including activation of the Emergency Alert System (EAS).
- Demonstrate the capability of the local EOC to coordinate the comprehensive response activities.
- Demonstrate the capability of management to conduct and coordinate an evacuation.
- Demonstrate responsible organization capability to identify shelters and mass care facilities for immediate use.
- Demonstrate the collection and dissemination of information to the public during emergency operations.
- Demonstrate the capability to conduct rapid situational assessment.
- Demonstrate the ability to identify immediate supplemental medical assistance to meet the health and medical needs of disaster victims.
- Demonstrate procedures for tracking assets and resources committed to response operations.
- Demonstrate the ability to prioritize and use jurisdictional resources and assets for maximum effectiveness during response operations.
- Determine the procedures for requesting assistance from higher levels of government.

Exercise Concept

Describe procedures before, during, and after the exercise to be taken by the various exercise development teams. Describe how each team will interact with other participants. List the procedures that each team's members will follow to fulfill their responsibilities.

Management Structure

Describe the exercise development team organizational structure as follows.

Overall exercise planning, conduct, and evaluation for the exercise is the responsibility of the [insert title] _____. [Title] _____ is responsible for coordinating all exercise planning activities between [Insert federal, state, and local departments and agencies and other participating organizations. Identify others in charge at each organizational level. Include those in charge of control and evaluation] _____

_____.

Exercise Team Staffing, Rules, and Procedures

For a large exercise, there may be an exercise director with assistants and other functional areas besides evaluation and control and simulation, such as support and coordination. Adapt the following text and charts to reflect your exercise management structure.

The team chiefs and personnel selected as exercise team members must be knowledgeable of emergency management and response functions. [Insert other qualifications identified by the

exercise management team leader.] _____
_____. They need this knowledge to understand ongoing exercise activities and to be able to track them. In order to meet this need, individuals who meet these requirements may be recruited from nonparticipating (or participating) emergency response organizations.

The exercise team will identify rules or guidelines for conduct during the exercise and will identify procedures of the exercise—before, during, and after.

The following team structure will be used. [*Identify exercise control team organization. Modify the chart below to reflect organization. Specific action sites should be added, such as state and local EOCs. If one simulation cell is used for all locations, modify the chart accordingly.*] _____

_____
_____

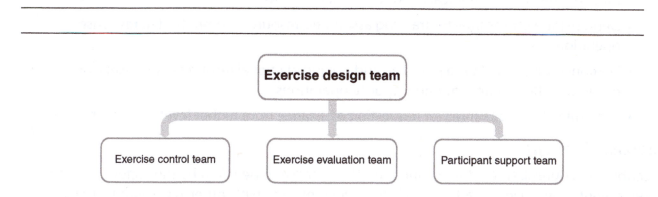

Exercise Design Structure

1. **Exercise Design Team:** Responsible for coordinating all exercise planning activities. The exercise director will assign exercise tasks and responsibilities, provide guidance, establish timelines, and monitor the development process. The team chief is responsible for developing the exercise objectives, concepts, scenarios, master scenario events list, exercise messages administrative support requirements, and communication methods.

2. **Control or Simulation Team:** The control or simulation team chief is responsible for the development of the control plan. The plan should include, but not be limited to, the following:

- Exercise control and simulation activity management
- Provisions for controller or simulator training and briefing
- Procedures for monitoring and reporting of exercise activities to include the flow and pace of the exercise
- Procedures to track the accomplishment of exercise objectives
- Procedures to record the responses of players
- Procedures for message injection, including the development of ad hoc messages to support exercise objectives
- A list of required exercise forms, including instructions for use and preparation
- Preparation for the critique

3. **Evaluation Team:** The evaluation team chief is responsible for the development of the evaluation plan. The plan should include all evaluation activities that should occur before, during, and after the exercise. Evaluation activities should include, but not be limited to, the following:

- Exercise evaluation activity management
- Provisions for evaluator training and briefing
- Procedures for monitoring and evaluating exercise activities
- Procedures to track the accomplishment of exercise objectives
- Procedures to record and evaluate the responses of players
- Procedures to track message injection, including the development of ad hoc messages to support exercise objectives
- A list of required exercise forms, including instructions for use and preparation
- Preparation for the critique

4. **Participant Support Team:** The participant support team is responsible for coordinating exercise support activities. This team works with the other teams to develop consistent staff briefings for the controllers, simulators, evaluators, and participants, and develops the player handbook. The handbook should contain a list of instructions for players and provide information regarding player responsibilities and functions to be performed during the exercise. The handbook should contain, but not be limited to, the following:

- A schedule of player exercise briefings
- Provisions for review of community or organization plans, policies, and procedures
- Scenario overview
- Exercise objectives
- Procedures for preparation of exercise-generated messages, logs, and reports
- Emergency operating center procedures
- Expected player actions
- Administrative requirements
- Recommended pre-exercise training events

Safety and Security

Describe the safety procedures, to include canceling of the exercise if an actual emergency occurs. Detail any special security issues involved with the exercise, location, or equipment.

Administrative and Logistical Support Requirements

Administrative and logistical support will be required to support all phases of the exercise. The level of support required will depend upon the complexity and length of the exercise, number of players involved, and the number of objectives being demonstrated. Administrative and logistical support consists of personnel, equipment, supplies, and facilities.

Describe the logistics and administrative support that will be provided at each exercise location. Examples of areas to consider when developing logistics and administrative support for the exercise are given below.

- Administrative support at exercise locations and action sites
- Personnel to assist with pre-exercise training registration, training, and packaging of training materials
- Information on facilities (rooms, etc.) for the exercise

Site Preparation and Support

Describe site preparations that may be necessary to meet exercise objectives and test plans and procedures.

Job Aids

List those aids that will assist the design team.

From S. Hall, W. Cooper, L. Marciani, and J. McGee, 2012, *Security management for sports and special events* (Champaign, IL: Human Kinetics). Adapted from Federal Emergency Management Agency, 2008, Introduction to exercise design.

Appendix 8.4
Exercise Checklist

- ☐ Identify exercise objectives
- ☐ Identify the appropriate type of exercise
- ☐ Establish a timeline for the planning and execution of the exercise
- ☐ Identify an exercise planning team and determine involvement of outside agencies
- ☐ Design the exercise scenario and define the functions to be tested
- ☐ Determine what resources are available and the cost of the exercise
- ☐ Confirm availability of facilities and equipment
- ☐ Test communications and necessary equipment
- ☐ Identify safety controllers and establish a code word for real-life emergencies (for operations-based exercises)
- ☐ Brief all participants and warn local media if appropriate
- ☐ Conduct an immediate debriefing focused on the events, coordination, and responses to developments
- ☐ Evaluate the exercise and prepare a final report
- ☐ Make recommendations and identify plans, policies, and procedures requiring improvement
- ☐ Distribute the report to all participating individuals and agencies

From S. Hall, W. Cooper, L. Marciani, and J. McGee, 2012, *Security management for sports and special events* (Champaign, IL: Human Kinetics).

Appendix 8.5
Debriefing Log

Exercise: _____

Your role: _____

Date: _____

Problem summary	Recommended action	Responsible agency

From S. Hall, W. Cooper, L. Marciani, and J. McGee, 2012, *Security management for sports and special events* (Champaign, IL: Human Kinetics). Reprinted from Federal Emergency Management Agency, 2008, Exercise evaluation.

Exercise Critique Form

1. Rate the overall exercise on the following scale:

   1   2   3   4   5

   Very poor   Very good

2. Compared with previous exercises, this one was

   1   2   3   4   5

   Very poor   Very good

3. Did the exercise effectively simulate the emergency environment and emergency response activities?   ☐ Yes   ☐ No

   If no, briefly explain why:_____

   _____

4. Did the problems presented in the exercise adequately test readiness capability to implement the plan?   ☐ Yes   ☐ No

   If no, briefly explain why:_____

   _____

5. The following problems should be deleted or revised: _____

   _____

   _____

6. I suggest that you add the following problems for the next exercise: _____

   _____

   _____

7. Please add any other comments or suggestions._____

   _____

   _____

   _____

   _____

   _____

References

Academy for Venue Safety and Security. (2006, August). Chapter 4 in *Training manual*. International Association of Assembly Managers.

Ammon, R., Southall, R. & Nagel, M. (2010). *Sport facility management: Organizing events and mitigating risks*. Morgantown, WV: Fitness Information Technology.

Ammon, R., Southall, R., & Blair, D. (2003). *Sport facility management: Organizing events and mitigating risks*. Morgantown, WV: Fitness Information Technology.

Appenzeller, H. (2000). Chapter 24: Risk assessment and reduction. In H. Appenzeller & G. Lewis (Eds.), *Successful sport management: A guide to legal issues*. Durham, NC: Carolina Academic Press.

Appenzeller, H. (2000). Risk assessment and reduction. In H. Appenzeller & G. Lewis (Eds.), *Successful sport management: A guide to legal issues*. Durham, NC: Carolina Academic Press.

Arquilla, J., Ronfeldt, D., & Zanini, M. (1999). Networks, netwar, and information-age terrorism. In I.O. Lesser, B. Hoffman, J. Arquilla, D. Ronfeldt, & M. Zanini (Eds.), *Countering the new terrorism* (pp. 39–84). Santa Monica, CA: Rand Corporation.

ASIS International. (2003). *General security risk assessment guideline*. Retrieved from www.asisonline.org/guidelines/guidelinesgsra.pdf

Atlanta Consulting Group. (1992). *Trust and teamwork training program*. Atlanta, GA: Author.

Australian National Security. (2010). *National terrorism public alert system*. Retrieved from www.nationalsecurity.gov.au

Baker, T.A., Connaughton, D., Zhang, J.J., & Spengler, J.O. (2007). Perceived risk of terrorism and related risk management practices of NCAA Division IA football stadium managers. *Journal of Legal Aspects of Sport, 13*(2), 145–179.

Beckman, L. (2006). *A system for evaluating emergency response capabilities at a university sporting venue*. Doctoral dissertation. Retrieved from ProQuest Digital Dissertations Database. (Publication No. AAT 3268436).

Bennis, W. (1997). Organizing genius: The secrets of creative collaboration. Reading, MA: Addison-Wesley.

Biringer, B.E., Matalucci, R.V., & O'Connor, S.L. (2007). *Security risk assessment and management*. Hoboken, NJ: Wiley.

Blake, R.R., & Mouton, J.S. (1964). *The managerial GRID*. Houston, TX: Gulf.

Broder, J.F. (2006). *Risk analysis and the security survey* (3rd ed.). Oxford, United Kingdom: Butterworth-Heinemann Business Books.

Buchholz, W. (2001). *Open communication climate*. Retrieved from http://atc.bentley.edu/faculty/wb/printables/opencomm.pdf

Bullock, J., Haddow, G., Coppola, D. & Yeletaysi, S. (2009). *Introduction to homeland security* (3rd ed.). Burlington, MA: Butterworth-Heineman.

Busowsky, G. (n.d.). *Risk management in facility management*. Retrieved from www.beims.com/fm_news/white_papers/Risk_Management_in_FM.pdf

Center for Venue Management Studies. (2002). *Best practices planning guide emergency preparedness*. IAAM Safety and Security Task Force.

Chelladurai, P. (2006). *Human resource management in sport and recreation*. Champaign, IL: Human Kinetics.

Chen, R. (2009, March). Large-scale stadiums set the standard. *A&S International*, pp. 56–62.

Collins, J. (2001). Good to Great. New York: Harper Business.

Commission on the Prevention of WMD Proliferation and Terrorism. (2008). *World at risk*. New York: Vintage Books, Random House.

Conger, J.A., & Kanungo, R.N. (1998). *Charismatic leadership in organizations*. Thousand Oaks, CA: Sage.

Contemporary Services Corporation. (2007, November). *Venue staff training*. Presented by Dane Dodd.

Continuity Central. (2009, August 27). *Exercising: The secret to successful business continuity plans*. Retrieved from www.continuitycentral.com/feature0696.html

Culf, A. (2006, January 19). The six-billion dollar sports security industry. *The Guardian.co.uk*. Retrieved from www.guardian.co.uk/sport/2006/jan/19/football.newsstory

Cunningham, G. (2007). *Security management capabilities in intercollegiate athletic departments*. Doctoral dissertation. Retrieved from ProQuest Digital Dissertations Database. (Publication No. AAT 3275010).

Decker, R.J. (2001). *Key elements of a risk management approach*. U.S. General Accounting Office. Retrieved from www.gao.gov/new.items/d02150t.pdf

Doukas, S.G. (2006, Spring). Crowd management: Past and contemporary issues. *The Sport Journal, 9*(2).

Drucker, P. (1988, Jan–Feb). The coming of the new organization. *Harvard Business Review*.

DuBrin, A.J. (2002). *The winning edge: How to motivate, influence, and manage your company's human resources*. Cincinnati, OH: South-Western.

Edwards, R., & Lemon, L.R. (2002) *Proactive or reactive? The severe storm threat to large event venues*. Preprints, 21st Conference on Severe Local Storms, San Antonio, TX, American Meteorological Society, 232–235. Retrieved from www.spc.noaa.gov/publications/edwards/lrgvenue.pdf

Federal Bureau of Investigation and U.S. Department of Homeland Security. (2009, September 21). *Potential threats to popular sport and entertainment venues*. Intelligence Bulletin No. 326 Joint FBI–DHS Bulletin.

Federal Emergency Management Agency, CitizenCorps. (2006). *Harris County, Texas, Citizen Corps response to hurricane Katrina*. Retrieved from www.citizencorps.gov/downloads/pdf/councils/llis/lessons-learned-tx-katrina-response.pdf.

Federal Emergency Management Agency, Emergency Management Institute. (2005a). Building and rebuilding trust. In *Leadership and influence: Independent study*.

Federal Emergency Management Agency, Emergency Management Institute. (2005b). Basic communication skills. In *Effective communication: Independent study*.

Federal Emergency Management Agency, Emergency Management Institute. (2005c). Communicating in an emergency. In *Effective communication: Independent study*.

Federal Emergency Management Agency, Emergency Management Institute. (2005d). Identifying decision-making styles and attributes. In *Decision making and problem solving: Independent study*.

Federal Emergency Management Agency, Emergency Management Institute. (2005e). The decision-making process. In *Decision making and problem solving: Independent study*.

Federal Emergency Management Agency, Emergency Management Institute. (2006a). The spectrum of incident management actions. In *Principles of emergency management: Independent study*.

Federal Emergency Management Agency, Emergency Management Institute. (2006b). *Developing and managing volunteers: Independent study*.

Federal Emergency Management Agency, Emergency Management Institute. (2008a). Introduction to exercise design. In *Exercise design: IS-139*.

Federal Emergency Management Agency, Emergency Management Institute. (2008b). The exercise process. In *Exercise design: IS-139*.

Federal Emergency Management Agency, Emergency Management Institute. (2008c). Exercise evaluation. In *Exercise design: IS-139*.

Federal Emergency Management Agency, Emergency Management Institute. (2009a). Establishing the foundation. In *An introduction to exercises: IS-120.A*.

Federal Emergency Management Agency, Emergency Management Institute. (2009b). Exercise basics. In *An introduction to exercises: IS-120.A*.

Federal Emergency Management Agency, Emergency Management Institute. (2010a, January 14). *Fundamentals of emergency management: IS-230.A*. Retrieved from http://training.fema.gov/EMIWeb/IS/IS230a.asp

Federal Emergency Management Agency, Emergency Management Institute. (2010b, July 22). *Special events contingency planning for public safety agencies: IS-15.B*.

Finch, B.E. (2008, June). *Decision raises serious liability concerns and emphasizes the need for SAFETY Act protections*. Dickstein Shapiro, LLP. Whitepaper.

Football Licensing Authority. (2007). *Exercise planning*. Retrieved from www.flaweb.org.uk

Fried, G. (2005). *Managing sports facilities*. Champaign, IL: Human Kinetics.

Gardner, W.L., & Avolio, B.J. (1998). The charismatic relationship. *Academy of Management Review*, January, p. 33.

Griffin, R.W., & Moorhead, G. (1986). *Organizational Behavior*. Houghton Mifflin Company: Boston, MA.

Hagmann, D.J. Black hole in America's heartland. *Northeast Intelligence Network*. 2005 Oct 30. Available at: www.homelandsecurityus.com/site/modules/news/article.php?storyid=16. Accessed July 20, 2006.

Hall, S. (2006). Effective security management of university sport venues. *Sport Journal*, 9(4), 1–10.

Hall, S., Cieslak, T., Marciani, L., Cooper, W., & McGee, J. (2010). Protective security measures for major sport events: Proposing a baseline standard. *Journal of Emergency Management*.

Hall, S., Marciani, L., & Cooper, W.E, & Rolen, R. (2007, August). Securing sport stadiums in the 21st century: Think security, enhance safety. Anser Homeland Security Institute. *Journal of Homeland Security*, pp. 1–7.

Hall, S., Marciani, L., & Cooper, W.E. (2008). Sport venue security: Planning and preparedness for terrorist-related incidents. *Sport Management and Related Topics Journal*, 4(2), 6–15.

Hall, S., Marciani, L., Cooper, W.E., & Phillips, J. (2010). Needs, concerns, and future challenges in security management of NCAA Division I football events: An intercollegiate facility management perspective. *Journal of Venue and Event Management*, 1(2), 1–16.

Hersey, P., & Blanchard, K.H. (1988). Management of organizational behavior: Utilizing human resources (5th ed.). Englewood Cliffs, NJ: Prentice Hall.

HSEEP. (2007a). Homeland Security Exercise and Evaluation Program - Volume I. The U.S. Department of Homeland Security.

Hui, S. (2010, January 22). U.K. terror threat level raised from substantial to severe. *Huffington Post*. Retrieved from www.huffingtonpost.com/2010/01/22/uk-terror-threat-level-ra_n_433519.html

Hurst, R., Zoubek, P., & Pratsinakis, C. (2007). *American sports as a target of terrorism: The duty of care after September 11th*. Retrieved from www.mmwr.com/_uploads/UploadDocs/publications/American%20Sports%20As%20A%20Target%20Of%20Terrorism.pdf

Ivancevich, J., & Matteson, R. (1999). *Organizational behavior and management* (5th ed). New York: McGraw-Hill.

Johnson, J.A. (2005). A brief history of terrorism. In G.R. Ledlow, J.A. Johnson, & W.J. Jones (Eds.), *Community preparedness and response to terrorism: Vol. 1. The terrorist threat and community response* (pp. 1–6). Westport, CT: Praeger Perspectives.

Kaiser, R., & Robinson, K. (2005). Risk management. In *Management of park and recreation services*. Washington DC: National Recreation and Park Association.

Kennedy, D.B. (2006). A précis of suicide terrorism. *Journal of Homeland Security and Emergency Management*, 3(4).

Kinney, J.A. (2003). Securing stadiums: Keeping them safe for successful special events. *Stadium Visions*, 2(1), 10. Retrieved from www.iapsc.org/uploaded_documents/stadiumPDF.pdf

Kotter, J.P. (1990). What leaders really do. *Harvard Business Review*, May–June, pp. 103–111.

Lencioni, P. (2002). *The five dysfunctions of a team*. San Francisco: Jossey-Bass.

Lindell, M.K., Prater, C., & Perry, R.W. (2007). *Introduction to emergency management*. Hoboken, NJ: Wiley.

Livingstone, N.C. (2008, September 24). Stadium and venue security. Domestic Preparedness.com. Retrieved from www.domesticpreparedness.com/Infrastructure/Special_Events/Stadium_and_Venue_Security/

Long, L.E., & Renfroe, N.A. (1999). *A new automation tool for risk assessment*. 15th Annual NDIA Security Technology Symposium. Session: Risk and Threat Assessment Techniques. Retrieved from www.dtic.mil/ndia/technology/smith.pdf

Madensen, T.D., & Eck, J.E. (2008, August). *Spectator violence in stadiums*. U.S. Department of Justice, Office of Community Oriented Policing Services, Center for Problem-Oriented Policing.

Marciani, L., Hall, S., & Finch, B. (2009). Intercollegiate athletics safety and security—concerns and responsibilities in the post 9/11 environment. *Athletics Administration*, 44(2), 14–17.

Marsden, A.W. (1998). Training railway operating staff to understand and manage passenger and crowd behavior. *Industrial and Commercial Training*, 3(5), 171–175.

Matheson, V. A., & Baade, R. A. (2006). Can New Orleans play its way past Katrina? College of the Holy Cross, Department of Economics Faculty Research Series, Paper No. 06-03. Retrieved from www.holycross.edu/departments/economics/RePEc/Matheson_NewOrleans.pdf.

National Counterterrorism Security Office. (2006). *Counter terrorism protective security advice for stadia and arenas*. Association of Chief Police Officers in Scotland. Retrieved from www.nactso.gov.uk/documents/Stadia%20Doc.pdf

Pantera, M.J., et al. (2003). Best practices for game day security at athletic and sport venues. *Sport Journal*, 6(4).

Pearson, G. (2006). *Fig fact-sheet four: Hooliganism*. Retrieved from www.liv.ac.uk/footballindustry/hooligan.html

Peck, S. (1988). *The different drum*. New York: Simon & Schuster.

Plochg Business Psychology Consulting. (2009). *Dysfunctional patterns in leadership*. Retrieved from http://businesspsychologistconsulting.com

Protective Measures Guide for U.S. Sports Leagues (2008). Department of Homeland Security. Washington, DC.

Ross, M.B. (1982). *Coping with conflict. The 1982 annual for facilitators, trainers, and consultants*. San Diego, CA: University Associates.

Sandia National Laboratories. (2008). *Risk assessment*. Retrieved from www.sandia.gov

Sauter, M.A., & Carafano, J.J. (2005). *Homeland security: A complete guide to understanding, preventing, and surviving terrorism*. New York: McGraw Hill.

Schwarz, E., Hall, S., & Shibli, S. (2010). *Sport facility operations management*. London: Butterworth-Heinemann.

Security and policing. (2005). In *U.K. sport, staging major sports events: The guide*. Retrieved from www.uksport.gov.uk/pages/major_sports_event_the_guide/

Sennewald, C.A. (2003). *Effective security management* (4th ed.). London: Butterworth-Heinemann.

Slack, T., & Parent, M.M. (2006). *Understanding sport organizations: The application of organization theory* (2nd ed.). Champaign, IL: Human Kinetics.

Spangler, J. (2001, September 30). Meeting the threat. *Deseretnews.com*. Retrieved from http://deseretnews.com/dn/sview/1,3329,320006966,00.html

State of Missouri Emergency Management Agency. (2009, October). *Special event considerations. Missouri hazard analysis*. Retrieved from http://sema.dps.mo.gov/HazardAnalysis/2009%20State%20Hazard%20Analysis/Annex%20K.%20%20Hazardous%20Materials.pdf

Steinbach, P. (2006, September). Storm: A year removed from the dark days of hurricane Katrina, college athletic departments are now being viewed in a new light—as disaster response specialists. *Athletic Business*, 38–46.

Stelter, L. (2009, September 1). From the uniform to the suit: Why education is so important. *Security Director News*. Retrieved from www.securitydirectornews.com

Stevens, A. (2007). *Sports security and safety: Evolving strategies for a changing world*. Sport Business Group.

Tarlow, P.E. (2002). *Event risk management and safety*. New York: Wiley.

Texas Engineering Extension Service (TEEX). (2005, January) *Threat and risk assessment* (*local jurisdiction*) (3rd ed.). College Station, TX.

Toohey, K., & Taylor, T. (2008). Mega events, fear, and risk: Terrorism at the Olympic Games. *Journal of Sport Management, 22*, 451–469.

U.S. Department of Homeland Security. (2002, July). *National strategy for homeland security*. Washington, DC. Retrieved from www.whitehouse.gov/homeland/book/nat_strat_hls.pdf

U.S. Department of Homeland Security. (2003a, February). *National strategy for combating terrorism*. Washington, DC. Retrieved from www.whitehouse.gov/news/releases/2003/02/counter_terrorism/counter_terrorism_stratgey.pdf

U.S. Department of Homeland Security, Office of Domestic Preparedness. (2003b, July). *Vulnerability assessment report*. Retrieved from www.ojp.usdoj.gov/odp/docs/vamreport.pdf

U.S. Department of Homeland Security. (2004). *Securing our homeland*. Washington, DC. Retrieved from www.hsdl.org/?view=docs/dhs/nps03-032404-07.pdf

U.S. Department of Homeland Security. (2005, April). *National planning scenarios executive summary*. Retrieved from http://cees.tamiu.edu/covertheborder/TOOLS/NationalPlanningSen.pdf

U.S. Department of Homeland Security. (2006, July). *Law enforcement prevention and deterrence of terrorist acts*.

U.S. Department of Homeland Security. (2007a). *Homeland security exercise and evaluation program* (*HSEEP*), Volume I.

U.S. Department of Homeland Security. (2007b). *Homeland security exercise and evaluation program* (*HSEEP*), Volume II.

U.S. Department of Homeland Security. (2007c). *Homeland security exercise and evaluation program* (*HSEEP*), Volume III.

U.S. Department of Homeland Security. (2008a). *Evacuation planning guide for stadiums*. Retrieved from www.dhs.gov/xlibrary/assets/ip_cikr_stadium_evac_guide.pdf

U.S. Department of Homeland Security. (2008b). *National incident management system*. Washington, DC.

U.S. Department of Homeland Security. (2008c). *Protective measures guide for U.S. sports leagues*. Washington, DC.

U.S. Department of Homeland Security. (2009a). *Department responsibilities*. Retrieved from www.dhs.gov/xabout/responsibilities.shtm

U.S. Department of Homeland Security. (2009b). *Homeland security presidential directives*. Retrieved from http://dhs.gov/xabout/laws/editorial_0607.shtm

U.S. Department of Homeland Security. (2009c, April). *Sport event risk management*.

U.S. Department of Homeland Security. (2009d). *State and local fusion centers*. Retrieved from www.dhs.gov/files/programs/gc_1156877184684.shtm

U.S. Department of Homeland Security, Office of Intelligence and Analysis. (2009e, January 26). *Threats to college sports and entertainment venues and surrounding areas*.

U.S. Department of Homeland Security. (2010). *Homeland security advisory system*. Retrieved from www.dhs.gov/files/programs/Copy_of_press_release_0046.shtm

Warfield, C. (2008). *The disaster management cycle*. Retrieved from http://gdrc.org/uem/disasters/1-dm_cycle.html

Yones, M. (2009). Dysfunctional leadership & dysfunctional organizations. *International Institute of Management Executive Journal*. Retrieved from www.iim-edu.org/dysfunctionalleadershipdysfunctionalorganziations/index.htm

Yukl, G.A. (2002). *Leadership in organizations* (5th ed.). Upper Saddle River, NJ: Prentice Hall.

Index

Note: The letters *f* and *t* after page numbers indicate figures and tables, respectively.

About the Authors

Stacey A. Hall, PhD, is associate director of the National Center for Spectator Sports Safety and Security (NCS⁴) and an assistant professor of sport management at the University of Southern Mississippi (USM), where she developed a graduate-level emphasis in sport security management for the master's program.

Hall's research on sport safety and security has been published in many journals on sport management, homeland security, and emergency management, and she has coauthored a textbook on global sport facility operations management. Hall has presented at international and national conferences and conducted invited presentations for U.S. federal and state agencies, college athletic conferences, and professional sport leagues, including Major League Soccer (MLS). She was also invited as a contributing expert in sport security to the first international sport security conference in Doha, Qatar, in 2011.

Hall has been the principal investigator on various external grant awards from the U.S. Department of Homeland Security in order to develop a risk management curriculum for sport security personnel at NCAA institutions, conduct risk assessments at college sport stadia, and develop training programs for sport venue staff. She has also been involved in several service projects, including development of a risk assessment tool for U.S. sport stadia in conjunction with the Department of Homeland Security and International Association of Assembly Managers and development of a disaster mitigation plan post-Katrina for the Mississippi Regional Housing Authority. Hall has completed training in assessment of threat and risk through the National Emergency Response and Rescue Training Center, training in terrorist bombing through New Mexico Tech Energetic Materials and Testing Center, and training in contingency planning of special events for public safety agencies through the FEMA Emergency Management Institute.

A competitive soccer player, Hall was team captain for the Northern Ireland international soccer team. She retired in 2008. Hall now resides in Hattiesburg, Mississippi.

Walter E. Cooper, EdD, is professor emeritus and director of training at the University of Southern Mississippi's National Center for Spectator Sport Safety and Security (NCS⁴). He holds certifications and has completed training in incident response to terrorist bombings, prevention and response to suicide bombing incidents, and incident response to campus bombing incidents (New Mexico Tech University); prevention, detection, and response to campus emergencies (NCBRT-Louisiana State University); enhanced threat and risk assessment (TEEX-Texas A&M University); and risk assessment methodology for chemical facilities (Sandia National Labs RAM-CFTM).

His research on emergency management and risk facilitator management for sporting events has most recently been published in the *Journal of Emergency Management* and the *Anser Homeland Security Institute: Journal of Homeland Security*. Cooper presents frequently on issues of emergency training within school environments at all levels (K-12 and collegiate).

Lou Marciani, EdD, is the director of the National Center for Spectator Sports Safety and Security (NCS⁴) at the University of Southern Mississippi. The NCS⁴ was founded with initial funding from the Mississippi Office of Homeland Security as the country's first academic center dedicated to spectator sports safety and security research, professional development, enhanced training, and outreach. At the NCS⁴, Marciani works with professional sport leagues, the NCAA, national collegiate directors of athletics, the private sector, and government agencies in enhancing sport safety and security.

Marciani is the principal investigator for research funded by grants through the Office of Homeland Security and U.S. Department of Education. His work at NCS⁴ focuses on the development and implementation of a sport risk management curriculum as well as a decision support system for sport venues to include simulation modeling for stadium evacuations.

Marciani's extensive career in sport management includes serving as intercollegiate athletic director at several universities and as executive director of two national sport governing bodies. He is an active speaker on sport safety and security at international and national sport organization annual conferences. Marciani also serves as a resource for the U.S. Office of Homeland Security on sport safety and security issues.

James A. McGee, MS, has 25 combined years of law enforcement experience and 21 years as a special agent with the Federal Bureau of Investigation (FBI). McGee is currently a senior consultant at the National Center for Spectator Sports Safety and Security (NCS⁴) and an adjunct professor in Department of Homeland Security studies at Tulane University in New Orleans, Louisiana. McGee teaches security and terrorism courses both at the university level and internationally. He is regarded as an expert in security measures associated with venues of mass gatherings, and he lectures frequently on this topic.

As an FBI special agent, McGee spent 16 years working in security management for sporting events, including several Super Bowls and the 2004 Olympic Games. During his tenure he was the FBI supervisory special agent for the New Orleans Division Joint Terrorism Task Force and the FBI security coordinator for the 2004 Summer Olympic Games in Athens, Greece.

In addition to his extensive field experience, McGee holds a master of science degree in criminal justice from Virginia Commonwealth University in Richmond, Virginia. As a Department of State Anti-Terrorism Assistance instructor, he teaches courses in major events security management and critical incident management. McGee is also the global security consultant for ESPN, providing corporate security consultation and surveillance operations for major sporting events such as Monday Night Football, Sports Nation, and College Game Day.

In 2010, McGee received an Independent Publisher's Book Award for his true crime book *Phase Line Green: The FCI Talladega Hostage Rescue*. In his free time, McGee enjoys spending time with his family, fitness training, and writing. He and his wife, Shawna, reside in Pass Christian, Mississippi.